The Memoirs Of Paul Kruger, Four Times President Of The South African Republic

Paul Kruger

Alpha Editions

This Edition Published in 2021

ISBN: 9789354419409

Design and Setting By
Alpha Editions
www.alphaedis.com
Email – info@alphaedis.com

As per information held with us this book is in Public Domain.
This book is a reproduction of an important historical work. Alpha Editions uses the best technology to reproduce historical work in the same manner it was first published to preserve its original nature. Any marks or number seen are left intentionally to preserve its true form.

PUBLISHERS' NOTE

Mr. Kruger dictated these Memoirs to Mr. H. C. Bredell, his private secretary, and to Mr. Piet Grobler, the former Under Secretary of State of the South African Republic. These gentlemen handed their notes to an editor, the Rev. Dr. A. Schowalter, who spent several weeks at Utrecht in constant colloquy with Mr. Kruger, elucidating various points with the aid of the President's replies to a list of some hundred and fifty to two hundred questions which Dr. Schowalter had drawn up.

The English and American edition has been translated by Mr. A. Teixeira de Mattos from Dr. Schowalter's revised German text, collated line for line with Mr. Kruger's original Dutch; with this difference that, in this edition, Mr. Kruger speaks in the first person throughout, whereas, in the Continental editions, the narrative is allowed to change into the third person from the point at which he begins to attain a prominent position in the affairs of his country. This latter arrangement, which appeared on reconsideration to be an artificial one, has been altered in this translation, and it has also been decided that, after Mr. Kruger's death, all subsequent Continental editions shall be printed in the first person throughout.

In the Appendix have been collected several documents in the shape of speeches, proclamations and circular dispatches, including the famous three hours' speech delivered by Mr. Kruger, after his inauguration as President for the fourth time, on the 12th of May 1898.

CONTENTS

CHAPTER I

EARLY DAYS AND PRIVATE LIFE

	PAGE
Homeless—In the new home—Hunting adventures—Kruger kills his first lion—The dead lion roars—Further lion-hunts—Panther and rhinoceros hunting—Under a rhinoceros—Buffalo hunting—A fight with a buffalo-cow—Elephant hunting—Race between Kruger and an elephant—Canine fidelity—Kruger amputates his own thumb	1

CHAPTER II

COMMENCEMENT OF PUBLIC ACTIVITY

Journey to the Sand River in 1852—The Sand River Convention—Punitive expedition against the Kaffir Chief Secheli—Kruger's life in danger—Vindictive raid on the Kaffir chiefs Makapaan and Mapela—Kruger alone in the cave among the besieged Kaffirs—He recovers Potgieter's body—Expedition against Montsioa—Kruger charges a band of Kaffirs single-handed 35

CHAPTER III

IN A POSITION OF COMMAND

The first Basuto War—Kruger assists the Orange Free State against the Basutos and negotiates the peace with Moshesh—Kruger as general in the field against the Kaffir chief Gasibone 53

CONTENTS

CHAPTER IV

The Civil War: 1861-1864

Kruger's protest against the violation of the constitution by Commandant General Schoeman—Assembly of the people at Pretoria—Kruger's declaration of war—Attempts at a settlement and their frustration by Schoeman—Kruger is nominated a voting member of the Reformed Church, in order that he may be qualified to hold office in the State without opposition—Fresh negotiations—Military preparations on both sides—The political contest develops into a religious war—Battle of Potchefstroom—Schoeman's flight—Renewed negotiations—The arbitration award of the Supreme Court rejected—Kruger insulted—Battle of Zwartkopje—Fresh negotiations—Mutual amnesty—The new elections—Kruger again Commandant General 67

CHAPTER V

Native Wars

The Transvaalers again come to the Orange Free State's assistance against the Basutos, under Moshesh, but break up in discord—Kruger's accident in 1866—Fighting in the Zoutpansberg—Lack of ammunition and support—Kruger alone among the Kaffirs . . . 93

CHAPTER VI

President Burgers

Dispute about Kimberley—Kruger's protest against the court of arbitration to which President Pretorius has yielded—Pretorius resigns the Presidency—T. F. Burgers elected by a large majority, notwithstanding Kruger's agitation—Explanation between Kruger and Bur-

CONTENTS

gers—Burgers's policy—War with Secucuni—Dispute about the arbitrary war-tax imposed by the President—Sir Theophilus Shepstone, the British Governor of Natal, arrives with his plans for annexation—Conferences with Shepstone—Burgers's difference with Kruger and the Volksraad—Kruger elected Vice-president—The annexation of the Transvaal—Protest of the Executive Raad against the annexation 103

CHAPTER VII

The Interregnum under the British Flag

Kruger's first visit to London with the deputation sent to procure the repeal of the annexation—Popular meetings and popular voting in the Transvaal—The second visit to London—The Kaffir chief Secucuni puts the English doctrine into practice—The British Governor seeks Kruger's assistance against Cetewayo, the Zulu king—Further assemblies of the people and protests against the annexation—Kruger pacifies the masses—The High Commissioners, Sir Bartle Frere and Sir Garnet Wolseley, interfere—The other Afrikanders ask for the freedom of their Transvaal brothers—Kruger suspected of treachery—The delegates of the burgher meetings arrested for high treason—Kruger once more allays the storm—Plans for confederation opposed by Kruger—Sir Bartle Frere tries to treat privately with Kruger—Kruger refuses on the grounds of Frere's double-dealing—Kruger and Joubert have recourse to Gladstone by letter—All hopes of a peaceful solution abandoned 123

CHAPTER VIII

The War of Independence: 1880–1881

The seizure of Bezuidenhout's wagon—Meeting of the burghers at Potchefstroom—The " Irreconcilables " at

CONTENTS

Paader Kraal elect a triumvirate, consisting of Kruger, Joubert and Pretorius, to carry on the government—The first shot—Battle of Bronkhorstspruit—Majuba Hill—Paul Kruger during the war—His negotiations with the Kaffir chief Magato, whom England was trying to gain as an ally—Armistice and peace negotiations—Protests in the Volksraad—" Transvaal " or " South African Republic " ? 147

CHAPTER IX

Paul Kruger's First Presidency

The election—The war with the Kaffirs in the Lydenburg district—Kaffir disturbances on the south-western frontiers of the Republic—Boer volunteers, in spite of the President's proclamation, enlist under the Chiefs Moshette and Mankoroane, for their war against other Kaffir chiefs, and found the Republics of Stellaland and Goshenland on the territory awarded them for their services—The Chiefs Montsioa and Moshette place themselves under the protection of the Transvaal—England protests against this arrangement—Negotiations regarding the western borders between Kruger, Sir Charles Warren and Cecil Rhodes—Kruger's third visit to London—Sir Hercules Robinson—Repeal of the suzerainty by the London Convention of 1884—Visits to the European Governments—Dr. Leyds—Internal situation of the Republic in 1885—The Delagoa Bay Railway—Unsatisfactory condition of the finances—Disturbances on the western frontiers—Discovery of the gold-fields—The population of the gold-fields: the " Uitlanders "—Negotiations with the Free State for a closer alliance—Incorporation of the " New Republic " 165

CONTENTS

CHAPTER X

PAUL KRUGER'S SECOND PRESIDENCY: 1888–1893

Dr. Leyds appointed State Secretary—Cecil Rhodes causes trouble on the northern frontiers of the Republic: the Chartered Company; Lobengula; Khama—Treaty of alliance between the Orange Free State and the South African Republic—Arrangements in favor of the Uitlanders: the Law Courts at Johannesburg; the Second Volksraad—Paul Kruger's "hatred of the Uitlanders"—The Swaziland Agreement—British perfidy—the Adendorff trek—Religious differences—Kruger the "autocrat"—The educational question—New elections 187

CHAPTER XI

PAUL KRUGER'S THIRD PRESIDENCY: 1893–1898

The Transvaal National Union—The second Swaziland Agreement—Difficulties with the Kaffir tribes in the Blue Mountains—The English immigrants refuse to perform military service—Sir Henry Loch at Pretoria—The President insulted—Annexation of Sambaanland and Umbigesaland by England—Solemn opening of the Delagoa Bay Railway and tariff war with Cape Colony—The Jameson Raid—Mr. Chamberlain's policy of provocation—The report of the Mining Commission—The struggle between the Government and the Supreme Court—Sir Alfred Milner—New elections—The Queen of England a "*kwaaie vrouw*"—Closer alliance with the Orange Free State 211

CHAPTER XII

PAUL KRUGER'S FOURTH PRESIDENCY

The Bunu Question—Sir Alfred Milner—F. W. Reitz—J. C. Smuts—The agitation of the South African

CONTENTS

League—The Edgar Case—The Crisis: the suffrage, the suzerainty—The Ultimatum—The War—President Kruger during the War—On the way to Europe—On foreign soil—Homeless—Conclusion 261

APPENDIX

A

Speeches delivered at the Solemn Inauguration of His Honor S. J. P. Kruger as State President of the South African Republic, on Thursday, 12 May 1898 . . . 333

B

Speech of State President Kruger in the First Volksraad on Monday, 1 May 1899 368

C

Two Speeches of President Kruger at the Decisive Sitting of the First and Second Volksraad of 2 October 1899 376

D

Opening Speech of President Steyn at the Annual Session of the Volksraad of the Orange Free State at Kroonstad, 2 April 1900 381

E

Opening Speech of President Kruger at the Ordinary Annual Session of the First and Second Volksraad of the South African Republic at the Joint Sitting of 7 May 1900 385

CONTENTS

F

Speech delivered on the 7th of May by President Kruger in explanation of his Opening Speech at the Ordinary Session of 1900 391

G

Circular Dispatch from State President Kruger to the Commandant Generals, Assistant Commandant Generals and Officers 399

H

Telegram from the State President to the Commandant General 403

I

Circular Dispatch from the State President to the Commandant General, the Assistant Commandants General and the Officers 405

J

Proclamation by President Steyn against the Annexation of the Orange Free State 409

Index 411

CHAPTER I

EARLY DAYS AND PRIVATE LIFE

CHAPTER I

EARLY DAYS AND PRIVATE LIFE

Homeless—In the new home—Hunting adventures—Kruger kills his first lion—The dead lion roars—Further lion-hunts—Panther and rhinoceros hunting—Under a rhinoceros—Buffalo hunting—A fight with a buffalo-cow—Elephant hunting—Race between Kruger and an elephant—Canine fidelity—Kruger amputates his own thumb.

MY recollections go back to the time when, as a boy of nine, I left the land of my birth with my parents and my uncles Gert and Theunis Kruger.

Till then we had lived at Vaalbank Farm, in the Colesberg district in Cape Colony, where I was born on the 10th of October 1825 as the third child of Caspar Jan Hendrik Kruger [1] and Elisa Steyn, his wife, daughter of Douw Steyn, of Bulhoek Farm, behind the Zuurberg in Cape Colony. My parents were simple farmers, and I grew up at the farm like other farmers' lads, looking after the herds and lending a hand in the fields. With the exception that an old woman prophesied to my mother that her son

[1] The President declares that his ancestors originally came from Germany, but his family do not know from which town. He only knows that the founder of the African branch of the family married a Frenchwoman, and was obliged to fly from the country on account of his religion.—*Note by the Editor of the German Edition.*

Stephanus Johannes Paulus was destined for a superior position in life, I do not know that any one could have had the least notion that God would entrust me with a special mission.

The first event of importance in my life was our departure from home, our *trek*. I was too young at the time to occupy myself much with the reason of the great emigration. But I know that my parents said they emigrated because the English first sold the slaves and, after they had got the money, set these slaves free again; and that the money which had been awarded in compensation was made payable in England, where it could be received either personally or through an agent. The expenses entailed by this method of payment in many cases amounted to more than the capital, so that a great many preferred to sacrifice what was due to them, rather than be put to so much trouble and vexation. But they refused to continue to live under such unjust masters. Added to this, the Kaffirs repeatedly raided the colony and stole the Boers' cattle, and the English general, after the Boers had themselves recovered their cattle, declared the collective herds to be so much booty, out of which the British Government must recover their war-costs before the rest could be distributed among the former proprietors, who had themselves joined in the fighting in order to get back their own. The discontent caused by this unjust proceed-

EARLY DAYS AND PRIVATE LIFE

ing took a firm hold of the Boer mind; especially since each child when quite young receives as his personal property a couple of sheep, oxen or horses from his parents, which he tends with special care and to which his heart becomes attached. Among the stolen beasts were naturally those belonging to the children, and when those presents, made sacred by custom, were detained in such an arbitrary way and used for the purposes of a war-indemnity, much bitterness was caused. And so my parents and relatives left house and home for a wild and unknown country, and set out, about twenty of them, with nearly thirty thousand African sheep and a few hundred horses and cattle, which they had received largely in exchange for the goods they left behind.

The exodus over the Orange River commenced in May 1835. Here my father sold about three thousand wethers, at a *dikketon*[1] (an old coin, worth a little over two shillings) apiece to a butcher, after which the expedition proceeded towards the neighborhood of the Caledon River, and there encamped. My occupation here, as well as on our further marches, was to drive the cattle and keep them together. The children of most of the emigrants had to do this work, for the black servants had nearly all remained in the Colony, and, just at that time, when

---

[1] Obviously a corruption of "ducatoon," the old silver ducat of Venice.—*Translator's Note*.

the whole property of the families consisted of herds of cattle, their services would have proved specially useful.[1]

Other burghers left their home at the same time as my parents and were also encamped near the Caledon River. But this was not the Great Trek. That took place during the following year, 1836, under Hendrik Potgieter, and was joined by the single groups of earlier emigrants. Immediately after this junction, a meeting was held, resolutions were passed to which all the emigrants had to submit, and a sort of government was instituted. But God's Word constituted the highest law and rule of conduct. Potgieter was chosen for the first position, that of commandant. The resolutions which came into general force contained, for example, the decree that it was unlawful to take away from the natives, by force, land or any other of their property, and that no sla-

---

[1] I am on this occasion able to confirm the authenticity of an anecdote which tells how a gentleman who introduced an English lord to President Kruger, thinking that the latter did not take sufficient account of his aristocratic visitor, and hoping to make a greater impression upon him, began to enumerate the important positions which this nobleman occupied, and to tell what his ancestors had been. Whereupon the President answered drily:

"Tell the gentleman that I was a cow-herd and my father a farmer."

The gentleman who introduced this nobleman was the proprietor of a large distillery at Zwartkop in the neighborhood of Pretoria.—*Note by the Editor of the German Edition.*

The anecdote is quite well known in England, where I have often heard it told of a certain noble duke who, at that time, had held no particular position outside the Court, but whose father, who was then living, had filled more than one important post under Government.—*Translator's Note.*

EARLY DAYS AND PRIVATE LIFE

very would be permitted. They now proceeded jointly to the Vet River and crossed the whole of the Free State without depriving the weak native races which lived there of a single thing. The land between the Vet and the Vaal Rivers was bartered in exchange for oxen and cows by the Kaffir chief who ruled there.

When the first emigrants arrived at the Vaal, and were encamped both here and on the Rhenoster River in small scattered parties, they were attacked unexpectedly and without having given the least provocation by the Zulu chief Moselikatse. This Moselikatse was at that time lord and master of the entire country west of the Lebombo and Drakensberg Mountains. All the Makatese tribes in this district had submitted to his sway. He treated them like dogs and called them so, and, when vultures passed over his " town," he gave orders to kill a few poor old men and women and throw them for food to his "children," as he called the vultures. The subjugated races hid from him in caves and gorges. When Moselikatse heard that men with white faces had come from the south, he sent a couple of thousand warriors with orders to massacre the invaders. The trekkers who were encamped along the Rhenoster and Vaal Rivers were divided into small parties, which was necessary on account of the dimensions of the herds, so as not to cause quarrels about the grazing lands. They were surprised by Moselikatse's robber band, and the greater number of them murdered.

After this massacre the Matabele went back to their town, taking the cattle with them; but they returned a fortnight later in great numbers and attacked the emigrants at Vechtkop, in the Orange Free State. But here Sarel Celliers had built a strong laager and, with the 33 men whom he had at his disposal, repelled the impetuous attacks of the Zulus, from his wagon fortress, causing them heavy losses. Women and children bravely assisted the defenders of the camp, casting bullets, loading the rifles and, in some instances, even taking rifle in hand themselves to shoot down the enemy. On their retreat to the Moselikatse Pass, near Pretoria, and to Marico, two of their principal places, the Kaffirs carried off all the emigrants' cattle, as naturally they could not be taken into the laager, and so were unprotected. They also took with them two white children and three half-breeds, of whom nothing was ever heard again.

A small party of burghers, under Potgieter, pursued the enemy as far as the Marico River: God was with them and gave them the victory at Zeerust. They continued to pursue the enemy further, and in the end entered into possession of his territory.

EARLY DAYS AND PRIVATE LIFE

They recovered part of their property and, when Moselikatse had fled, the commando returned.

A small number of the emigrants now proceeded to Natal. To develop the conquered country and make it independent, it was necessary to be in communication with the outer world, and, in Natal, where already a number of emigrants had settled and were in treaty for the necessary acquisition of land, they hoped to obtain the harbor of Durban. But after the treacherous murder of Piet Retief and the attack on the settlers by Dingaan's hordes, most of the emigrants, including my father, returned to the district which is contained within the Free State and Transvaal of to-day. My people settled at Liebenberg Vlei, in what has since become the Orange Free State; a tract of country which became so well known through Kitchener's operations against De Wet.

A commando again crossed the Vaal, in 1839, to find and punish Moselikatse, who continued to rob and plunder, and also to recover the stolen cattle. I took part in this expedition. Potgieter left the wagon laager behind at Wonderfontein, in what is now the Potchefstroom district, and, with a mounted commando, pursued Moselikatse, who continued to fall back. The whole country had been devastated and all the settlers murdered. Potgieter discovered the Chief Magato at Klein Bueffelshoek, near the well-known Elephant River in the Magaliesberg, where he was hiding. We shall hear of him again, for he settled, later, in the neighborhood of Rustenburg. He had only a few followers with him and, when Potgieter asked him where Moselikatse was, he told him that he had already crossed the Crocodile River. Asked why he had remained behind and was in hiding, he said that he had escaped during the night on the march to the north, and was now hiding because he stood in fear of Moselikatse's bands which had been left behind on the Moselikatse Pass. Seeing that it was impossible to overtake Moselikatse and that an attack on the entrenched position at Moselikatse Pass was out of the question, the commando returned to the women's camp on the Rhenoster and Vaal Rivers. But as early as the following year, 1840, Potgieter started with another commando, and this time went direct to Moselikatse Pass. I took part in this expedition too. Potgieter there found a large Kaffir town, which he stormed. When it was in our hands we recovered a number of things which had formerly belonged to the trekkers who had been murdered by Moselikatse's orders.

During the pursuit of Moselikatse, the chief Mamagali told Potgieter that there was still a force of Moselikatse's savages at Strijdpoort in the Waterberg district. Potgieter went there at once and at-

EARLY DAYS AND PRIVATE LIFE

tacked the Kaffir camp. But it turned out that we were fighting the wrong people. They were not Zulus but Rooi, or red Kaffirs who had been forced to join Moselikatse's hordes. Directly Potgieter was informed of this fact he put a stop to the fighting. Mamagali, who had been the cause of this battle, was arrested and, after a regular trial by court martial, was sentenced to six months' imprisonment. He would not have got off so cheaply had he not been able to prove that the Rooi Kaffirs had always been associated with Moselikatse on the war-path, and that he had taken them for Zulus.

At last the wanderers had found a comparatively safe home. It is obvious that the disturbed life which they had led till then must have occasioned great losses. To institute schools or churches, or a firm and regular management of external affairs, was out of the question. But the Boer fathers and mothers, for all that, looked after the education of their children to the very best of their ability. They knew that they lived in a country where anything that was once neglected was difficult to recover, and that to neglect the rising generation meant the ruin of their nationality. Therefore every Boer taught his children to read and write, and, above all, instructed them in God's Word. At dinner and supper, as the children sat round the table, they had to read part of the Sacred Scriptures, and to repeat from memory or write down now this and now that text; and this was done day by day unless unusual circumstances made it impossible. That is how my father taught me the Bible, and instructed me in its teaching during the evenings. My other course of instruction was covered altogether by a period of about three months, with frequent interruptions. My master's name was Tielman Roos, who found much difficulty in carrying out his mission. Whenever the trek came to a resting-place and we out-spanned, a small hut was built of grass and reeds, and this became the school-room for the trekkers' children. This was done during the whole journey to the Magaliesberg, where my father settled.

When I was sixteen years old I was entitled to choose two farms like any other independent member of our community; one as a grazing-place and the other for sowing with crops. I lived at Waterkloof, and, in 1842, fetched Miss Maria du Plessis, from the country south of the Vaal, to be my wife.[1]

---

[1] During a journey which he had undertaken in order to visit his betrothed, young Kruger found that the torrential waters of the Vaal were so swollen as to render it impassable. But his ardor was greater than the danger, and his strength mightier than the force of the stream. He drove his horses into the water, and, dressed as he was, swam with them across the river under conditions which threatened almost certain death. The old ferryman, who had not dared to cross the river that day with his boat, read him a fine lecture. But it was thrown away. Fortunately the engagement did not last long enough to render a repetition of this hazardous enterprise necessary.—*Note by the Editor of the German Edition.*

EARLY DAYS AND PRIVATE LIFE

The wedding took place in the village of Potchefstroom, which began to flourish at that time.[1]

After a period of rest, a new expedition was fitted out, in 1845, in order to colonize the conquered country. Every participant received the promise of another farm in that part of the country. A commission, to which my father belonged, had gone to Delagoa Bay during the previous year in order to come to an understanding with Portugal regarding the mutual frontier, and had agreed that the ridge of the Lebombo Mountains should form the frontier between Portugal and that part of the country which the Boer emigrants wished to colonize. I accompanied this expedition, as deputy field cornet, with my father and the other members of our family. We went as far north as the present Lydenburg district, and there founded the village of Ohrigstad. But we found no abiding-place there. Fever, cattle-sickness and other evils determined us to return to the Magaliesberg, where I continued to live and acquired several farms by barter. Here, in January 1846, I had the misfortune to lose my wife and the little baby

[1] There was at that time as little opportunity for church weddings as for school instruction or proper preparation for confirmation. The Boer was obliged to be, more or less, his own schoolmaster, minister and civil servant. Even as in the late war, a landdrost had often to appoint himself, so as to provide for an official qualified to "legalize" marriages. Perhaps that accounts for the fact that the otherwise so religious Boers looked upon civil marriage as a perfectly natural rite for many years before we began to fight for it as a "necessity of our enlightened times."
—*Note by the Editor of the German Edition.*

to whom she had given birth. God gave me another life-companion in Miss Gezina Suzanna Frederika Wilhelmina du Plessis. From this marriage sprang nine sons and seven daughters, of whom three sons and five daughters are still alive.

The first care of the new settlers was to secure reliable labor and to induce the black inhabitants of the country to undertake it. That was not an easy matter. For, although the Kaffir was willing enough to work, he was always endeavoring to cheat his master in one way or another. And, as soon as he had learned his work, his arrogance often became unbearable. We had constantly to fight this difficulty in great ways and small, and the contest sometimes had its humorous side. For instance, one New Year's Day, I sent a Kaffir from my farm at Waterkloof to my mother's farm (I had lost my father in 1852) to fetch some raisins. My mother sent me about five or six pounds, and said so in a note, which the Kaffir conscientiously delivered. But the letter was a proof that the Kaffir had robbed me, for the raisins which he brought weighed much less than the quantity mentioned in the letter. I asked him what he meant by trying to cheat me and why he had eaten nearly all the raisins.

"The letter tells me," I said, "that there were a great many more than you brought me."

"Baas," he replied, "the letter lies, for how could

it have seen me eat the raisins? Why, I put it behind the big rock under a stone and then sat down on the other side of the rock to eat the raisins."

After I had convinced him that the letter knew all about it nevertheless, he humbly acknowledged his fault; still the thing was not quite clear to him.

I had a very faithful Kaffir, called April, on one of my other farms at Boekenhoutfontein in the Rustenburg district. During the winter I traveled with my cattle to Saulspoort, near Pilaansberg. Before going away I called him aside and said:

"I will teach you how to read a letter."

I then took a piece of paper and drew lines on it.

"The longest lines," I continued, "stand for melons, the next oranges and the shortest lemons," and I added that he was to send me from time to time just as many of each of these as were indicated by the number of strokes in the letter which I should send by a messenger. He was also to send back a letter by the messenger and inform me, by means of similar lines, how many he had sent of each sort, and to close the letter carefully. The Kaffir was immensely proud of his scholarly attainments, and from that moment considered himself immeasurably above every other Kaffir. There was really no need to tell him not to give my secret away; nothing would have induced him to do so. Later on, I sent two messengers to him and said simply:

"Give this letter to April; he will give you what I want."

This was done; and when they returned, bringing a letter from April, I said:

"Give me the letter which April has written, so that I may see if you have cheated me or not."

They were simply amazed, and April's scholarship roused their unbounded envy and admiration. They told everybody about the wise April who had suddenly learned to read and write.

At that time there were no missionaries in our country; but a pious Kaffir, called David, went round among his countrymen in order to teach them religion. When this David wanted to teach the Kaffirs in my district the Bible and how to read it, they refused to learn to read or write.

"Why," they asked, "should we first learn the 'book' and then bother to learn to write, in order to be able to read again what we have already learned, when Paul Kruger's Kaffir reads and writes without knowing the book and without having learned to write?"

David came to me and told me his difficulties, and, in order to break down the resistance of the Kaffirs, I was obliged to let David into my secret. April did not forgive me for a long time, for his importance and the admiration of his comrades were now things of the past.

EARLY DAYS AND PRIVATE LIFE

During the first years of our settlement as well as during our wanderings it was our task to clear the recently acquired land of wild animals, which had hitherto roamed about unrestrained side by side with the wild races, and thus to protect our pastures. Every Boer took an active part in this work, and the rising youth, in whom the love of adventure had turned hunting into a passion, did a great deal, in this way, to make the country habitable.

It is, of course, impossible that I should be able to tell to-day how many wild beasts I have killed. It is too much to remember the exact number of lions, buffaloes, rhinoceroses, giraffes and other big game; and, besides, it is nearly fifty years since I was present at a big hunt. Nor can I recall to mind all the details connected with those hunts. As far as I know, I must have shot at least thirty to forty elephants and five hippopotamuses. And I know that I have killed five lions by myself. When I went hunting I always took a companion with me, as well as good horses; and I made it a rule, on larger hunting expeditions, to allow two or three wagons of our poor people to accompany us, so that they might have the game.

I shot my first lion in the year 1839. I was then 14 years of age. A lion had attacked our herds and robbed us of several head of cattle that were grazing by the banks of the Rhenoster River in what has since become the Orange Free State. Six of us started (I was the seventh, but did not count) to find that lion. We were all mounted and rode in two parties of three, with a good distance between the parties. The lion sighted us before we were face to face with him, and came on with a wild rush. The three adults with whom I had come, my father, my uncle and my brother, quickly tied the horses together and then turned them round, with their heads in the opposite direction to that from which the lion was bearing down upon us. This is the regular procedure at a lion hunt; for, if the horses catch sight of a lion, there is always a danger lest they should get frightened and bolt.

My relatives placed us. I was told to sit behind —or, from the lion's point of view, in front of— the horses, with my rifle covering him. His last bound brought him close to me; then he crouched, with the intention, as it seemed to me, of jumping right over me on the horses. As he rose, I fired, and was fortunate enough to kill him outright, so that he nearly fell on top of me. My companions ran to my assistance; but I needed no help, for the lion was dead. He was a strong beast.

Hearing the shot, the other three hurried up, and then we all stood round the lion and talked the adventure over. A certain Hugo knelt down to mea-

EARLY DAYS AND PRIVATE LIFE

sure the lion's teeth, which were extraordinarily big. Thinking no harm, I jumped on the lion's stomach. As I did so, the air shook with a tremendous roar, which so frightened Hugo that he forgot his tooth-measurements and fell down flat upon his back. The others shook with laughter, for every hunter knows that, if you tread upon a lion's body within a short time of his death, he will give a short last roar as though he were still alive. The breath still in him, being forced from the stomach through the throat, produces the roar. Hugo, of course, knew this, but he had forgotten it, and was greatly ashamed of his fright. In fact, he was so angry that he turned on me to give me a good hiding. But the others stepped good-naturedly between us and made him see that it was only my ignorance that had given him so great a fright.

I shot my second lion behind the Magaliesberg on the Hex River. My uncle Theunis Kruger and I were after a herd of antelopes when, my horse being done up, I was left behind, alone. Riding at a foot-pace, I came upon a herd of lions. Escape on a tired horse was out of the question. Suddenly one of the lions left the herd and made a dash for me. I allowed him to come within twenty paces and then shot him through the head. The bullet passed through the head into the body. The lion fell, with his head turned away from me, but jumped up again immediately and returned to his companions, while I reloaded. The moment he reached the herd, he fell down dead. Encouraged by my success, I fired upon the others. But in vain. They escaped into the nearest mountain, and I was not able to follow them. A few years later, I had another encounter, on the same spot, with a herd of lions which had killed several of our oxen. These also escaped into the same mountain; but I succeeded in first shooting two of them. My companions, who were not so swift of foot, lost their quarry.

I shot my fifth lion in the Lydenburg district, when on a trek towards the Elephant River. We were pursuing a brute that had robbed us of several oxen. I at that time had a good and faithful dog, which was my constant companion, and which used to track the lions through the bushes. When he found the lion, he stood still, loudly giving tongue till the lion roared angrily back at him. When the dog saw me coming, he stood aside a little. Now the lion got ready for me; but, at the moment of springing, the dog seized him from behind, and a bullet at close quarters dispatched him quickly. This made the fifth lion that I killed by myself. In company with others, I have of course shot a great many more.

During a march against Moselikatse, who, a short time previously, had surprised and cut down our

EARLY DAYS AND PRIVATE LIFE

people, I was ordered to set out with a strong patrol from Wonderfontein, where we left our wagons, to reconnoiter the enemy's position. At Elephant's Pass, in the neighborhood of Rustenburg, we came across a big herd of elephants. The pass owes its name to this encounter. My father went after them, but Commandant Potgieter stopped him from shooting, as the enemy might be nearer than we knew. Those were the first elephants I saw.

My first rhinoceros I encountered during that same expedition. As I was slightly in advance of the others, my uncle Theunis Kruger gave me permission to fire, and I was so fortunate as to bring him down with the first shot. I had an ugly experience on the next occasion that we—my brother-in-law and faithful hunting companion, N. Theunissen, and I—hunted rhinoceros. I must mention that we had made an agreement by which that one who behaved recklessly or, through cowardice, allowed game which was only wounded to escape should receive a sound thrashing. There was something wrong with my rifle on the morning we started, and I was obliged to take an old two-barreled gun, one barrel of which was injured; consequently its driving power was considerably lessened. I knew that a shot is thrown away on a rhinoceros unless you manage to send it through the thin part of its skin. We came across three of them, a bull and two cows.

They were *witharnosters*,[1] the most dangerous brutes. I told Theunissen to follow the two cows and not lose sight of them. It was my intention to kill the bull, and then join in pursuit of the cows. My comrade fired from time to time to let me know where he was, for he was soon out of sight in the thick undergrowth of the wood. When I had passed the rhinoceros, I jumped from my horse to shoot him. I placed myself so that he had to pass me within ten paces; this would give me a good opportunity to hit him in a vulnerable place. One bullet killed him outright. I mounted and rode as fast as I could go in the direction whence I heard Theunissen's gun, loading my rifle as I galloped. He had just sent a second bullet into one of the cows as I came up. The brute stood quite still. I saw that the animal was trying to get away through the underwood, which was less dense here than anywhere else, and I went after her. As I rode past my comrade, he called out:

"Don't dismount in front of the beast; she's awfully wild and can run like anything."

I did not pay much attention to the warning, knowing Theunissen to be over-cautious, but jumped off my horse and ran obliquely past the rhinoceros. She had scarcely caught sight of me

---

[1] *Rhenoster* is the Afrikander for rhinoceros. *Witharnoster* is a white rhinoceros.—*Translator's Note.*

EARLY DAYS AND PRIVATE LIFE

before she was in hot pursuit. I allowed her to come within a distance of three or four yards. When I fired, the percussion-cap refused, and there was no time for a second shot. The animal was close upon me, and there was nothing to be done but to turn round and run for dear life. In attempting to do so, my foot struck against the thorn roots, and I came down flat on my face. The beast was upon me; the dangerous horn just missed my back; she pinned me to the ground with her nose, intending to trample me to death. But, at that moment, I turned under her and got the contents of the second barrel full under the shoulder-blade, right into her heart. I owed my life to not letting go my hold on the gun during this dangerous adventure. The rhinoceros sprang away from me, but fell down dead a few yards away.

My brother-in-law hurried up as fast as he could, for he thought I had been mortally wounded by my own gun in this deadly combat. When he saw, however, that I was standing up safe and sound, he took his sjambok, and "according to contract" commenced to belabor me soundly, because I had, he said, acted recklessly, in disregarding his warning. Soft words and attempts to justify my conduct were thrown away on him; it availed me nothing to point out to him that the beast had already hurt and bruised me to such an extent that I might well be let off my hiding. I was eventually obliged to entrench myself behind the thorn-bushes. But this was the first and last time that Theunissen had occasion to thrash me.

I brought down my first buffalo very near the above spot. A flying herd of buffaloes came up from the valley by the bank of the stream. We hunted them, and I led. A buffalo-cow left the herd and made a rush for me as I jumped from my horse to shoot. I was ready, however, and, when she had come very near, shot her through the shoulder. The impetus of her onset knocked me down, and she rushed on over my body, fortunately without stepping on me. She took refuge on the opposite bank of the river, where we killed her.

My next adventure with buffaloes took place near Bierkraalspruit Farm. The underwood was from four to five feet high, and contained a number of buffaloes. Six of us came to hunt them. I forced my way alone through the bushes to see if it was possible to get a shot there, and passed a herd of buffaloes without being aware of them; but before long I came right upon a second herd of the beasts. A big buffalo at once turned his attention to me, but fortunately his horns were so wide apart that, in butting, the trees and bushes got mixed up between them, which not only broke the force of his attack, but hid me very effectually, if only for a few mo-

EARLY DAYS AND PRIVATE LIFE

ments, from his sight. Trying to get out of the wood, I found myself suddenly amongst the herd which I had passed a little while ago, without noticing them at the time. Even now I only realized the position when I ran right up against a buffalo that was just getting up from the ground. Angered at being disturbed, the beast tore my clothes from my back with his hoof. My comrades, as they stood outside the wood, took the buffalo's hoof for his horns, so high did he raise it in attacking me. Fortunately I escaped with a fright.

My brother-in-law N. Theunissen and I were hunting near Vleeschkraal, in the Waterburg district, when I had a most unpleasant encounter with a buffalo. I had hit a buffalo-cow, and she had escaped into the dense thorn-bushes. As it was impossible to follow on horseback, I gave my horse to my brother Nicholas, and followed the buffalo on foot. The great thing was not to lose sight of her in the thick undergrowth. Believing myself to be the pursuer, I was unpleasantly startled to find her suddenly facing and attacking me. I got ready to shoot, but my flint-lock missed fire, so I had to run for it. The rains had been heavy, and just behind me was a big swamp into which I fell as I jumped out of the enraged animal's way. The buffalo fell in after me, and stood over me in a threatening attitude before I had time to get up.

THE MEMOIRS OF PAUL KRUGER

My rifle was in the water and useless; but, fortunately for me, as the buffalo butted at me, she rammed one of her horns fast into the ground of the swamp, where it stuck. I got hold of the other and tried with all my strength to force the animal's head under the water and so suffocate her. It was a difficult thing to do, for the horn was very slippery on account of the slimy water, and I needed both hands and every atom of strength I had to keep her head under. When I felt it going, I disengaged one of my hands to get at the hunting-knife, which I carried on my hip, in order to rid myself of my antagonist. But, if I could not hold the brute with two hands, I certainly could not hold her with one, and she freed herself with a final effort. She was in a sad plight, however, nearly suffocated and her eyes so full of slime that she could not see. I jumped out of the swamp and hid behind the nearest bush, and the buffalo ran off in the opposite direction. My appearance was no less disreputable than the buffalo's, for I was covered from head to foot with mud and slime. Theunissen, hearing the row we made, knew that something was amiss, but he could not come to my assistance. It was impossible to get through the undergrowth of thorns on horseback.

When I had cleaned myself down a little, I got on the track of the rest of the herd, and succeeded in shooting two.

EARLY DAYS AND PRIVATE LIFE

I was never so near losing my life as once during a race with an elephant. One day, Adrian van Rensburg and I were on the veldt looking for elephants. Van Rensburg was behind me, when the first herd came in sight. I galloped on to get a good shot at them. I could not wait for van Rensburg, for the horse I was riding that day was a particularly spirited animal, and had the habit of running round me in a circle after I dismounted. This necessitated my quieting and holding him, and so some time was lost before I was ready to shoot. As I jumped down, one of the elephants caught sight of me, and came through the bushes as fast as she could go. At the moment of dismounting, I knew nothing of my danger, and had not the least idea that an elephant was after me. Van Rensburg, however, saw everything, and called out as loudly as he could to warn me. I turned and saw that the elephant was flattening the bushes behind me with her heavy weight as she broke though the underwood. I tried to mount, but the elephant was already upon me, and the weight of the underwood, trodden down and held together by the bulk of the elephant, pinned me to the ground. I found it impossible to mount. I let go of my horse, freed myself with a tremendous effort, and sprang right before and past the elephant. She followed, trumpeting and screaming, hitting out at me fiercely with her trunk. Now came a race for life or death. However, I gradually increased the distance between us; but that was a race I am never likely to forget.

The Kaffirs who were with us were about a hundred yards away. When they saw what was happening, they too commenced to run; so there we were: the Kaffirs first, I after them, and after me the elephant in furious pursuit. While running, the idea came to my mind that I would catch the Kaffir who was the poorest runner, and, in case the elephant bore down on him, step suddenly aside and kill her at close quarters. I had kept hold of my rifle, a big four-pounder. But the elephant was so tired out by this time, that she herself put a stop to the hunt by standing still. Just then van Rensburg came up, but his horse stepped into a hole covered with grass, and both horse and rider came down, for van Rensburg's foot had caught in the stirrup. Meanwhile, the elephant had disappeared. After van Rensburg had found his legs again, I said to him:

"Hunt in that direction," pointing with my finger, "and try to catch my horse!"

The elephant, in making her escape, had turned first to the north and then to the west, the direction in which the herd had moved on. I said to van Rensburg:

"When you have found my horse, bring it after

EARLY DAYS AND PRIVATE LIFE

me. Meanwhile, I will follow the herd of elephants, and not lose sight of them till you join me."

I soon came up with the female elephant that had pursued me. The calf ran a little way behind her. I passed it quickly to get near the mother; but it screamed when it saw me, and the mother, who turned round quickly at the cry, just caught sight of me as I jumped into the bushes. I ran as fast as I could through the underwood, and came suddenly upon van Rensburg, who had caught my horse.

"There are tse-tse flies here," he said; "we must turn back."

"Very well," I answered, "you go on, but I must get a shot first at these elephants which have given me so much trouble."

The mother and her calf had meanwhile disappeared, but, before I made my way back, I was so lucky as to shoot two of the herd. Unfortunately my horse, whose name was Tempus, had been stung by the poisonous flies, and shortly after our return, at the commencement of the rainy season, it sickened and died.

When quite a youth I encountered a tiger or panther. My Uncle Theunis, his son and I were hunting antelope, or elands, near Tijgerfontein Farm, in the neighborhood of Ventersdorp, and we soon found an antelope in the cover. My cousin rode in front and my uncle followed him; there was a distance of about forty yards between them. Suddenly, a panther appeared and made for us at a furious rate, although we had given him no provocation whatever. He overtook my uncle; but the latter's well-aimed shot brought the panther to the ground at the very moment when he was leaping on the horse which my uncle was riding.

A big lion-hunt, in which several of us took part, gave me the opportunity of witnessing a remarkable instance of canine fidelity. We had a whole pack of hounds with us. When they had found the herd of lions, they surrounded it, barking furiously. One of the hounds would go no further from us than about twenty paces. There he stood barking; but nothing could induce him to join the pack: he was too frightened to do that, and too faithful to leave us. One of the lions made for us and then the poor terrified hound was the only one that did not run away. He stuck to his post. He trembled and howled with fear, to say nothing of more visible signs of distress, and every second he looked round anxiously at his master to see if he were still there, hoping, I dare say, that he would fly, and that the dog might follow at his heels. But the master stayed and so the dog stayed. The lion was within ten paces of the dog when we shot him. And even now the timid dog was the only one of all the noisy pack that attacked him as he fell

EARLY DAYS AND PRIVATE LIFE

under our fire. He nearly died of fear, but remained at his post for love of his master.

In the year 1845, my two brothers Douw and Theunis, Douw's wife, my own wife and I were making a halt near Secucuni's town, not far from the place where the Spekboom River joins the Steenpoort River, in the north of the Transvaal. We outspanned, and I went, in the course of the day, on the veldt to shoot some game. I was mounted, and carried my old big four-pounder. After about an hour's ride, I came across a rhinoceros and shot at it. But I only succeeded in wounding the animal, and it fled into the wood. I dismounted quickly, ready to shoot again, but moved only a few steps away from my horse, lest the rhinoceros should turn to attack me, in which case it would be necessary to remount at once. I succeeded in getting a second shot; but, at that very moment, my rifle exploded just where I held it with my left hand, and my left thumb, the lock and the ramrod lay before me on the ground and the barrel of the gun behind me. I had no time to think, for the furious animal was almost upon me; so I jumped on my horse and galloped away as fast as I could, with the rhinoceros in fierce pursuit, until we came to the ford of a little spruit, when my pursuer came to the ground and so allowed me to ride quietly in the direction of our wagons. During the next day, our people, guided by the track of my horse, went to the spot, and there they found the rhinoceros still alive, and, following the trail of blood, discovered the remains of the rifle and my thumb.

My hand was in a horrible state. The great veins were torn asunder and the muscles lay exposed. The flesh was hanging in strips. I bled like a slaughtered calf. I had succeeded in tying a large pocket-handkerchief round the wound while riding, to save the horse from being splashed with blood. When I got to the wagons, my wife and sister-in-law were sitting by the fire, and I went up to them laughing so as not to frighten them. My sister-in-law pointed to my hand, which looked like a great piece of raw meat, the handkerchief being saturated with blood.

"Look what fat game brother Paul has been shooting!" she said.

I called out to my wife to go to the wagon and fetch some turpentine, as I had hurt my hand. Then I asked my sister-in-law to take off my bandolier, and she saw that my hand was torn and noticed how white I was, for I had hardly any blood left in my body. I kept on renewing the turpentine bandages, for turpentine is a good remedy to "burn the veins up," as the Boers say, and thus to stop the bleeding. I sent my youngest brother—he was still really young at the time—to borrow as much turpentine as he could get from the nearest farm, which was about half an hour's ride away. Herman Potgieter, who

EARLY DAYS AND PRIVATE LIFE

was afterwards so cruelly murdered by the Kaffirs, came over with his brother. The former got into the wagon and, when he saw the wound, cried out:

"That hand will never heal; it is an awful wound!"

He had to get down again as quickly as possible, for he was nigh fainting. But his brother said, possibly to comfort me:

"Nonsense; I have seen worse wounds than that: get plenty of turpentine."

We inspanned and drove to the farm. Every one there advised me to send for a doctor and have the hand amputated; but I positively refused to allow myself to be still further mutilated of my own free will. The two joints of what was once my thumb had gone, but it appeared that it would still be necessary to remove a piece of bone. I took my knife, intending to perform the operation, but they took it away from me. I got hold of another a little later and cut across the ball of the thumb, removing as much as was necessary. The worst bleeding was over, but the operation was a very painful one. I had no means by me of deadening the pain, so I tried to persuade myself that the hand on which I was performing this surgical operation belonged to somebody else.

The wound healed very slowly. The women sprinkled finely-powdered sugar on it, and, from time to time, I had to remove the dead flesh with my pocket-knife; but gangrene set in after all. Different remedies were employed, but all seemed useless, for the black marks rose as far as the shoulder. Then they killed a goat, took out the stomach and cut it open. I put my hand into it while it was still warm. This Boer remedy succeeded, for when it came to the turn of the second goat, my hand was already easier and the danger much less. The wound took over six months to heal, and, before it was quite cured, I was out hunting again.

I account for the healing power of this remedy by the fact that the goats usually graze near the Spekboom River, where all sorts of herbs grow in abundance.

CHAPTER II

COMMENCEMENT OF PUBLIC ACTIVITY

CHAPTER II

COMMENCEMENT OF PUBLIC ACTIVITY

Journey to the Sand River in 1852—The Sand River Convention—Punitive expedition against the Kaffir chief Secheli—Kruger's life in danger—Vindictive raid on the Kaffir chiefs Makapaan and Mapela—Kruger alone in the cave among the besieged Kaffirs—He recovers Potgieter's body—Expedition against Montsioa—Kruger charges a band of Kaffirs single-handed.

I WAS appointed a deputy field cornet as early as 1842, but my position was not one of any importance until 1852, when I was elected a full field cornet. In this capacity, I accompanied, in that year, old Commandant General A. W. J. Pretorius[1] to the Sand River, where the famous Sand River Convention was concluded.

In that same year, the expedition against the Bechuana chief Secheli took place. I took part in it as a commandant. This Secheli was protecting an-

[1] After Pretorius, who had commanded during the War of Independence against England in the Free State, came to the Transvaal, the popular assembly of 1849 elected Potgieter Commandant General for life; but eventually, in order to avoid unpleasantness, it became necessary to appoint three commandants general all possessing equal powers. Pretorius, accordingly, became Commandant General of the Potchefstroom and Rustenburg districts where Kruger lived.—*Note by the Editor of the German Edition.*

other Kaffir chief, called Moselele, who had committed several murders in the South African Republic, and refused to deliver him up. The demand for Moselele's surrender was received with the insolent reply:

" Who wants Moselele can come and fetch him out of my stomach."

Secheli meant to convey that Moselele was as safely hidden with him as the food which he had eaten. A commando under Chief Commandant Scholtz, with myself as deputy-commandant, was sent to punish him. When the commando arrived before Secheli's town, the Kaffir chief sent a messenger to Commandant Scholtz to say that he would do nothing to him on the morrow, as that was a Sunday, but that he would duly settle his account on the Monday. At the same time, he very artlessly asked for some coffee and sugar, probably in return for his amiability in "letting us off" for Sunday. Commandant Scholtz sent back word to Secheli that he had coffee and sugar, but none to give away. He promised, however, to give him pepper on Monday.

On Monday morning the battle began. I was well in front, and brought down a number of Kaffirs with my four-pounder, which I had loaded with coarse shot. When the mountain on which Secheli's town lay was already partly taken, Louw du Plessis, who was serving the guns, accidentally hit a large rock, and the

PUBLIC ACTIVITY

ball, rebounding, struck my head with such force that I fell to the ground unconscious. A certain van Rooyen had to help me to my feet, and at the same time bound up my aching head in a cloth. While I was lying unconscious and van Rooyen was busying himself about me, a Hottentot servant of my brother's, thanks to his accurate aim, kept the Kaffirs at a safe distance. When I came to myself, the first thing I saw was that the Kaffirs were creeping up behind rocks and boulders, and I realized the danger to which my burghers would be exposed if they were not warned in time. I at once got up to lead the attack on the dangerous points, although my wound prevented me from carrying my musket. The Kaffirs kept up a hot fire from every cave and gorge, but, after a sharp fight, the burghers succeeded in driving them from the mountain.

My life was in danger for a second time during this same battle. One of the enemy's bullets, fired from a huge rifle, struck me on the chest and tore my jacket in two. The artful Secheli afterwards said that he had, up to the last, had it in his power to drive us back, but that, when I had once laid my hands on his brandy-bottle, I became invincible. As a matter of fact, I have never tasted a drop of brandy.

After hostilities were concluded, Commandant Scholtz sent up to the house of Livingstone, the English missionary, which was not far from the Kaffir town. Here Theunis Pretorius found a complete workshop for repairing guns, and a quantity of materials of war which Livingstone was storing for Secheli. This was a breach of the Sand River Convention of 1852, which prescribed that neither arms nor ammunition should be supplied to the Kaffirs, and that they should not be permitted to provide either for themselves. Scholtz accordingly confiscated the missionary's arsenal, and in consequence the Boers were abused by Livingstone throughout the length and breadth of England, and slandered in every possible way as enemies of the missionaries and cruel persecutors of the blacks.

As a matter of fact, the Boers were neither opposed to the mission nor enemies of the natives. Their principle was to allot a certain district to every tribe that kept quiet and peaceful and was willing to accept civilization; such district to be proportionate to the size of the tribe. The missionaries who wished to labor among the natives also received free grants of land for the erection of churches and for private purposes. Even before the arrival of the missionaries beyond the Vaal, some of the Boers had instructed their native servants in the Gospel. But they were often brought into unpleasant contact with the native tribes owing to the engagement into which they had entered to deprive the natives of the arms which the latter were constantly smuggling into the

PUBLIC ACTIVITY

country. This engagement was faithfully kept so that England might have no opportunity to accuse them of violating the treaty and, consequently, to annul the Sand River Convention, which guaranteed the liberty of the emigrants north of the Vaal.[1]

[1] The missionaries seem often to have failed to understand that, for the Boers, the native question was, necessarily, not only religious and humanitarian, but also political. South Africa has room for only one form of civilization, and that is the white man's civilization; and, where there was only a handful of white men to keep hundreds of thousands of black natives in order, severity was essential. The black man had to be taught that he came second, that he belonged to the inferior class which must obey and learn. Lest it should appear as though the friendly and reasonable position adopted by the Boers in this matter had only developed gradually in recent years, I may point out that, in 1882, Mr. Kruger spoke to the following effect in his program issued before his first election and, afterwards, in the name of his people, as President :

"Native politics in a Republic such as ours, where so many Kaffir tribes live among us and all around us, offer very exceptional difficulties. The chief principle that must always be borne in mind is that savages must be kept within bounds, and always overruled by justice and morality."

And again:

"Much is being said about a universal native policy for the various states of South Africa. All who know the difficulties of this problem will most certainly agree with me when I say that the greatest benefactor of South Africa would be the man who could provide a completely satisfactory solution to this question. That man is perhaps as yet unborn. Meanwhile, as regards our Republic, her duty, or, rather, her mission is clear and simple. Every Kaffir tribe within our boundaries must be taught to respect the authority of our Government, and, in order that the laws, by which these tribes also benefit, may be equitably administered, they must bear their share of the public burden. When once the disastrous influence of foreigners and enemies of the Republic, who now so often try to persuade these unfortunate Kaffirs that they need not consider themselves subjects of the Republic, when once this influence has been done away with, then the time will have come when the native tribes will reap the prosperous fruit of the old principle of the Republic, by which every tribe of any importance has a fixed territory appointed to it, under the protection of the Government. For what was determined in the Convention regarding

THE MEMOIRS OF PAUL KRUGER

The next war in which I took part under Commandant General Pretorius was that of 1853, against the Kaffir chiefs Mapela and Makapaan, in the Waterberg district, near Makapaanspoort. This was an expedition to avenge the foul murder of Herman Potgieter, brother of the late Commandant General.[1] This Potgieter was a splendid shot and a great elephant-hunter. Mapela had sent for him, saying that there happened to be an exceptionally large number of elephants in his territory. More-

this distribution of territory is nothing more than the old law of the Republic. As for the future, I cherish the hope that some time, under God's blessing, it will come to this, that order, industry and the fear of God will make the Kaffir also a happy and contented subject of the South African Republic."

At the end of the speech delivered at his inauguration as State President in 1888, in connection with his admonition to the children and teachers to profit by the advantages of the education provided by the Republic, he added these words:

"You colored people,

"A short word to you too. You have a right to the protection of the laws of this Republic. Whether you make use of the opportunities given you to acquire civilization depends upon yourselves. You are free to accept civilization or to reject it. For you also I pray for the blessing of Almighty God."

Kruger was elected President upon the first of these declarations, and he called down a blessing upon the blacks, on a solemn occasion, in his official character. This, therefore, permits us to draw definite conclusions as to the attitude of the people in regard to this question.—*Note by the Editor of the German Edition.*

[1] Commandant, afterwards Commandant General Hendrik Potgieter, who is so closely connected with the history of the Kruger family, had, in the meantime, died, at the beginning of March, 1855, and his son Piet had been appointed to succeed him as Commandant General for the Lydenburg and Zoutpansberg districts.—*Note by the Editor of the German Edition.*

PUBLIC ACTIVITY

over, he asked Potgieter to come to see to his cattle, which were in Mapela's charge, the latter receiving the milk of the cows in return for his trouble: an arrangement which had been made at Mapela's request. On receiving this message from Mapela, Potgieter set out with his son Andries, a few burghers and his colored groom. When they arrived at Mapela's, the wagons were, as usual, deposited in the Kaffir town. At first, the Kaffirs were very friendly in their conversation with Potgieter and his companions, and described to him the place where the elephants were to be found. Suddenly, however, they fell upon the whole company, killed Potgieter's son and companions and dragged Potgieter himself to the top of a hill, where, shouting and dancing for joy, they skinned him alive in the presence of his groom. The poor man was not released from his sufferings until his murderers had torn the entrails from his body. The groom, who was allowed to go free, afterwards showed me the spot where this butchery had taken place.

While Mapela was engaged in this horrible business, Makapaan, in a time of peace, when nobody suspected any harm or danger, suddenly attacked a number of women and children who were quietly traveling from Zoutpansberg to Pretoria. The two chiefs had arranged that they would between them murder all the white people in their respective districts. When these foul deeds became known, it was decided that the Kaffir chiefs should be punished.

General Piet Potgieter, the nephew of the so cruelly murdered Herman Potgieter, set out with 100 men from Zoutpansberg to avenge the murder. At the same time, Commandant General Pretorius left Pretoria, with 200 men, on the same errand. I was second in command of the latter's commando. Before these two commandos had united, the Kaffirs made a night attack on Potgieter's laager, but were fortunately repelled. After the two commandos had joined forces, the Kaffirs were driven back into their mountains, where they hid in caves and ravines. The joint commandos kept them imprisoned in these caves in order to starve them into surrender.

After the Kaffirs had been besieged for some time and suffered greatly from famine, without our getting any nearer to effecting our object, I endeavored to end the matter and bring about a surrender by stratagem. With this object in view, I crept in the dark, unseen, into the cave where the Kaffirs lay hidden. I sat down among them and began to talk to them in their own language, as though I were one of themselves, and suggested that it would surely be better to surrender than die of hunger. I also said that I was certain that the white men would not kill us, and offered myself to go to the white men to

PUBLIC ACTIVITY

treat with them. Suddenly an armed Kaffir exclaimed:

"*Magoa!*" (White man!)

But this dangerous moment also passed, for, when the Kaffir shouted "*Magoa!*" all the others fled deeper into the cave, and I jumped up and ran after them, right into the back of the cave. The Kaffirs now began to hunt for the white man, looking for him in every direction, except where he was, in their very midst. When they had quieted down a little, I once more addressed them in their own language, and urged them to surrender. Finally, I succeeded in bringing 170 or 180 women and children out of the cave, and it was not until I was outside that they perceived that it was I and not a Kaffir who had been talking to them. My intention had really been to effect a voluntary surrender of the Kaffirs, and thus to get hold of their guilty captains. But I was unable to attain this object and we had to continue the siege.

Commandant General Pretorius was very angry at my imprudence, punished me severely for venturing to go alone among the Kaffirs in their caves, and ordered me away from the caves. Before the siege was over, I had one more narrow escape from death. In one of the fights, Commandant General Potgieter was hit by a shot fired from a crevice in the rocks. He was standing close to the edge of a rocky wall, giving directions to his Kaffir, when the fatal shot struck him. Potgieter fell down into the midst of a Kaffir trench. I saw this happen, and rushed down at once to try at least to save the body. The Kaffirs aimed a furious fire at me from the loop-holes in their entrenchments, but the burghers answered the fire no less heartily; and I was able to leap over the wall of the entrenchment, to lift the body over the wall, leap back, protected by the smoke of the powder, and bring the body safely back with me. Potgieter was a big, heavy man, and I had to exert all my strength to carry my dead friend back to his people.

One of the Kaffirs who had been captured said that he could show us some hidden caves where elephants' tusks lay in heaps. Pretorius sent me with this Kaffir to fetch the tusks. While on this expedition, I came upon a number of blood-stained garments which had belonged to the women and children murdered by the Kaffirs, as well as remains of portions of human bodies which the Kaffirs had roasted on the spit: roasted shoulders, arms, etc. The Kaffir who was to show me where the tusks were hidden also wore clothes which had clearly belonged to murdered white men. When at last we reached the cave where the ivory was supposed to be, the Kaffir tried to escape, and it cost me a great effort

PUBLIC ACTIVITY

to recapture him. The elephants' tusks were a mere cheat.

Soon after this, the resistance of Makapaan's men came to an end. It had been found impossible to induce them to leave their caves, and they had shot every one who approached. There was therefore nothing for it but to starve them out. Many hundreds died of hunger. A small portion of them escaped through underground passages into the mountains. Several were captured and brought before the court-martial. I was out hunting at the time, and before I came back they had all been shot under martial law. It was absolutely necessary to shoot these cannibals, especially as none of the culprits were delivered up and the chief had disappeared. The children of the tribe, as soon as they fell into the hands of the Boers, were *ingeboekt*, that is to say, portioned out among Boer families and kept under strict legal supervision until they came of age.

The commando now turned its attention to Mapela, Makapaan's ally. I did not join this expedition at first. Commandant General Pretorius sent me with a small commando to Maraba's town, where we had heard that a large number of Makapaan's cattle had been stored. I was to look into this matter and attack Maraba's town if it offered any resistance. But I met with none. Some of the Kaffirs fled, and the remainder surrendered. The latter declared that they had some of Makapaan's cattle, that they had never shared in his crimes, and that they were quite willing to restore such of his stolen cattle as were in their possession. This was done, but only a thousand head were discovered. As soon as I had possession of the cattle, I returned, leaving Maraba's Kaffirs unharmed. I reached the other commandos in time to join them on their march against Mapela. But Mapela's Kaffirs had also fled for the greater part, so that there was practically nothing to do. A few wagons, some chests, and other things which had belonged to the murdered whites were discovered on a kop near Mapela's town. These goods the commandos carried back with them.

Mapela's punishment was not effected until many years later, in 1858. Meanwhile, he had committed several other outrages; and it had also become necessary to take away the fire-arms which he had managed to obtain. A commando under General Schoeman, with myself as assistant general, set out against him. But Mapela had entrenched himself on the summit of a high kop, consisting of sheer rocky walls on every side. I called for volunteers to storm this fortress, and about 100 men came forward. With these, I went in the night, unseen, to the foot of the mountain. The commando now took off their *veldschoen*, so as noiselessly to climb the steep gorge that formed the only way to the top, and thus surprise

PUBLIC ACTIVITY

the Kaffirs. I went first with a patrol, and had got half-way up the mountain when we were discovered. A sentry allowed me to come up quite close to him, and then fired. Fortunately the gun refused. I did not notice the man until I heard the click of the trigger; I aimed and shot him dead at my feet. Thereupon the Kaffirs who held the gorge began to fire from every side. My gun-carrier fell. I myself ran back as fast as I could to my comrades.

"Forwards!" I shouted. "On with your *veldschoen*, and have at them without mercy!"

So the pass was seized and we took up our positions on the top until daybreak. The Kaffirs had retired still further, but charged when they caught sight of the first group of burghers, consisting of about 15 men, preparing for the attack. By the time, however, that they were still fifty paces off, this handful of burghers had been reinforced and now numbered about 100 men. Our fire mowed down the blacks in rows, and they rushed away in wild flight. From the rocky plateau, another road, or rather a ladder of trees, led down to the further side. Here the fugitives flung themselves down, and more were killed in this way than fell in the actual battle. The trees were hung with dead men, for all was thick forest below. Mapela himself escaped.

I had hardly returned from the first unsuccessful expedition against Mapela when, in December 1853, I had again to go on commando, this time against the chief Montsioa, who lived on the *hoogeveld* between Schoonspruit and Marico, on the Harts River. This chief had taken advantage of the very severe weather, accompanied by a heavy fall of snow, to steal a large number of cattle from the Boers, and had, at the same time, murdered one of the cattle-owners and then fled to Setlagoli in British Bechuanaland. When the Boer commando which had been sent against him reached the neighborhood of Setlagoli, it suddenly found itself in the midst of an enormous swarm of locusts. The Kaffirs had also seen this swarm, and when they saw the dust raised by the approaching commandos, they thought it was the locusts, and allowed the enemy to approach their town without preparing to receive him. When the commando was close to the town, Commandant General Pretorius sent me[1] to the captain to explain why the commando had come, and to demand that Montsioa should come out to justify himself. The captain, however, was not in the town, and I had to go on to the capital; and, before I had reached it, the Kaffirs suddenly attacked me and my escort. I was some distance in front of the others, and my position was most critical. My horse was

[1] Kruger was a commandant, but, in this case, acted as an adjutant to the general.—*Note by the Editor of the German Edition.*

PUBLIC ACTIVITY

quite exhausted. Flight was out of the question. I rode on at a walking-pace, so as not to attract the attention of the Kaffirs. When the foremost Kaffirs were quite close to me, four burghers came hurrying up, and this first drew the Kaffirs' attention to my person, and they turned against me. I now forced my horse into one last gallop and charged the Kaffirs, to make them think that my horse was still in good condition. This stratagem succeeded; the Kaffirs turned and fled, and I and my four companions got safely away. I took my exhausted horse back to the other cattle belonging to the commando, and proposed to go on foot, with the others, against the Kaffirs. Commandant Schutte tried to persuade me to relinquish this plan, as, being on foot, the Kaffirs might easily take me prisoner; but I replied:

"Most of the Kaffirs are on foot too, and, if it comes to running, the Kaffirs will not catch me easily."

When Schutte saw that I was not to be persuaded, he told his groom to give me his horse and return to camp. So I rode on to the battle. The Kaffirs numbered about 500, while the burghers who had gone on ahead to oppose them were only 40 men in all, and of these a few had remained behind with the wagons and the cattle. Our small band, however, managed to cause the Kaffirs considerable loss and to put them to flight. Our losses were only a few wounded.

The commando also succeeded in recapturing the cattle. With the cattle were several Kaffir boys, who were sent back to their town by the general that same evening, under my protection. I was also instructed to tell the chief that the Boers had not come to fight him, but only to fetch the stolen cattle, and that we would come the next day to negotiate about this. I went close up to the town, set the boys free and returned to camp. The released captives delivered their message correctly, but it never came to negotiations, for the chief fled that same night. We did not pursue him, but returned to our farms with the cattle which we had recovered.

CHAPTER III

IN A POSITION OF COMMAND

CHAPTER III

IN A POSITION OF COMMAND

The first Basuto War—Kruger assists the Orange Free State against the Basutos and negotiates the peace with Moshesh—Kruger as general in the field against the Kaffir chief Gasibone.

AFTER our return from the expedition against Montsioa, Commandant General A. W. J. Pretorius fell seriously ill. When he realized that the end was at hand, he sent for me, but I had just gone on a hunting expedition in the Rustenburg district, and the messengers, unfortunately, did not reach me in time, so that, when I returned, I found that this great leader of the emigrants had passed away. This was most deplorable, for who knows what he might still have wished to discuss in his last moments. On the return journey from Montsioa's town, he had talked much to me on religious matters, and he might have had more to say to me on this subject.

A few days after his death, a letter arrived, addressed to the deceased, from the British Commissioners, Owen and Hogge,[1] in which Pretorius was

[1] These were the special commissioners who had been appointed by the Queen of England to settle relations on the eastern and northeastern

requested to take over the Orange Free State from the British Government on behalf of the emigrants. But that was now impossible, and the assumption of the government of the country of the Orange Free State from the hands of the English was now effected by Messrs. Venter, Boshoff and a few other burghers of the Free State. This, afterwards, led to serious differences between the younger Pretorius and the Orange Free State, for the communication was to the effect that the Free State should be transferred to Commandant General Pretorius and the emigrants. Young Pretorius, like many other burghers, was of opinion that the land had been handed over to his father and therefore to himself as his successor. The question led almost to civil war between the Free State and the South African Republic.

Marthinus Wessel Pretorius, the eldest son of the deceased Pretorius, was appointed Commandant General of the South African Republic in his father's stead, and, after a law had been passed providing for a president, he was also elected to the office a few years later. This title, however, did not then mean that he was president of the Republic, for the new statute was not universally recognized. He was merely president of the Government which he repre-

frontiers of the Cape of Good Hope, and who made the agreement with the Boer emigrants by which both the Free State and the South African Republic obtained their independence.—*Note by the Editor of the German Edition.*

IN A POSITION OF COMMAND

sented. He now began to put forward his pretended claims on the Free State, and, in 1857, issued a call to arms, because he was offended that his claims had been rejected. I was away on business, but was asked to return at once. I disapproved most strongly of the conduct of Pretorius, whom I found encamped with his troops on the Vaal River, and I told him very plainly what I thought. But, when I heard that the President of the Free State had made an agreement with Commandant General Schoeman, in the north of the Transvaal, which was that part of the country where the new law was not yet acknowledged, that the latter should come to the Free State's assistance I advised prompt action and that we should attack Boshoff without delay. We crossed the river to meet Boshoff, who was advancing with a large commando. When the opponents were close to one another, Boshoff sent one of his officers with proposals for a peaceful settlement. Pretorius was much in favor of this; nor were his men at all in a warlike mood. When the adversaries' messenger arrived, they were practising buck-jumping, so that the officer exclaimed in astonishment:

"Do they hold us so lightly?"

Pretorius sent me as negotiator; and I told Boshoff my opinion just as openly as I had told it to Pretorius:

"You are quite as guilty as your adversary," I

said. "Why do you take up arms, instead of impeaching Pretorius before the Volksraad? He would certainly have been punished."

Koos Venter, a big, strong man, who was standing by, began to rage against Pretorius, and kept on shouting:

"If I only had him here, I would wring his neck for him like a bird's."

At last my blood was up too, and I said:

"Mr. Boshoff, the matter can easily be settled. Let Koos take off his coat and I will take off mine, and we will fight it out. If he is beaten, you must submit to our conditions, and if he beats me, it will be the other way about."

But Venter would have none of this; he had no grudge against me, he argued. But I said:

"That has nothing to do with it. You stand up for your President and I for mine."

However, there was no duel, but Venter kept quiet after that, and a commission was appointed to meet on the Vaal River to settle the difference. Here, although I did not at all approve of it, I was called upon to defend the action of my President, who was himself violently attacked. In the end a compromise was arrived at, and Pretorius relinquished his unjust claims.

It was agreed in the contract that each section of the Boers should have the right to punish offenders

IN A POSITION OF COMMAND

in its own country. Now, however, two burghers who had sided with Pretorius in the Free State were charged with high treason and condemned to die on the gallows. Once again I had to go to act as mediator:

"Why do you again break the compact?" I asked Boshoff.

"We break the compact? What do you mean?" he retorted.

"Well, are you not going to hang two of your people?"

"Yes, we have the right to do so: it says so in the agreement."

"Nothing of the sort. You have the right to punish certainly; but 'punish' means to 'chastise,' to admonish, to warn, and to correct by means of the chastisement."

And, when Boshoff would not allow this, I fetched a Bible and showed him that the Holy Writ distinguished between punishing and chastising. We may chastise a man with the prospect of death, but we may not kill him in order to punish him. The Free Staters gave in after this, and so the matter was finally settled.

Shortly afterwards, I had the opportunity of rendering the Free State a service. Ever since the Declaration of Independence, they had had difficulties with Moshesh, and these difficulties at last led to open war between Moshesh and the Free State. Moshesh was no contemptible adversary, and he had a large force at his command. His bands were continually making plundering inroads into the southern portion of the Orange Free State, and, when this came to my knowledge, I decided to go to the Free State and offer my services to the Government. President Pretorius accompanied me with about 50 men, under Field-cornet Bodenstein. At Osspruit, on the Upper Sand River, we came upon the first camp of the Free Staters. That same night, the Kaffirs robbed the herds of this camp. I sent Field-cornet Bodenstein with his men in pursuit, and they succeeded in regaining the cattle. From here we marched on by Winburg to Bloemfontein.

On our arrival, I offered myself to go to Moshesh to negotiate a peace. The Free State Government accepted my offer and gave me General Fick and Marthinus Schoeman as an escort. Moshesh lived on Thaba Bosigo Mountain. When we came to the foot of the mountain, I sent up a message to Moshesh that we had not come to fight him, but that I wanted to talk to him about peace. Moshesh sent back word:

"I will come down directly to speak with Mr. Kruger."

I was not disposed to wait, however, and at once climbed the mountain so as to go straight to Mo-

IN A POSITION OF COMMAND

shesh's town. When we reached the top, Moshesh was just coming to meet us. Magato, the Kaffir captain from the Rustenburg neighborhood, whom we knew and who happened to be with Moshesh, introduced me to him, saying:

"This is Paul Kruger."

Moshesh gave me his hand, and said:

"Is that Paul Kruger? How is it possible? I have heard tell of him for so many years, and now I am so old. How, then, can he still be so young?"

He took hold of my arm and led me to his house and into a room which no black dared enter, but which was always ready for the reception of white men.

After taking some refreshments, we at once proceeded to business. I began:

"Why do you kill one another for such a trifle? Why not, rather, arrange the matter amicably? You must surely see that war does you damage and makes you block the highroads for other nations with whom you are living at peace."

After much argument on both sides, Moshesh said at last:

"What you say is true, for everything I want in this house I have to buy from other nations. And, when the roads are blocked by war, of course I can get nothing." Then, changing the subject, "Are you the man," he asked, " who fetched Mapela down from his mountain? "[1]

I said:

" Yes."

Then Moshesh proceeded:

" Are you aware that two of my daughters were married to Mapela? " adding, after a moment's silence, " You need not think that it was your courage that brought Mapela down from his mountain, but it was the dispensation of God that punished Mapela for committing so foul a murder."

Now, as Moshesh was at every moment speaking of the dispensation of God and using pious words, I said to him:

" But if you are so devout, how do you come to have more than one wife? "

Moshesh replied:

" Yes, I have just about two hundred; but that is not half so many as Solomon had."

To which I made answer:

" Yes, but you surely know that, since Christ's time and according to the New Testament, a man may have only one wife."

Moshesh reflected for a moment and then said:

" Well, what shall I say to you . . . it is just nature."

---

[1] The trial of Mapela had just taken place.—*Note by the Editor of the German Edition.*

IN A POSITION OF COMMAND

In the evening, I sent for Moshesh again to come to me. Moshesh came, but this time dressed like an ordinary Kaffir, that is, not in European clothes. When he came in, I called to him:

"Why is Moshesh so long coming? Can't he come when I send for him?"

Moshesh answered:

"I am Moshesh."

"Oh," said I. "Are you Moshesh? Then why are you dressed like a woman?"

Moshesh laughed heartily.

That same evening, we made an agreement that the war was to stop at once. Moshesh agreed to call in his Kaffirs as soon as he received word that the Orange Free State had accepted the terms. A peace document was drawn up, and signed the following morning.

Moshesh then invited me to stay with him a little longer, as he wanted to pick me out a fine saddle-horse. I accepted the invitation, but my companions Fick and Schoeman did not care to wait any longer and went back alone. Moshesh then brought me an excellent saddle-horse as a present. The Government of the Orange Free State afterwards accepted the treaty drafted by Moshesh and myself, and this brought the first Basuto War to an end.

Before leaving Moshesh's town, I received a message from President Pretorius asking me to return at once and set out as general or, rather, assistant general, with a commando, against Gasibone, a Kaffir chief on the Harts River. This chief had stolen the white men's cattle, killed some of the men and carried off an old woman and a girl of eighteen. On receipt of this message, I at once jumped on my horse and rode to my home in the Magaliesberg, in the Rustenburg district. In three days, I spent over fifty hours on horseback. The commando had meantime assembled and was waiting for me near Klerksdorp, where I joined it after spending one day at my farm. On reaching the meeting-place, I found that the burghers had hardly any ammunition and no cattle for food. But we set out, nevertheless, in the hope of being able, on the way, to procure both from private sources. I also sent a message to the Orange Free State requesting them to provide us with what was necessary. But I did not obtain much here, as I had no money and had to buy on the promise of future payment. Our shortness of ammunition was such that we could not shoot any game, but I nevertheless devised a means of providing meat for my commando, by instructing the burghers to surround the game, drive it into the bends of the Vaal River and there kill it by beating it with sticks.

The whole commando was about 200 strong. When we approached Gasibone's place, Commandant Piet Venter came to our support from the Orange Free

IN A POSITION OF COMMAND

State with about 100 men, white and colored. It soon became evident that Gasibone had taken refuge with one of his subordinates, called Mahura, who lived in a mountain fastness, filled with ravines, further up the Harts River Gorge. I sent word to Mahura that I was coming in pursuit of Gasibone and that I should keep to the south side of the Harts River, also that Mahura was not to interfere with Gasibone, unless he was prepared to capture him and deliver him up. On receiving this message, Mahura, with the assistance of an interpreter, set free the old woman and the young girl who had been carried off by Gasibone. When our commando came to within a few thousand paces of the place where we knew Gasibone's camp to be, the two chiefs attacked us with united forces. We defeated them, and they fled into the caves and rocks with which the place abounded. The following morning, the commando attacked them there and hunted them out of their hiding-places. Gasibone fled in the night in the direction of British Bechuanaland, but, on the following day, he was found in the brushwood by a patrol, and fell after a sharp fight. Part of the men with him were taken prisoners, but afterwards released.

Meanwhile, the missionary who was with Mahura wrote to me on his behalf to say that he had done wrong in helping Gasibone, that he deserved to be punished, but begged for forgiveness and was willing to submit. I sent back word that I would gladly forgive him all, but that he must come to me to receive instructions as to his subsequent behavior. Mahura, however, did not come personally, on the pretence that he was too ill to travel, but sent one of his captains. I nevertheless appointed him chief of that particular Kaffir tribe, in Gasibone's place. The cattle which Gasibone had stolen were restored forthwith. Then the commando returned home again. For me it had been a year of hard work.

CHAPTER IV

THE CIVIL WAR: 1861–1864

CHAPTER IV

THE CIVIL WAR: 1861-1864

Kruger's protest against the violation of the Constitution by Commandant General Schoeman—Assembly of the people at Pretoria—Kruger's declaration of war—Attempts at a settlement and their frustration by Schoeman—Kruger by an act of the Reformed Church is qualified to hold office in the State—Fresh negotiations—Military preparations on both sides—The political contest develops into a religious war—Battle of Potchefstroom—Schoeman's flight—Renewed negotiations—The arbitration award of the Supreme Court rejected—Kruger insulted—Battle of Zwartkopje—Fresh negotiations—Mutual amnesty—The new elections—Kruger again Commandant General.

IN the year 1860, Pretorius visited the Orange Free State to settle public affairs there. He had become State President of the Republic two years previously, after the acceptation of the constitution, and now, on the retirement of President Boshoff, was also elected President of the Orange Free State. He owed his election to the Unionist Party there, since his chief aim was to amalgamate the two Republics. On attaining the second presidency, he was granted leave of absence for six months by the Volksraad of the South African Republic, of which he was also President, for the purpose of visiting the Free State. He probably expected to be able, within that time, to accomplish the union which he so much desired. During the President's absence, in accordance with an earlier resolution of the Volksraad, the oldest unofficial [1] member of the Executive Raad became Acting President of the South African Republic. In this case, the office fell to Johannes Grobler. He was associated, as the law required, with another member unconnected with the Government, and these two, together with the Commandant General, composed the Executive Raad. Towards the end of 1860, the Volksraad passed a resolution that the State President should hold no other office. Therefore Pretorius, who refused to renounce the Presidency of the Orange Free State, resigned that of the South African Republic.

But, when Grobler assumed the office of Acting President, Schoeman, the Commandant General,[2] opposed him, declaring that the post should have been his. He held public meetings to get this power transferred to himself and to obtain a vote of censure on the Volksraad. Finally, he summoned all the military officers to Pretoria, and, having assembled them,

[1] The official members were the President, the State Secretary and the Commandant General. The two others were non-official, or auxiliary members, whose presence was not required at every sitting.—*Note by the Editor of the German Edition.*

[2] After the Constitution had been accepted, there was as yet only one Commandant General.—*Note by the Editor of the German Edition.*

THE CIVIL WAR: 1861-1864

proposed to abolish the Volksraad and to confer legislative power on the Executive Raad. I, with some other officers, protested against this proposal, on the ground that it ran counter to the constitution, and eventually won over the majority of the officers to my view. But this did not in the least disturb General Schoeman. He went to the Government Office and demanded of Grobler the papers and documents belonging to the Government. Grobler offered strong opposition, but was finally forced to retire. I now proposed that a general public meeting should be summoned for the purpose of deciding the matter, and this proposal was also accepted by Schoeman's party. His supporters, however, came to the meeting armed, while their leader had, in the meantime, on his own responsibility, appointed a certain Johannes Steyn to be Commandant General. Neither I nor my adherents, of course, carried arms. I had no idea that the other side intended to bring weapons, but, even if I had known of their intention, I should still have gone unarmed with my men, for party feeling ran so high that a hand-to-hand encounter might easily have ensued, which would have led to civil war.

When I had gone as far as Daspoort, on my way to Pretoria, I received an order from General Schoeman to advance no further, but to remain where I was. I replied that I would certainly not turn back before reaching Pretoria, having once accepted an invitation to attend the meeting. As a matter of fact, I rode into the town and went at once to Schoeman's house. I asked him how it was that he wished to hinder my coming to Pretoria, although he had himself agreed to the plan of summoning a general meeting, to which all burghers were invited. I added that this meeting was the sole object of my visit. Now, just as I entered, a council of war happened to be taking place in Schoeman's house, under the presidency of Steyn, whom Schoeman had appointed Commandant General. As soon as he saw me, Steyn said:

" You must give in with a good grace. It's the best you can do."

I made him no answer, but turned to Schoeman and reproached him for having come armed to the meeting with his followers, while the other side had refrained from doing so. After I had spoken my mind plainly, I told him that I would inspan at once and return home with my burghers. But, when I turned to leave the room, some of Steyn's officers tried to seize me, while others signified their disapproval of such treatment and prevented my arrest. After I had left the house, Steyn ordered a gun, loaded with shrapnel, to be pointed at the laager of the opposition party and threatened to shoot unless a certain Jeppe were handed over to him. This

THE CIVIL WAR: 1861-1864

Jeppe was at that time the only printer in the Republic. His printing-press was at Potchefstroom, and Schoeman's party wished to have proclamations printed so that they might be quickly distributed and thus influence the burghers. I, of course, refused to grant this request; but the threat of Steyn's people, that they would open fire, made such an impression on Jeppe, who was standing behind me, that he rushed forward and gave himself up to the other side. I now inspanned to return to Rustenburg. I cried out at parting to Schoeman's men:

" Once I have crossed the Magaliesberg, you must look on me as an enemy."

Just as our wagons were moving away, President Pretorius arrived at Pretoria on his return journey from the Orange Free State and at once rode up to our wagons with a number of Schoeman's men, in order to speak to me and induce me to go no further. Schoeman's followers now declared that they would sooner throw away their guns than allow them to be a cause of strife. They were also willing that I should make a proposal to be submitted to the vote of the Volksraad. I therefore outspanned again and suggested that Pretorius, Proes the State Attorney, and myself should elaborate a proposal. This met with universal assent. At a meeting of us three men, it was agreed that a commission should be appointed to summon the Volksraad, which should then decide who had acted rightly and who wrongly. The public meeting endorsed this suggestion and at once appointed a commission with Stephanus Lombard as president. The commissioners now entrusted three members of the Volksraad, including the president, Christian Klopper, with the task of summoning that assembly. Thus, at length, a properly-convened Volksraad met, declared, after thorough investigation, that Schoeman was guilty of breaking the law, and deposed him from the office of Commandant General. The Volksraad resolved further that a special court should settle all the resulting points of dispute. It nominated W. van Rensburg as acting State President, and Theunis Snyman as Commandant General. When, however, the special court sat to deal with these matters, Schoeman violently put an end to its proceedings.

I had returned home after the session of the Volksraad and happened to be on a hunting expedition on the Crocodile River, when the new complications arose. Messengers were sent to recall me. Now during the recent disputes many members of the *Hervormde* Church had reproached me with having no right whatever to meddle in public affairs. According to the constitution of the Republic, the *Hervormde* Church was the state church. Its members alone were entitled to exercise any influence in public affairs. Whoever was not a member of the *Her-*

THE CIVIL WAR: 1861-1864

vormde Church was not a fully-qualified burgher. Now I belonged to the *Christelijk-Gereformeerde* Church, recently founded, in 1859, by Dr. Postma, at Rustenburg. It is generally known in South Africa as the *Dopper,* or Canting Church. The actual derivation of the word *Dopper* cannot be stated with certainty. At that time, it was derived from the word *dop,* a damper or extinguisher for putting out candles. The meaning would seem to be that, just as a *dop* extinguishes a candle, so the *Doppers* extinguished all new thoughts and opposed all progress. As for the peculiar tenets of the *Dopper* Church, they consist in a strict adhesion to the decrees of the Synod of Dordrecht, of 1618 to 1619, and share the point of view of the Old Reformed Church. The service differs from that of the other Evangelical bodies in this particular, that no hymns except psalms are sung by the worshipers. The members of this Church were not recognized by the constitution, for, when it was drafted, they did not form an independent community.

Now when I was asked to give help in these fresh difficulties, I replied that people must put up with Schoeman's conduct. At any rate, I could not do or suggest anything, for I had no political standing. As a result of this, Acting President van Rensburg, who had been put in office by my party, caused a meeting to be called of the Council of the *Hervormde*

THE MEMOIRS OF PAUL KRUGER

Church, which passed a resolution conferring equal rights on the burghers of all Evangelical churches. As soon as I heard of this resolution, which was subsequently confirmed by the Volksraad, I rode to Pretoria, where I found President van Rensburg with a portion of his followers and also Schoeman with a number of his adherents.

The two parties were on hostile terms. I went at once to Schoeman's people, with the intention of persuading them to come to a peaceful understanding. I suggested that a meeting should be summoned of burghers from every part of the Republic and that all should acquiesce in whatever resolution the majority of the meeting might adopt. Both parties agreed to this proposal, and a meeting was called at Pretoria. Hither came a mass of burghers from all parts of the Republic, and it was resolved, by a large majority, to carry out the proposal which had been already accepted by the Volksraad: namely, that a special court should settle each separate question. But Schoeman resisted this proposal and called up all his men, who were still outside Pretoria, to rally round him. Thereupon van Rensburg, in his turn, ordered Commandant General Snyman to call a council of war and at once posted sentries to prevent Schoeman from sending out any more messages.

Pickets were now stationed at various points around Pretoria—a particularly strong one at

THE CIVIL WAR: 1861-1864

Aapjes River, where the suburb of Arcadia is now situated. The veteran Jacob Malan was in command of this post. He notified the Commandant General, on the following day, that his presence there was superfluous, as Schoeman's messengers easily made their way through the pickets and rode people down, if they did not get out of the way. Snyman then gave orders, that, if one of Schoeman's messengers should again come and refuse to halt when the challenge to do so was repeated, the watch must fire at his horse. Soon after this order was issued, a messenger came riding at full speed and paid no heed to the injunction to halt. The outpost thereupon shot the horse with a charge of large shot. The messenger turned, but as he was turning, his horse dropped. He himself was wounded by a shot in the arm. Thus was the first shot fired that began the Civil War.

On the same evening, the Commandant General, in conjunction with the military officers, issued an order that all burghers must assemble in the town in order to surround Schoeman and take him prisoner on the following day. But, during the night, Schoeman found a way of breaking through with his men as far as Potchefstroom. All who remained behind were visited with punishment by the Council of War. Schoeman then mustered a commando at Potchefstroom, to which spot General Snyman's commando now hastened. The Acting President and myself accompanied Snyman.

Schoeman's party now spread a report that I, Paul Kruger, was out with my men on commando to compel the recognition of my own church, the *Christelijk-Gereformeerde* Church, as the state church, instead of the *Hervormde* denomination. These rumors occasioned many to join Schoeman's side. Even in the district of Marico, he obtained adherents, including Jan Viljoen, the commandant of that district. As soon as the Government's commando, numbering about 500 or 600 men, reached Potchefstroom, President van Rensburg sent a message to Schoeman with a proposal that a joint commission should be appointed from both sides to find a way out of their difficulties. Schoeman agreed to this proposal, and appointed, on his side, Jan Kock, the father of General Kock, who fell in the late war, together with other burghers, to serve on the commission, while I, together with some others, was entrusted with the conduct of the peace negotiations by the Government party. The delegates met half-way between the two camps. Scarcely had we met, when Jan Kock said to me:

"So you want to make your church the state church?"

I answered quietly:

"Oom Jan, I need not take much trouble to contradict you. If you think a little, you must see for yourself that such a statement must be untrue. Here is the Government's laager. The President and all the officers belong to the *Hervormde* Church, and I scarcely know whether, out of 500 or 600 men, as many as twenty belong to my church. Therefore what you say about the churches cannot be true."

Afterwards I added:

" I have never thought of making the church to which I belong the state church. Nay, even if you were to offer to make it so, I should decidedly refuse, for our principle declares that Christ and no other must be the Head of the Church."

The commission was, however, unable to come to a decision, and the members separated without accomplishing any result.

On the following day, General Snyman sent me with a gun and a number of burghers to bombard the town from the south side. As soon as I arrived, I at once opened fire with the gun, and succeeded in disabling one of the enemy's guns with my third shot. General Schoeman replied from the town with artillery and rifle-fire. This duel of the guns lasted all day. On the following night, Schoeman, with his commando, quitted the town for a plateau on the northern side, in order thence to attack the Government party. But I had suspected Schoeman of this intention, and crept alone up the hills in order to observe the enemy's movements. When, at daybreak, I saw Schoeman's commando approaching, I hastened back to my men and gave them orders to get ready and follow me to the hills. That no time might be lost, I led the way with fifteen to twenty men, while the rest completed their preparations, and charged with them to within fifty or sixty paces of Schoeman's followers, who opened fire with shot and bullets. Of course, I and my men replied, and the firing grew so fierce that neither party could see the other for the smoke and we were obliged to take aim by instinct. I had three wounded, while the other side had to lament the loss of one killed and about fifteen wounded. General Schoeman, who was slightly wounded himself, fled on the same day into the Orange Free State, but was pursued by us and lost yet a few more followers, whom we took prisoners. On his farm in the Orange Free State, his people rallied once more, and General Snyman took the necessary steps to have his opponents arrested there. The Government of the Orange Free State was asked if it would allow such arrests to take place on that ground and territory. It replied that it had no objection, and even sent Landdrost Truter, of Kroonstad, to assist in making the arrests. But Schoeman was too quick for them. He retreated in the night in the direction of Wakkerstroom, and

THE CIVIL WAR: 1861-1864

once more rallied his commando on a farm at the junction of the Klip Stream and Vaal River.

The Government commando, which had at first withdrawn rather to the north, on the assumption that Schoeman would make for Pretoria, pursued him first to the farm I have mentioned, thence to Potchefstroom, and fell in with his laager at the Mooi River between the Loop Stream and Potchefstroom. Just as fighting was about to begin, a small band of Schoeman's people came up, among them being President Pretorius. He proposed that yet another commission should be appointed to settle our differences. The Government party agreed to this and laagered a few thousand paces above Schoeman's men, opposite Potchefstroom, on the Mooi River. The Government once more sent me with a few other burghers to serve on the commission, while Schoeman's party nominated President Pretorius and others. The place of meeting lay half-way between the laagers. I proposed that we should now definitely recognize the resolution of the Volksraad appointing van Rensburg Acting President and entrusting the punishment of the guilty to a special tribunal. One of the most hotly-debated points in our discussion was, who should sit as judge of this tribunal? But at last this question, too, was decided, after a debate of many hours, in accordance with my ideas. I had proposed to establish the tribunal in exact conformity with the requirements of the constitution. It was further resolved that President van Rensburg should summon the special court without delay. The decisions of the commission were accepted by both commandos; the members separated; the war seemed at an end.

President van Rensburg at once acted on this decision and summoned the special court. But, although the court was composed in equal parts of members drawn from both factions, the first case, which happened to be that of Andries du Toit, belonging to the Schoeman party, was given against him. This was enough. The remaining members of the party rode away. The costs of the court, as well as those of the commando, were given against Schoeman's party, and a council of war was to be held, to which his officers were also to be invited. It so happened that I had meantime been elected Commandant General, and was charged by the Government with the task of collecting the costs of the commando from the opposite side and, at the same time, bringing the officers to the council of war. I summoned a meeting for this purpose in the Heidelberg district, where I met with a most friendly reception from the field-cornet of that district, named Roets, a member of the opposite faction. I also succeeded in collecting, by peaceful means, a portion of the fines imposed, and in inducing a number of the officers opposed to me, including Commandant Jan

THE CIVIL WAR: 1861-1864

Marais, to accompany me to Pretoria. On my way to the meeting at Heidelberg, a young Boer perpetually rode in front of me and announced that " Paul Kruger was coming." To this he invariably added that he would not advise him to come, as it would go badly with him. Now, since I traveled by night as well as by day, I overtook this young man and, on the following morning, turned back from a farm, which he was just going to visit. The young man came straight up to me and began to rattle off his usual speech. I let him finish his say and then said to him:

" Young man, let me give you some good advice: do not repeat this foolish stuff any longer! Your whole party has already been guilty of quite enough disobedience against the administrative authority."

" Yes; but who are you, Oom? " asked the young man.

" Paul Kruger," I replied.

To hear these words and lay hold of his horse was for the young man the work of an instant. He trembled so violently in every limb that he could scarcely mount his horse. But, once he was in the saddle, he did not wait a moment. I tried at least to discover his name but could get no reply save a cry of terror, and then away he flew!

On my return from Heidelberg to Pretoria, I had a still more amusing experience. I was traveling with the above-mentioned Jan Marais to the farm of a certain Strydom in the Pretoria district. Mrs. Strydom knew Marais very well, and was aware that he belonged to Schoeman's party. But she did not know me, and thought I was one of his officers. Her husband had been summoned to serve as a magistrate in the local court, but had failed to appear, and had accordingly been condemned to pay a fine of £100, whereupon he had taken to flight. Mrs. Strydom told her visitors with complete unconcern that her husband had been obliged to fly from his house, because "this Paul Kruger" had condemned him to pay a fine of £100 on account of his failure to preside in the local court. Of course this fine was not imposed by me, but by the court itself. Yet she directed all her wrath upon "Kruger," and spoke without restraint in a most unpleasant manner about the Government party and specially about myself, who, "so to speak, was the head of the party." After she had continued these tirades against myself and my party for about half an hour, there arrived from Pretoria a certain Jan Bantjes, who was attached to the side of the Government. He saluted me, and, coming up, said:

"What, you here too, General? Are you taking Marais as your prisoner?"

"No," I answered, "he is going with me of his own free will to the council of war."

THE CIVIL WAR: 1861-1864

A light began to dawn on Mrs. Strydom, and her tongue was silenced by apprehension. In tones of earnest entreaty she said to me:

"Oh, General, I did not know who you were. Do not be angry at what I have said. I am so nervous by nature that I always talk to people as they talk to me, to avoid all unpleasantness. I only speak like that when I think people belong to the other side; but, if people of your party come, I speak quite differently. I have the sum here, which my husband was fined. I can fetch it you, if the general will only take it."

To this I, of course, replied that I had nothing to do with the money; neither could I take it, for the matter was one which concerned the court. But, from that moment until the time of my departure, Mrs. Strydom was more than amiable.

The council of war in Pretoria passed off without any noteworthy results. Shortly afterwards, I was instructed by President van Rensburg to go to the Orange Free State to settle the question of determining the boundary between the two States. When I reached Potchefstroom, I learned that Jan Viljoen, of Schoeman's party, the Commandant of Marico, was approaching with a commando to capture me. I rode to meet him with my small escort to ask what he wanted. Some of my men, including Field-cornet Sarel Eloff, dashed forward to seize a kopje, which seemed to be Viljoen's objective, and succeeded in reaching it before Viljoen. When they had secured this advantage, they cried out to Viljoen's men that they had no hostile intentions, but only desired a friendly conference. The others rode continually nearer, until they completely surrounded Eloff with his small band of comrades, whereupon they captured the whole company and rode off with them to their camp. When they were nearly opposite the place where I had remained with the rest of my men, Field-cornet Eloff suddenly put spurs to his horse and rode up to me. His guards of course set after him, as soon as they had recovered from their surprise, but they could not catch him on his good horse. The other prisoners were taken to the enemy's laager and afterwards declared that they had been threatened with all sorts of punishments, if I did not yield to the demands of Schoeman's party. They did not dare to make a prisoner of me, although I had only a few men with me. My camp had been surrounded, but it was impossible to surprise me, for I was prepared for everything. However, considering their overwhelming superiority in numbers and in order to avoid injuring the prisoners, I had resolved, if it came to a fight, to avoid an encounter. So I and Eloff determined to continue our journey to the Orange Free State, while the other burghers might better disperse to their homes. As

THE CIVIL WAR: 1861-1864

a matter of fact, we arrived without hindrance at Bührmann's farm, in the neighborhood of the Rhenoster River, in the Orange Free State, while several more of our burghers were made prisoners on their way home by Viljoen's men.

I was continually kept informed of the plans and intentions of Viljoen's commando by trusty messengers, and I made use of the same messengers to convey to the enemy the following intelligence. I allowed them to suppose that I never intended to return to the South African Republic, but should settle down in the Orange Free State, because there were so many disputes in the Transvaal. I even bought a farm in the Orange Free State, on condition of being allowed to give it back again, and sent for a team of oxen: nay, I even caused my family to prepare themselves for a trek, so as to make the news seem more probable. I had recourse to this stratagem chiefly that I might set free my imprisoned burghers. Shortly afterwards, I received a message that a large commando of the Opposition was on the way to Pretoria for the purpose of attacking a Government commando encamped on the Crocodile River. A small portion of the hostile commando had remained at Potchefstroom to guard the prisoners. When I learned that the prisoners had been set free and were dispersed, and when, at the same time, a messenger from the Government party came to me to ask what my plans were, I resolved to return immediately and join the Government commando on the Crocodile River. Pretorius, who in the meantime had resigned the office of President of the Orange Free State, happened at this moment to be at Potchefstroom. I let him know that I would pay him a visit, if it were at all possible, but found no time to do so. I did, however, push on in the night to Stompoorfontein Farm, in the Potchefstroom district, which belonged to Wolmarans, a member of the party. But I stayed there only about half an hour and journeyed on again to my farm, called Waterkloof, in the Rustenburg district, which I reached in the afternoon of the same day. Field-cornet Sarel Eloff, who had been with me the whole time, parted from me on the *hoogeveld*, and went straight to the Zwartruggen district to commandeer the burghers there. He promised to rejoin me in a few days with his men.

On the day after my arrival at the farm I rested, as it was Sunday, but the same night I pushed on to Zwartkopje, where President van Rensburg, with part of his burghers, was encamped. Here I met him, having hurried up on the news of the advance of a strong commando. On the following day, which was Tuesday, the enemy's commando was sighted. I had set a good watch and was early informed of their approach. The enemy seemed intent on occupying

THE CIVIL WAR: 1861-1864

Zwartkopje, while my men hurried to outstrip them and be the first to take up their stand on the kopje. Now began a race on both sides for the nearest kopje. Both sides came into collision at the top. I, with a man named Enslin, was in front. As he got off his horse, Enslin was already prepared to fire, but some one from the enemy's ranks called across:

"Don't shoot; let us talk: why need we kill one another?"

Enslin lowered his gun, but, just as he did so, received a bullet and fell dead into my arms. Thereupon a general engagement ensued, but, before it had lasted half an hour, the enemy made for their horses and fled in the direction of Pretoria.

My burghers now mounted their horses to pursue the enemy, but I stopped them by pointing out that they had not to do with enemies, but with brothers. Just at that moment, Field-cornet Eloff came up with 50 men, and wanted to continue the fight. But I would not let him, and, though dissatisfied at this, he listened to my arguments. President van Rensburg greatly appreciated this conduct on my part. When the enemy's burghers saw that they were not being pursued, they turned back to bring their wagons to a safe place. They encamped on a group of kopjes a few thousand paces distant from my men.

In the evening, I sent Eloff with some men to keep

THE MEMOIRS OF PAUL KRUGER

watch in the neighborhood of the enemy's laager. They got so close to the laager that they could hear the people talking there, and could see how busy they were in putting their artillery into position by the light of lanterns. None of them observed that the enemy was in close proximity.

That night, ex-President Pretorius entered the enemy's laager, and at once sent a message to me, in which he asked for a conference to discuss the terms of peace. As I had entertained the same plan, I readily agreed to it. Delegates were appointed on both sides for this conference: Grobler, Prinsloo and myself for the Government, and ex-President Pretorius, Menitjes and Fourie for the enemy. As soon as we met, I again proposed, as at a previous conference, that the Government elected must, in accordance with the constitution of the country, be first recognized as legal by the Volksraad. In proof of our peaceful intentions, I told the enemy that one of our pickets, on the previous night, had come so close to their laager that it might have attacked them quite unawares, had it wished to do so. This fact did not fail to make an impression, and after a discussion that lasted several days, we agreed on the following points:

    1. The Government to be recognized by the Volksraad.

    2. A new presidential election to take place.

THE CIVIL WAR: 1861–1864

> 3. The mooted points still existing to be referred to a court of arbitration composed of judges of the Free State. With this object, the Free State should be asked to assign such judges as were necessary.

The Opposition proposed, moreover, that a commission should be nominated from their side whose duty it should be to see that the arrangement was strictly kept by the Government, and that they must have free access to President van Rensburg's office. To this no objection was raised, and ex-President Pretorius and another burgher were elected members of this commission. At the same time, Fourie and myself, with Jan Kraep as secretary, were dispatched to the Orange Free State, in order to ask for judges from the Government of this State, who, in accordance with the arrangement, might constitute the court.

The burghers dispersed and went to their homes. When our deputation reached the Orange Free State, where President Brand had just taken his oath of office, the latter advised both parties to settle the matter amicably rather than bring it before a court. He pointed out to us that an impartial court of law would pass sentences on too many burghers, and that an understanding on both sides would be much better; finally, he even refused to appoint the judges of his country for the purpose. I now sought for a precedent for settling a matter of this kind, and at last discovered that an old jurist had laid down the principle that charges of rebellion in a country torn by civil war could, by general consent, be dismissed by a general amnesty, so long as the chief parties concerned were discharged from their official positions. The Volksraad resolved in this sense, and peace was thus fully restored. The Volksraad also agreed to the proposal that a new presidential election should be held. At the same time, at my own instance, as I wished to give the burghers the opportunity of choosing another commandant general if they were dissatisfied with me, a new election for Commandant General was held, at which I obtained more than two-thirds of the votes.

CHAPTER V
NATIVE WARS

CHAPTER V

NATIVE WARS

The Transvaalers again come to the Orange Free State's assistance against the Basutos, under Moshesh, but break up in discord—Kruger's accident in 1866—Fighting in the Zoutpansberg—Lack of ammunition and support—Kruger alone among the Kaffirs.

IN 1865, the great Basuto War broke out in the Free State. Robbing and plundering, the Basutos penetrated far into Free State territory. They also murdered some Transvaalers, among others a certain Pretorius and his family, who was returning home in his wagons, across the Drakensberg, from a journey to Natal. As assistance was required in the Orange Free State, I was dispatched with about 300 men [1] supplied by Pretorius. From Malap, that is, from the settlement of the Chief Malap and his tribe, near Moshesh's town, I sent a message to the head chief to deliver up the murderers. Moshesh replied that he was prepared to do so, but asked for a few days' delay. Before the short time which was now

[1] I desire here to state that these figures are absolutely correct, notwithstanding that they differ entirely from those given in the historical works on South Africa that have so far appeared.—*Note by the Editor of the German Edition.*

allowed to him had expired, he treacherously fell upon the Boer camp with 3,000 Kaffirs and about 4,000 Zulus who had come to his assistance. Under cover of the darkness, aggravated by a continuous soft rain, and a rising mist, the Kaffirs came right into the camp and naturally occasioned great consternation. It was not till daybreak that we managed to drive them from the camp.

I had at that time a certain Nyhoff for my secretary, who had been drunk on the evening before the fight, and had been tied to a wagon-wheel for a punishment. He there slept so soundly that he noticed nothing of the fight, and, the next day, when he at last awoke, he looked round in astonishment and asked:

"Have you people been fighting during the night?"

Our commando pursued the enemy into the mountains in the direction of Malap's town. At the same time, I dispatched a message to Fick, the Chief Commandant of the Orange Free State, who had about 600 men with him, to ask him also to advance towards Malap's town, with his commando, and join me there. This was done, and we held a council of war in which it was decided that the burghers of the South African Republic should receive farms in the territory which was now about to be freed of the enemy and hold them under the laws of the Orange Free State. The

NATIVE WARS

Government of the Free State was informed of this resolution. An attack was made on the Malap Mountains and met with perfect success. The enemy was driven off, a large number of his men killed and wounded and a quantity of cattle captured.

From there the commando marched further in the direction of Moshesh's town. On the way, near the Katskatsberg, we came upon a strong Kaffir force of about 20,000 men. The strength of the enemy may be estimated to some extent from the following observations. When we Boers first saw the Kaffir forces, who were all mounted, we noticed some loose cattle among them, but these seemed so few compared with the number of the Kaffirs that we concluded they were cattle which the Kaffirs had brought with them for food. But, when we had succeeded in capturing the cattle, we counted no less than 8,000 head. The Kaffirs made their way back to the town, pursued by our men, and, after some more fighting, we managed to capture 30,000 more sheep, 8,000 oxen and a few hundred horses.

Commandant Fick here received word from President Brand of the Free State that he could not consent to the resolution, which had been passed at the council of war, by which Transvaal burghers were to obtain grants of ground in the reconquered territory to be held under the laws of the Free State. In consequence of this the burghers of the South African

Republic refused to fight any longer and went home.

I had hardly reached home, after this expedition, when I had to go to Potchefstroom to attend the Session of 1866 of the Volksraad. On my return journey after the sitting, I met with a serious accident. At Schoonkloof Farm, in the Rustenburg district, just beyond Elephant's Pass, I had to cross a *sloot*, or ditch. The ditch was dry, but the road which led across the ditch was thoroughly soaked and cracked, so that it was impossible for wagon or horse to get through. Now, rather than turn back and go a long way out of my road, I went back a little way with my two-wheeled cart and then urged the mules to a full gallop towards the ditch, intending to make them jump the ditch and drag the cart after them. But the cart upset and I broke my left leg at the knee. With my broken leg and assisted only by the small Kaffir boy whom I had with me, I had to get the cart up again, lift it on to the wheels, and, without being able to bind up my leg, drive for an hour and a half to get home. The jolting of the cart caused me terrible suffering, and my broken leg compelled me to nine months of inactivity, during which time I only managed to crawl about on crutches. My left leg has ever since been a little shorter than the other, but it was hardly noticeable after a time.

Before I had quite recovered, in 1867, I had to

lead a commando against the rebel Kaffirs of the Zoutpansberg district. But, through lack of ammunition, this expedition was able to do but little. President Pretorius had promised to send me ammunition, but could not keep his word, as the goods were stopped at the frontier. In the Zoutpansberg district the village of Schoemansdaal had suffered especially from the attacks of the Kaffirs. I went there, and twice attacked the Kaffirs in order to drive them from that neighborhood. But, in these two attempts, all my ammunition was exhausted, and, much against my will, I was obliged to abandon the village. I offered to remain until help and ammunition should come from Pretoria, where I had sent a mounted messenger to inform the President of our plight. But only one field-cornet with his men was willing to stay with me, the others refusing to hear of any further delay. I called the villagers together, and held a meeting in which I told them that I would remain with them, but the villagers declared that they would rather not stay there under such conditions, but would go back with the commando, as they could then at least take their most valuable possessions on the wagons of their relations in the commando, while otherwise, if the Kaffirs were not driven away, they would have to flee later on, and then, for want of transport, would have to leave all their property behind them. So there was nothing for it but to escort the inhabitants of Schoemansdaal to Marabastad, which place thus, for the time being, became the chief settlement in the Zoutpansberg district.

On the return journey across Makapaanspoort, the inhabitants of that district complained that the Kaffir captain Machem had stolen much cattle from them and that he had acted altogether in so aggressive a manner that they lived in constant fear of attack.

Machem was summoned to appear before me, as he had changed his quarters, and I could not go to him to speak with him. His present habitation was a mere nest of caves, ravines and earth-holes, where his people lived on stolen cattle and could easily escape pursuit. Machem answered the summons, but many of his people would not leave their caves. I therefore went myself, accompanied by the captain, to fetch the rebels. On arriving at the kraal, I sent messengers to announce the object of my visit. But the Kaffirs refused to listen to the messengers and attacked them. When I heard the firing, I ran to the rescue. The Kaffirs fired at me also, but, after a short fight, we succeeded in capturing those of the cave-dwellers who had not escaped. This band, together with the others who had first obeyed the summons, were then taken to their new home, five or six miles up the Nile River. At Makapaanspoort,

NATIVE WARS

a small guard was also left to protect the inhabitants.

This affair with Machem had caused a great to-do. While we were besieging the refractory Kaffirs in their caves, the girls of the tribe brought them water and food. In order not to harm the women and yet to prevent them from prolonging the men's resistance, I had them all captured, as they were going to the caves, and placed under supervision. We took them with us to Pretoria, there to be delivered, and left to the decision of the Executive Raad, whose confirmation I also had to obtain of my choice of the place allotted to Machem and his people for their new settlement (I had full authority and orders to make him leave his old quarters). If Machem's tribe should not have submitted and promised to behave better, the girls, according to English (and afterwards also Boer) custom, would have been *ingeboekt,* that is, portioned out to Boer families under legal supervision until they came of age. Machem, however, behaved so well that the Executive Raad soon after restored all the girls to him.

In the following year, 1868, I set out again, and, accompanied by only one burgher, made for the Waterberg and Zoutpansberg districts, to see how matters stood there. At Makapaanspoort, I found all the Kaffir chiefs of the neighborhood assembled.

They all seemed greatly surprised at my unexpected visit. They knew I was to come, but had thought that I would summon them by messenger to come to me; and they now consulted as to how they should act in this case. They had never thought that I would venture among them alone. Without displaying the least distrust, I dismounted in their town, and they all kept quiet. They greeted me with the words:

" When it is peace, it is peace; and when it is war, it is war," which implied that my arrival without an escort showed them that my disposition towards them was friendly, that I expected the same from them, and that therefore they must keep the peace. From Makapaansport, I went on to Zoutpansberg, where one of the captains who had fought against me in the previous year now offered his submission. The object of this journey was not merely that I might see the captains personally and admonish them to keep the peace, but also, as is the duty of a commandant general, take a census of the Kaffirs, a valuation necessary for the purpose of taxation.

CHAPTER VI.

PRESIDENT BURGERS

CHAPTER VI

PRESIDENT BURGERS

Dispute about Kimberley—Kruger's protest against the court of arbitration to which President Pretorius has yielded—Pretorius resigns the Presidency—T. F. Burgers elected by a large majority, notwithstanding Kruger's agitation—Explanation between Kruger and Burgers—Burgers' policy—War with Secucuni—Dispute about the arbitrary war-tax imposed by the President—Sir Theophilus Shepstone, the British Governor of Natal, arrives with his plans for annexation—Conferences with Shepstone—Burgers' difference with Kruger and the Volksraad—Kruger elected Vice-President—The annexation of the Transvaal—Protest of the Executive Raad against the annexation.

IN 1870 diamond fields were discovered in West Griqualand, at Kimberley and in the west of the South African Republic, near Barkly West. I myself went to regulate matters in those which lay within Transvaal territory, but was very uncivilly received by the English miners who had gathered there. These people had arbitrarily established a kind of republic, with a certain Parker as president and threatened Pretorius with war unless he left them alone.

Pretorius complained to the British Government about the behavior of its subjects. He was told that the districts in which the diamonds were found did not belong to the Republic but to the Kaffir chiefs Montsioa and Gasibone. This was one of those false statements with which the British Government is always prepared when it suits its purpose; for Gasibone had now for some time been deposed by the Government of the South African Republic and Mahura put in his place. His district was within the borders of the South African Republic. About this there had never been the slightest doubt or dispute. Waterboer himself only laid claim to the territories at the instigation of the English. He had no right to them whatever.

In order to avoid the difficulties, President Pretorius agreed to arbitrate with Mahura, Montsioa and Waterboer. This was a mistake and very much against my wish, as I maintained that the Republic did not need and should never accept arbitration regarding her own possessions or between herself and her subjects. President Pretorius asked Keate, the Governor of Natal, to arbitrate, and the latter decided in favor of the Kaffir chiefs, declaring them to be the independent proprietors of the disputed districts.

One of the witnesses in this business was the Kaffir chief Mobilo. He was asked if he intended to make any claims, as he had assisted in clearing the district and making it habitable. He answered:

"Yes, I did help, but I only followed the white man like the jackal which follows a herd, to watch if it can't pick up a lamb here and there."

He was told that he too might have a part of the district. The Kaffir was lost in thought for a few moments, and then answered:

"No, *baas,* I dread Malimo's (God's) anger. When Moselikatse's Kaffirs were murdering us, Malimo sent the white men to save us. Shall I now place my foot upon the neck of my deliverer?"

He spoke some time and reminded them how Moselikatse used to put the old people to death, when he saw the aasvogels hovering over his kraal, and how he threw them to the aasvogels. He refused to injure the rights of the white men who had delivered the Kaffirs from these horrors.

The Government of the South African Republic had appointed a commission to attend the discussions of the arbitration court. I was a member of this commission, which protested against Governor Keate's judgment and lodged its objections with the Volksraad against the proceedings of President Pretorius. The Volksraad joined in the protest and Pretorius resigned. The protest at least effected this result, that the Republic retained a small piece of the territory—that part, namely, which contains the village of Christiania.

The resignation of President Pretorius necessitated a new election. A number of burghers asked me to become a candidate. But I refused and with my party supported Robinson as our candidate for the Presidency. The Opposition candidate was Thomas François Burgers. The latter had just returned from a tour through the country and was chosen State President by a large majority, although we made every effort to secure Robinson's election. The inauguration of the new President took place in the old Government Buildings at Pretoria.

I was present. After the President had taken the oath of office, I rose and addressed him in the following words:

"Your Honor, I have done my best to prevent your election, principally, because of your religious views, which appear to me to be mistaken. But as you have now been elected by the majority, I submit as a good republican to this vote of the people, trusting that you are a more earnest believer than I thought, in which case I will congratulate you with all my heart."

To this the President answered:

"Burgher, who voted against me for conscience' sake, you are as dear to me as those who voted for me."

Many burghers now came up to me to express their delight at my outspokenness; many had thought I would keep my own counsel.

PRESIDENT BURGERS

President Burgers was without doubt a man of keen intelligence and of very great gifts. He endeavored without delay to improve the government of the country and to enter into commercial relations with foreign countries. Another favorite project of his was the construction of a railway from Lorenzo Marques to Pretoria, and he personally undertook a journey to Europe to borrow money for this purpose. This loan was only partially successful, but he had the good fortune to discover in Europe a few prominent men whom he brought back with him. One of them was Dr. Jorissen who afterwards rendered so many useful services to the country. The only thing to be said against Burgers' government was, that his views differed too much from those of the burghers. And this was the case not only in religious questions, but also in other matters which he considered necessary for the development of the Republic, whereas his burghers were of a different opinion. It must be admitted that the Republic of that day was not ripe for T. F. Burgers' advanced ideas. Even if, for instance, he had succeeded in collecting the money for the railway from Delagoa Bay to the Republic, the scheme could not have been termed a success, for the resources of the Republic were not yet sufficiently developed to make such a line a paying concern.

His plans, which were in advance of the times, and

his liberal views regarding religion soon won him a host of adversaries. But what cost him nearly all his influence and made him almost impossible to the majority of the burghers was the unfortunate Secucuni War of 1876.

This war was brought about in the following way. The Government had leased a farm in the neighborhood of Secucuni's town to a certain burgher, whose cattle were seized by one of Secucuni's subordinates. When the Government sent to make inquiries, Secucuni returned an insolent answer, summoned his troops and threatened the Lydenburg district. The Republic was therefore obliged to bring back Secucuni to a sense of his duty. President Burgers wished personally to accompany the burgher commando. I was very much opposed to this, as I considered it my duty as Commandant General to lead the expedition. When Burgers insisted on accompanying the commando I refused to go. Burgers asked the reason of my refusal, and I replied:

"I cannot lead the commando if you come; for with your merry evenings in laager and your Sunday dances the enemy will shoot me even behind a wall; for God's blessing will not rest on our expedition."

Burgers answered that it was in my power as Commandant General to forbid anything that I did not approve of. But I said:

"Do you think that the burghers would listen to

anything I might say, once you, as President, have set them the example?"

Then he asked me whom I advised him to take with him as fighting General. I recommended Nicholas Smit, afterwards Vice-President of the South African Republic, and Ex-President Pretorius. Burgers accepted my recommendations and marched with a fairly strong force against Secucuni. Before coming to close quarters with him they attacked one of his subordinates called Magali, who lived in a very ugly rocky fastness. But the commando succeeded in driving the Kaffirs out of their caves and gorges, whereupon Burgers flew into such an ecstasy that he exclaimed:

" Now, Gibraltar is mine! "

After this attack they advanced against Secucuni. But in consequence of discords and the absence of combined efforts, the attack on his entrenchments failed. A certain number of burghers, under Commandant Joubert, of Pretoria, had already captured the position, but were obliged to retire for want of reinforcements. They were attacked from all sides by between four and five thousand Kaffirs. This incident, joined to other causes of discontent, exasperated the burghers to such a degree that, in the end, they refused to fight or to remain where they were. And, although the President employed all his eloquence to persuade them to stay with him, he did not succeed and was at last obliged to let the commando return home. He left three strong outposts of volunteers behind, however, under a Boer commandant and a German officer in order to hold Secucuni in check. Later on, the latter sued for peace and paid a war indemnity of 1,000 oxen.

Meanwhile the President and the burghers had returned home without bringing the war to a conclusion. The outposts cost money, and the President, for this purpose, levied a special tax of £5 on every burgher. This measure brought him into violent conflict with myself, for I considered the tax unlawful as it was imposed without the consent of the Volksraad. A considerable number of the burghers refused to pay.

During the session of the Volksraad, after the war, in 1877, the President made a violent attack on the burghers who refused to pay the extra tax, and this in the presence of Sir Theophilus Shepstone, the British Special Commissioner who was already in Pretoria waiting to see how he could put the English plans for the annexation of the Republic into execution. I defended the burghers who resisted the illegal impost. During the adjournment, I was chatting with other members of the Volksraad on the veranda, when President Burgers joined us, slapped me on the shoulder and said:

" Mr. Kruger, you can't deny that the burghers

who refuse to pay the taxes are in a state of rebellion against their Government?"

I answered:

" I deny it absolutely, on the grounds which I have already stated. They don't refuse to pay their taxes; but they do refuse to pay a tax which you have added, without authority, to the already existing taxes. But even if the fact were as you say, I should like to ask you a question. Would you consider it a proof of affection to accuse your wife—no matter what her faults—openly before her bitterest enemy? That is what you have done to the Republic in the presence of her enemy, and this is to me a proof that you do not love but hate the Republic."

The President was silent and left us.

All the difficulties which President Burgers encountered, through his own fault, were employed by the English to bring about and justify annexation. A large majority of the burghers who lived in the plains were, as has already been stated, dissatisfied with the President's government, while the inhabitants of the villages,[1] who consisted almost entirely of foreigners, and of whom a large number were not even burghers, were contented with Burgers' rule, above all because they expected great things from the proposed railway. When they now realized how

---

[1] The Boer always speaks of villages, or *dorpen*, where we should say towns. He knows the term "Kaffir town," or *stad*, but to him even the capital is only a "village," or *dorp.—Translator's Note.*

THE MEMOIRS OF PAUL KRUGER

strong the opposition was they gradually came to the conclusion that annexation by the British Crown would not be at all a bad thing for them. It was from these men that Shepstone received petitions in favor of annexation. These petitions were signed almost entirely by the village populations.

Shepstone, the Governor of Natal, was authorized by the British Government to discover the best means for annexing the country. He left Natal for Pretoria with an escort of twenty-five men, for the purpose, as he pretended, of discussing the Kaffir difficulties and other questions. He added openly, which was the case, that the Republic had not defeated Secucuni, and that this fact would be a dangerous incitement to rebellion on British territory. I clearly foresaw Shepstone's intentions, and asked President Burgers not to permit him to enter the town with his armed body-guard, except under the escort of an armed burgher force. President Burgers paid no attention to my request.

The President's term of office had at this time expired, and a new election had become necessary. I was asked by a great number of burghers to present myself as a candidate, and, although I at first refused, I at last consented in order to put a stop to the dissatisfaction which the burghers had shown at my refusal to stand. But I made this condition with the election committee, that, if Burgers obtained a

PRESIDENT BURGERS

majority, they must rest content and obey him, so as not, through open discords, to give England an excuse for carrying out her plans of annexation. Already in the first week in which the votes of the several parties (not the official election) were recorded, it became evident that I should have a large majority. I went to President Burgers and said to him:

"President, I promise to bring over the majority of the burghers to your side, if you will promise me to take strong measures against the annexation and to defend our independence. If this is your intention, you must make it plain, so that I can emphatically assure the burghers that the independence of our country will be powerfully guarded. Otherwise my arguments will, of course, make no impression. There is my hand on it, that I shall do what I have offered to do."

Before the election took place, however, the British flag waved over the once free Republic.

Shortly after the above conversation, on the 21st of January 1877, Shepstone arrived at Pretoria with his armed body-guard and a few wagons. A number of "loyal" and excited inhabitants were foolish enough to take the horses out of his carriage and draw him to the house where he was to stay. The population as a whole, on the other hand, took the matter very quietly. People who were present and, therefore, in a position to know, say that there were not ten burghers at his reception. [The first conference between the President and his Executive Raad and Shepstone took place on the 26th of January 1877, when Shepstone at once made a great point of the "inherent" weakness of the Republic and of the fact that it had been unable to subjugate Secucuni.] The weakness displayed towards the Kaffir chiefs on the part of the white men gave him grave cause to fear, he said, that difficulties with the Kaffirs might also arise in Her Majesty's territories. The Executive Raad appointed a commission to discuss matters more fully, and chose State Attorney Jorissen and myself as members. I absolutely refused, however, to discuss any questions at this conference which affected the independence of the Republic; and nothing, therefore, came of it. Shepstone had several interviews besides with President Burgers, who finally decided to call an extraordinary meeting of the Volksraad, which took place in February.

The first subject discussed was Secucuni's petition for peace. As already mentioned, President Burgers had left several strong volunteer corps behind when the burgher commandos retired, and these had harassed Secucuni so closely that he was now suing for peace. But this did not suit Shepstone's plans; for, if peace were concluded, the principal argument in favor of the annexation of the Republic to the

PRESIDENT BURGERS

British Crown fell through. There would then be an end to his talk about the general incapacity of the Republic to master the Kaffirs, or, as he phrased it, its "inherent" weakness. It was against my will that Burgers now agreed to his proposal to send two envoys to Secucuni in order to investigate matters on the spot. This "duumvirate" commission, which consisted of Englishmen, of course brought back the desired answer, namely, that Secucuni had no idea of making peace. This dishonesty cost the English dear, as will shortly be seen.

The second matter for discussion was that of a confederation with the British dominions in South Africa. An overwhelming majority of the burghers sent in memorials declaring against the measure. I myself made a violent speech against any such plan, in which I said that this confederation would mean the absolute loss of our independence.

Burgers now resorted to a strong measure. He pointed out that several of the most violent of the opposition in the Raad had refused to pay the aforesaid tax of £5 per head, and were consequently debarred from taking part in the present discussion, and requested these members to withdraw from the Raad as unqualified. Although the State Attorney, Dr. Jorissen, was on the President's side, the Raad refused to accede to his request, which was certainly a great blow to Burgers. It seems that this incident confirmed him finally in his opinion that the existing constitution of the South African Republic did not give him sufficient power, and that it was therefore incumbent upon him to draw up another which would fetter him less. At any rate, he did draw up a new constitution and submitted it to the Raad. It provided for the institution of responsible ministers, a supreme court, and extension of the powers of the State President. At the same time, an alteration was made in the arms of the Republic by the addition of a gnu. Although this measure met with the strongest opposition in the Volksraad, the proposed constitution was at last accepted, and before the Raad broke up I was elected Vice-President. The people, however, as the highest authority, rejected the new constitution.

The Volksraad did not break up in a very happy mood. Most of the members feared that the thread by which the sword of Damocles was suspended over the head of the Republic would break and end its independence. Although many hoped that the various new measures which the Volksraad had passed in its extraordinary session might avert the danger, it soon became evident that the pessimists were right. Shepstone seemed to be only waiting for the arrival of the High Commissioner, Sir Bartle Frere, before proceeding to the annexation of the South African Republic. Frere arrived in Cape Town at the be-

PRESIDENT BURGERS

ginning of April 1877; and as early as April the 7th, Shepstone had an interview with the Executive Raad, in which he openly declared that he had been authorized and was prepared to annex the country on behalf of the British Government. I at once told him that I would never give my consent to any such step, as I was bound by my oath to uphold the independence of the Republic. I must submit if the Volksraad agreed to the annexation and thus absolved me from my oath, but not otherwise. Shepstone thereupon asked me how long it would take to call the Volksraad together. I told him that I thought it would not take long if the President issued the summons at once. But here President Burgers intervened, saying that it would not do to try Shepstone's patience too far; and so the plan fell through. Burgers proposed instead, that we should at once draw up a protest against the annexation whilst the Government of the Republic still existed, and appoint a commission to take the protest to England. This was done; but Burgers had never expected it to succeed, nor was he a member of the commission. In the meanwhile, on the 12th of April 1877, Shepstone executed his plan and annexed the Republic.

This annexation cannot be too strongly branded as an entirely iniquitous act on England's part. It was in flagrant contradiction with the Sand River Convention of 1852, by which England solemnly undertook to acknowledge the unrestricted independence of the South African Republic, and never to encroach upon the districts north of the Vaal. But as soon as it suited her convenience, perfidious Albion broke her solemn peaceful promise, as she always has done, and as she will always continue to do when it serves her purpose. What misery has come upon South Africa through this breach of treaty! The late war, which has reduced the whole country to ruins,—quite apart from costing hundreds of men and thousands of innocent women and children their lives,—this war, in which England has behaved in so uncivilized and base a fashion as to draw down upon herself the contempt of all civilized nations, had its origin partly in Shepstone's annexation. I say partly, for the war had two causes. The first and principal cause was the wealth of the gold-fields of the Republic; the second, "revenge for Majuba Hill." But if it had not been for Shepstone's annexation there would have been no Majuba Hill, and no "revenge for Majuba Hill" would have been called for.

The exasperating influence which the annexation was likely to have upon the relations between the two nations was foreseen by the Executive Raad of the South African Republic, which for that reason published the following protest against the annexation:

PRESIDENT BURGERS

Whereas Her Britannic Majesty's Government, by the Sand River Convention of 1852, has solemnly pledged the independence of the people to the north of the Vaal River, and whereas the Government of the South African Republic is not aware of ever having given any reason for hostile action on the part of Her Majesty's Government, nor any grounds for such an act of violence;

Whereas this Government has ever shown its readiness and is still prepared to do all which in justice and equity may be demanded, and also to remove all causes of dissatisfaction that may exist;

Whereas, also, the Government has repeatedly expressed its entire willingness to enter into such treaties or agreements with Her Majesty's Government as may be considered necessary for the general protection of the white population of South Africa, and is prepared punctually to execute such agreements;

And whereas, according to public statements of Her Majesty's Secretary of State for the Colonies, Lord Carnarvon, there exists no desire on the part of the British Government to force the people of the South African Republic against their wish under the authority of the British Government;

And whereas, the people, by memorials or otherwise, have, by a large majority, plainly stated that they are averse to it;

And whereas, this Government is aware that it is not in a condition to maintain the rights and independence of the people by the sword against the superior power of Great Britain, and moreover has no desire in any way to take any steps by which the white inhabitants of South Africa would be divided in the face of the common enemy against each other, or might come in hostile contact with each other, to the great danger of the entire Christian population of South Africa, without having first employed all means to secure in a peaceful way and by friendly mediation the rights of the people:

Therefore the Government *protests* most strongly against this act of Her Majesty's Special Commissioner.

It is also further resolved to send, without delay, a Commission of Delegates to Europe and America, with full power and instruction to add to their number a third person, if required, in order to endeavor in the first place to lay before Her Majesty's Government the desires and wishes of the people, and in case this might not have the desired effect, which this Government would deeply regret and cannot as yet believe, then to appeal to the friendly assistance and intercession of other Powers particularly of those who have acknowledged the independence of this State.

As members of this Commission are appointed, the Hon. the Attorney General, Dr. E. J. P. Jorissen, and S. J. P. Kruger, Vice-president of the South African Republic.

Dr. Jorissen was appointed by my wish, as he was a lawyer, and I was anxious to have some one with me who could speak foreign languages.

After appointing this deputation, the Executive Raad ceased to exist. President Burgers returned to his home in Cape Colony, and the Republic was left without a president. I had to act in his place; for, as Vice-President, it would have been my duty, even in other circumstances, to conduct the business of the state in the absence of the President from the country.

CHAPTER VII

THE INTERREGNUM UNDER THE BRITISH FLAG

CHAPTER VII

THE INTERREGNUM UNDER THE BRITISH FLAG

Kruger's first visit to London with the deputation sent to procure the repeal of the annexation—Popular meetings and popular voting in the Transvaal—The second visit to London—The Kaffir chief Secucuni puts the English doctrine into practice—The British Governor seeks Kruger's assistance against Cetewayo, the Zulu king—Further assemblies of the people and protests against the annexation—Kruger pacifies the masses—The High Commissioners, Sir Bartle Frere and Sir Garnet Wolseley, interfere—The other Afrikanders ask for the freedom of their Transvaal brothers—Kruger suspected of treachery—The delegates of the burgher meetings arrested for high treason—Kruger once more allays the storm—Plans for confederation opposed by Kruger—Sir Bartle Frere tries to treat privately with Kruger—Kruger refuses on the grounds of Frere's double-dealing—Kruger and Joubert have recourse to Gladstone by letter—All hopes of a peaceful solution abandoned.

THE commission appointed to take the protest to England consisted of Dr. Jorissen and myself. We took Mr. W. E. Bok with us as secretary and left, in May 1877, for Port Elizabeth, thence to set sail for England. Shortly after our departure, Shepstone wrote to Lord Carnarvon, the then Colonial Secretary, stating that I myself had told him that, if the deputation failed, I would become a loyal subject of the new Government, even as I had been of the old. He also knew that Dr. Jorissen had declared that the annexation was inevitable and that its repeal would be a public misfortune. As far as I am concerned, I declare this statement to be absolutely untrue. I never told Shepstone this nor anything of the kind; moreover, my further actions of themselves give the lie to any such assertion.

On arriving in England, we found that the rumor had been spread, by means of newspapers and letters, including a letter of Dr. Jooste, of Potchefstroom, first published in the *Zuid Afrikaan*, that only a handful of irreconcilables, with myself at their head, had declared against the annexation. I denied this report with the greatest emphasis and said that it was easy to arrive at the truth by taking a *plébiscite* of the whole Republic, which would show for certain whether the majority were for or against the annexation. I personally wrote a letter in which I denied the imputation touching the "handful of irreconcilables" and suggested a *plébiscite* of the whole population. Dr. Jorissen had scruples against signing this letter, and I sent it alone, on my own responsibility. The British Government rejected the proposal with the foolish statement that a vote of this kind would involve too much trouble and expense. This shows

THE INTERREGNUM

that England always remains true to herself: she makes assertions and, as soon as she is given the opportunity of convincing herself of their inaccuracy, resorts to cowardly and insipid evasions, but at the same time repeats her assertions, until she herself, and sometimes the world with her, begins to believe in their truth.

In November 1877, the deputation left England and, on the homeward journey, visited Holland, France and Germany, to try to move those Powers to intervention, but, of course, without result, in spite of the friendly reception accorded to us. About the end of December, I reached my home in the Rustenburg District and, in January of the following year, went to Pretoria, where some thousand burghers were waiting for my report. The proceedings at this meeting were not a little stormy when it became known that we had failed to receive a satisfactory reply from the British Government. One of the burghers, M. W. Vorster, moved a resolution, which was passed unanimously, that an universal *plébiscite* should be taken, so that the burghers might express their general opinion on the annexation. At a subsequent meeting, at Nauwpoort, in the Potchefstroom District, this resolution was again brought forward and passed, and a committee was appointed to institute the *plébiscite* and to sign an eventual petition. Ex-President Pretorius was elected chairman of the committee.

Shepstone was greatly dissatisfied with this resolution, declared that he could not allow the *plébiscite* to be held and demanded that I should give up this plan. I thereupon rode to Pretoria, accompanied by Messrs. Pretorius and Viljoen, and, in an interview with Shepstone, told him that I could not interfere with the *plébiscite*, as I had said, during my stay in England, that this measure would prove that the majority were against the annexation, and I did not wish to be branded as a liar. I added:

"If you admit that I was right and that the report which you sent to England on the feeling of the people was untrue, then the vote will be quite unnecessary."

Shepstone then gave his consent to the holding of the meetings, provided that the burghers came unarmed; and the members of the committee were requested to take strict care that none but burghers who were really entitled to vote should vote at the meetings.

Our committee met at Doornpoort in April 1878, when it appeared that 125 petitions, with 6,591 signatures, had been handed in against the annexation, and 31 petitions, with 587 signatures, in its favor. This clearly showed the feeling of the people, the more so when one remembers that the total male

THE INTERREGNUM

white population of the Republic, as given in Shepstone's report to the Colonial Secretary, numbered only about 8,000, and among those who had not been able to attend the meetings there must have been many more opponents of the annexation. The committee now resolved to send a new deputation to England, with instructions to hand in the proofs of the objection of the majority of the people to the annexation of the Republic. Piet Joubert, the future general, and myself were chosen to form this second deputation; and Mr. W. E. Bok again accompanied us as secretary. The expenses of the journey were to be defrayed by a collection among the burghers, and £1,900 was subscribed for this purpose before the meeting broke up. The deputation took with it a petition, addressed to Lord Carnarvon, declaring that the people of the Republic were convinced that the British Government was misinformed as to the real feeling of the Boer population, that they could not believe that England would wish to govern another nation against its wish, that they had therefore decided to prove to her that the great majority were opposed with heart and soul to the annexation, and that they hoped that the Government, after examining the accompanying memorials, would repeal the proposed annexation on the grounds of incorrect information. How little our people knew England at that time! To-day no one would presume to reckon on England's acceptance of any such argument as that set forth above.

On our way to England, we asked for an interview with the High Commissioner and Governor of Cape Colony, Sir Bartle Frere, at Cape Town. He was very amiable, but absolutely refused in any way to support us in our endeavors, declaring that he saw no reason to do so, as the Boers would be very happy under the British flag.

In July 1878, the deputation landed in England and found that, in the meanwhile, Lord Carnarvon had been succeeded as Colonial Secretary by Sir Michael Hicks-Beach. The change was anything but favorable to the people of the Republic. Moreover, on our arrival in London, we received a letter from Sir Theophilus Shepstone in reply to the petition which we had handed to him personally on our departure. In this letter, Shepstone made a violent attack on Joubert and myself and threw it in our teeth that, if there was any dissatisfaction in the country, we were the cause of it. In our first interview with Sir Michael Hicks-Beach, he declared that he would only treat by correspondence, and so a long and strongly-worded memorial was drawn up, setting forth the right of the Republic to an independent existence and the iniquity of the grounds on which it had been sought to justify the annexa-

THE INTERREGNUM

tion. A protest was also made against the annexation as a breach of the Sand River Convention, which the British Government had concluded with the Boer emigrants in 1852, and, lastly, we expressed the hope that the sense of justice of the British Nation would no longer oppose the restitution of an independence which had been recognized by the great powers. Sir Michael's reply, as was to be expected, was a complete disappointment to us. The Colonial Secretary only promised to introduce a sort of self-government as soon as the condition of the country permitted, and added that the pursuance of that policy of reconciliation would depend above all on the attitude of the delegates. We replied briefly that we could not believe that a policy such as that which England was now adopting could serve to allay the existing dissatisfaction and to bring about friendly feelings. Later, in a longer memorandum, we again defended the Republic's title to its independence; but all to no purpose. The delegates had to return to South Africa without accomplishing any results.

On the occasion of this second visit to England, I was presented by an English friend of the Boers with a gold ring, engraved with the words: " Take courage, your cause is just and must triumph in the end." The inside of the ring is engraved with the figures which represent the result of the *plébiscite* on the acceptance or rejection of the annexation. I still wear this ring as my only ornament.

On our return journey, in the autumn of 1878, we again visited the Continent. In Paris the great International Exhibition was in progress. On this occasion, I saw my first balloon and took part in an ascent. High up in mid-air, I jestingly asked the aeronaut, as we had gone so far, to take me all the way home. The aeronaut now asked who his passenger was and, when we returned to the earth, presented me with a medal to remind me of my journey through the air. Our deputation landed at Durban in December 1878.

In the meantime, the situation in South Africa had assumed a very serious aspect. Secucuni, who had formerly been persuaded by the English, when it served their turn, to declare that he would not make peace, had not troubled his head about the change of government and kept to the lesson under the new Government which he had learnt under the old. Whereas formerly he had always been supported in his refusal to recognize the sovereignty of the South African Republic over his territory, he was now required to keep the peace, as his territory belonged to the Transvaal. At last, an expedition consisting of volunteers and blacks, under Colonel Rowlands, was dispatched against him, but without effecting much. And the worst of all was that the Zulu king,

THE INTERREGNUM

Cetewayo, was also in rebellion against the British Government. England had equally refused to acknowledge the Republic's claim on his territory, but, immediately after the annexation, herself laid claim to it as constituting an unquestionable part of the dominions of the erstwhile Republic. Sir Bartle Frere asked me, on my arrival at Durban, to assist the British Commander-in-chief, Lord Chelmsford, with information as to the best ways and means of waging war against the Zulus. I gave a ready and sincere compliance with this request. I advised the British commander to make every halting-place into a camp, by collecting the wagons together, as the Boers had been used to do, and always to be well provided with good spies and scouts, so as to keep thoroughly informed of the enemy's movements. Sir Bartle Frere asked me to accompany one of the Commander-in-chief's columns as adviser and leader. I at first refused. But, when he pressed me and declared that I might name my own reward for this service, I said:

"Very well, I accept. I will take 500 burghers and hand Zululand over to you, if you will give me the reward I want."

Sir Bartle Frere was a little offended when I offered to do with 500 men the work for which the English had placed so many soldiers in the field, and asked:

THE MEMOIRS OF PAUL KRUGER

"Do you mean to say that your people are so much better than our soldiers?"

"Not that," I replied, "but our method of fighting is better than yours, and we know the country."

Sir Bartle now asked what reward I required. I said, "The independence of my country and people," whereupon the High Commissioner refused to discuss the subject further. Later, Shepstone also asked me, by letter, to come to the assistance of the English with a Boer commando. I replied that the annexation and the breach which this had caused between the people of the South African Republic and the British Government made a friendly co-operation of the two races impossible. I could not but refuse my assistance to those who paid no attention to the urgent entreaty of the people that their independence should be restored to them.

With their usual arrogance, the English despised the Zulu impis, and the result was the bloody defeat of Isandlhana (22 January, 1879), in which about 1,200 English soldiers were cut to pieces. This taught them wisdom; they went to work more cautiously and, in the Battle of Ulundi (July, 1879), Lord Chelmsford succeeded in completely defeating the Zulus. Later, Cetewayo was taken prisoner and the war brought to an end. It was generally stated in Africa, at the time, that the English had bribed Cetewayo's general to surrender his king to them.

THE INTERREGNUM

According to this account, the general thereupon persuaded Cetewayo to go to a certain spot which he declared to be safer than that in which Cetewayo then was. Cetewayo listened to this proposal and was easily surrounded and taken prisoner by the English. Whether all this, however, happened as related is not certain.

In the meanwhile, in March 1879, Sir Theophilus Shepstone had been replaced by Sir Owen Lanyon, a man absolutely unfitted for this difficult post. As a soldier, Sir Owen, of course, had no knowledge of civil administration; and, moreover, he was totally unacquainted with the manners, language and nature of the Boers.

After our return to the Transvaal, our deputation called a mass meeting to report on the results of our mission. This meeting was held on the 10th of January 1879, at Wonderfontein. About 3,000 Boers assembled and more would undoubtedly have come, if many had not been prevented from attending the meeting by the swollen state of the rivers and by the prevailing horse-sickness, which always rages at its worst at that season of the year. Meanwhile, Sir Bartle Frere had distributed among the burghers an open letter to myself and Joubert in which he said, among other things, that he hoped that we would make it clear to the people that the annexation was irrevocable. At the meeting, after first thanking the burghers for their numerous attendance and for the welcome which they had given the deputation, I exhorted them to remain unanimous and to allow no discord or differences of any kind to come between them, as only unanimity, obedience and combined efforts would enable them to regain their freedom. The meeting passed a resolution thanking us for the trouble and sacrifices which we had made, and declaring that the people would not rest content with the decision of the British Government.

Some of the burghers thought that the time had now come to seek to obtain from the British Government by force what they were not inclined to give of their own free will; but I explained to them that the time had not yet come, and was supported in my endeavors to maintain peace by Joubert and Pretorius. A burgher stepped forward and said:

"Mr. Kruger, we have been talking long enough; you must now let us shoot the English."

I asked him, in reply:

"If I say, '*sah*,'[1] will you bite? And if I say, 'bite,' will you hold tight?"

The man made no reply.

At the same meeting, it was resolved to send Piet Joubert to Natal, where Sir Bartle Frere then was, in order to communicate to him the determination of

[1] "*Sah!*" is the ejaculation employed in South Africa in setting on a dog to bite.—*Translator's Note*.

THE INTERREGNUM

the people not to submit to England. This mission, however, had not the smallest result, except that Sir Bartle Frere promised to come to the Transvaal in order to convince himself in person of the state of affairs. With this intent, a new meeting was called at Kleinfontein Farm, and Sir Bartle Frere was invited to attend.

On the appointed day (18 March, 1879) four or five thousand burghers met at Kleinfontein. Joubert gave an account of his mission and its failure, and ended with the words:

" The question which the people has now to put to itself is, Shall it submit or not? "

I also made a speech in which I impressed upon my hearers that they must not disturb the peace by taking imprudent steps, but leave the matter to the committee which would not fail to let them know as soon as it thought that all peaceful measures had been exhausted. This admonition was very necessary, for many of the burghers were greatly excited and spoke openly of the need for " shooting the English." More voices were raised at the meeting proposing that the burghers should help the Zulu king, Cetewayo, with whom England was then at war, in order jointly with him to overwhelm the English. I combated this proposal with all my might, and said that the thing was not Christian and that one must never join with savages in war against a civilized nation. And thus this plan was stifled at its birth.

Meantime, Sir Bartle Frere, who had promised to attend this meeting, had not arrived. He had left Natal for Kleinfontein, but was traveling very slowly. Possibly he hoped that the delay would discourage the Boers, or that we would return to our homes without its being necessary for him to appear. From Heidelberg he sent word to inform the meeting that he would have no time to stop at the camp as he had to go to Pretoria. He received an answer, however, saying that we had long been waiting for him and relied upon seeing him. He then determined to come. As he approached the camp, the leaders of the committee rode out to meet him and escorted him into the camp. The burghers stood closely gathered and preserved a deathly silence. No one saluted him, although at first he bowed to the burghers to right and left. In the course of a debate that ensued, it was decided to meet again a few days later, and then to discuss the several points at issue. Sir Bartle then went on to Pretoria.

Frere attended the new meeting, escorted by the Governor, Sir Owen Lanyon, a number of officials and an armed body-guard. He reproached the committee with being the cause of the dissatisfaction. The committee took little notice of this remark and its only reply was that the people were not content

THE INTERREGNUM

to accept the annexation. Finally, the High Commissioner struck another note, and said that he must admit that he had been misinformed, for he now saw that the opposition to the annexation was a powerful one and that it proceeded from the best men among the Transvaal people. The committee suggested to him that it should again set forth the objections of the people in a petition to the British Government, and asked him to forward this petition accompanied by a report on what he had seen and heard. He declared that he was prepared to recommend the petition to the earnest consideration of the British Government, although personally he was opposed to the repeal of the annexation. Shortly after, the meeting broke up. It appeared afterwards, however, that Sir Bartle Frere wrote to the British Government that he regretted he did not have enough guns to disperse the rebels. How typically English!

After Sir Bartle Frere's visit, the committee sent letters to the Orange Free State and Cape Colony asking them to support the request for the repeal of the annexation. The Volksraad of the Orange Free State, by a large majority, passed a resolution in which the hope was expressed that the endeavors of the burghers to recover their independence might be crowned with success. In Cape Colony, a deputation waited on Sir Bartle Frere with the same object. Of course, it received, together with many fine speeches, the stereotyped reply of the English statesmen, that the thing was past and done with. In the meanwhile, Sir Garnet Wolseley had been sent to South Africa with special powers. He was appointed High Commissioner beside Sir Bartle Frere with special instructions to settle Zulu and Transvaal matters. This is the man who uttered the famous phrase:

" So long as the sun shines, the Transvaal will be British territory; and the Vaal River shall flow back to its sources before the Transvaal is again independent!"

At about that time, Sir Garnet was engaged in suppressing Secucuni, an enterprise in which he at last succeeded with the aid of his greatly superior force.

After the Kleinfontein meeting, the Committee announced that a new meeting would be held at Wonderfontein. This caused Sir Garnet Wolseley to issue a proclamation in which he pointed to the danger to which those who attended the meeting would expose themselves, their families and property. He also threatened to punish all such persons for high treason. This proclamation, however, was quite ineffective, for five to six thousand persons attended the meeting, which was held at Wonderfontein on the 10th of December. The burghers were enthusiastic in the highest degree. They

THE INTERREGNUM

thought that the time had now certainly come to begin the war; but, while rejoicing at the unanimity that prevailed among the burghers, I thought it my duty to address one more word of warning to them. I pointed out to them that England was a powerful nation, and expressed the fear that many of them, once the war had broken out, would become discouraged and go back to their farms. It was not safe to decide on war at this moment of excitement.

Late that night, I walked through the camp to listen to the conversations which the burghers were holding at their camp-fires. I was anxious to ascertain how my warning had been taken. Many of the remarks that fell upon my ears were very characteristic. For instance, I heard one man say:

"I think Kruger is betraying us."

"No," said another, "I will never believe that of him, for he has done too much for us and he is still working too hard that he should be accused of such a thing."

"But," replied the first, "if he doesn't intend to betray us, why won't he let us shoot the Englishmen?"

"Ay," said the other, "I think his plans are wrong, but I won't believe that he's betraying us."

Very well satisfied with my observations, I returned to my tent and thanked God that my people

THE MEMOIRS OF PAUL KRUGER

were so firmly determined to recover their independence.

At the same meeting, a popular resolution was passed which declared that the people demanded to remain free and independent; that the burghers had never been subjects of Her Majesty and never wished to become so; that they asked for the restitution of their independence and the restoration of the Volksraad; and that the last-named body must take the necessary measures to ensure that independence. Pretorius and Bok were sent as delegates to acquaint Sir Garnet Wolseley with this resolution. However, these two gentlemen were arrested on a charge of high treason, Pretorius at Potchefstroom and Bok at Pretoria.

It goes without saying that this incident aroused great dissatisfaction. A large number of burghers at once determined to set Pretorius free by force. But the latter wrote a letter in which he begged them to abandon that intention. In consequence of these events, I went to Potchefstroom. On my way, I learnt that, in spite of Pretorius' request, a number of armed burghers were on their road in front of me, with the intention of setting Pretorius free. I galloped after them as fast as my horse could carry me and caught them up close to the village. After many arguments I at last succeeded in persuading them to give up their plan.

THE INTERREGNUM

That same evening, Pretorius and Bok were released on bail. But the British authorities now pressed Pretorius until he at last consented to travel through the country and read out a proclamation of the British Government intended to convince the burghers of the error of their ways. At the same time they supplied him with horses for his journey.

The burghers whom I had persuaded to turn back were still gathered in a body at Nauwpoort, not far from Potchefstroom, and I with them, when Pretorius came up and read out the proclamation of the British Government. The burghers must submit peacefully, it said, for their freedom had not been taken from them and the present situation was only the bridge by which they might attain self-government. When Pretorius had finished, I turned to the burghers.

"Burghers," I asked, "do you understand what the British Government offers you? I will try to explain to you what this self-government, in my opinion, means. They say to you, 'First put your head quietly in the noose, so that I can hang you up: then you may kick your legs about as much as you please!' That is what they call self-government."

The burghers entirely agreed with this view, and, on the next day, Pretorius wrote to Sir Garnet Wolseley that he must give up the idea of continuing his journey, since the burghers were firmly determined to recover their independence, and it was of no use to try to persuade them to a different way of thinking.

Shortly after these occurrences, a scheme for the confederation of South Africa was down for discussion in the Cape Parliament. The Transvaalers considered it of the highest importance, in the interest of the freedom of their country, to bring about the failure of this project for a united South Africa under the British flag, since, in the event of its acceptance, there would be no chance left for the repeal of the annexation. Joubert and I were, therefore, sent to Cape Town to urge our friends in the Cape Parliament to oppose this proposition. On our way to Cape Town, we were received everywhere with the greatest heartiness. At Cape Town itself we had an interview with a number of members of Parliament, at which I insisted, in the strongest terms, on the need for rejecting the plan and declared that the Republic would never accept a federation arrived at in this manner, above all as the burghers themselves had no voice in the matter and would not allow foreigners to determine their future for them.

"Do not wash your hands in the blood of your brothers!" were the words with which I parted from the members.

Fortunately the plans for a confederation were rejected.

During our stay at Cape Town, a member of the

THE INTERREGNUM

Upper House came to Joubert and me to invite us to pay a visit to Sir Bartle Frere. We refused; but, when the invitation was repeated, and it was added that Sir Bartle wished to speak to us privately, I said:

"I will come, if you can tell me which Sir Bartle Frere it is that wishes to see us; for I know four of them. The first came to us at Kleinfontein and assured us that he had not come with the sword, but as a messenger of peace. But, later on, I read in an English Blue Book that, on the same day, a Sir Bartle Frere, the second, therefore, had written to the British Government, 'If only I had had enough guns and men, I would soon have dispersed the rebels.' I made the acquaintance of the third Sir Bartle Frere through his answer to our petition for the repeal of the annexation: he then said that he had informed the British Government that he had met some five thousand of the best Boers at Kleinfontein and that he recommended their petition to the Government's earnest consideration. Afterwards, I saw in the English Blue Book that, on the same day, a Sir Bartle Frere, obviously a fourth, had informed the British Government that he had met only a handful of rebels. Now these four cannot possibly be one and the same man; if, therefore, you can tell me which of the four Sir Bartles wishes to see us, we will think about it."

It is needless to add that Sir Bartle Frere's emissary was unable to answer the question and returned with his mission unfulfilled.

During the stay of our deputation at Cape Town, the Tory Ministry fell, and Gladstone, who had often spoken against the annexation, became Premier of the new Cabinet. Joubert and I now formed new hopes, and, in May 1880, wrote to Gladstone from Cape Town, laying the situation before him and earnestly requesting him to do justice to the country, to repeal the annexation and to restore the Sand River Convention of 1852. We were bitterly disappointed on receiving an answer from the Liberal statesman informing us that he was unable to annul the annexation or to advise Her Majesty to abandon her suzerainty over the Transvaal. We returned to the Transvaal and reported to the committee on our mission. The general conviction was now arrived at that further meetings and friendly protests were useless. The best course appeared to be to set quietly to work and to prepare for the worst by the purchase of arms and ammunition. The greatest prudence and the strictest secrecy had to be observed in order to avoid suspicion: this was the only possible way of preparing for the decisive struggle.

CHAPTER VIII

THE WAR OF INDEPENDENCE
1880–1881

CHAPTER VIII

THE WAR OF INDEPENDENCE: 1880–1881

The seizure of Bezuidenhout's wagon—Meeting of the burghers at Potchefstroom—The "Irreconcilables" at Paader Kraal elect a triumvirate, consisting of Kruger, Joubert and Pretorius, to carry on the Government—The first shot—Battle of Bronkhorstspruit—Majuba Hill—Paul Kruger during the war—His negotiations with the Kaffir Chief Magato, whom England was trying to gain as an ally—Armistice and peace negotiations—Protests in the Volksraad—"Transvaal" or "South African Republic"?

THE first sign of the approaching storm was the incident that occurred at the forced sale of Field-Cornet Bezuidenhout's wagon, on which a distress had been levied. The British Government had begun to collect taxes and to take proceedings against those who refused to pay them. Among these was Piet Bezuidenhout, who lived in the Potchefstroom district. This refusal to pay taxes was one of the methods of passive resistance which were now employed towards the British Government. Hitherto, many of the burghers had paid their taxes, declaring that they were only yielding to force. But when this was explained by the English politicians as though the population were contented and peacefully paying their taxes, some asked for a receipt showing that they were only paying under protest and others refused to pay at all. The Government then levied a distress on Bezuidenhout's wagon and sent it to public auction at Potchefstroom. Piet Cronjé, who became so well known in the last war, appeared at the auction with a number of armed Boers, who flung the bailiff from the wagon and drew the wagon itself back in triumph to Bezuidenhout's farm. Bezuidenhout and another burgher were sent to me at my farm of Boekenhoutfontein, in the Rustenburg District, to ask me to come at once to Potchefstroom, as the burghers were ready to commence the war of independence. I obeyed this request and found the burghers collected not far from Potchefstroom. The officer in command of the English troops at Potchefstroom sent to ask if he could speak to me, and, when I answered in the affirmative, he came out, described what had happened at the sale of the wagon and ended with the words:

"You must admit that this is open rebellion."

I answered:

"I should agree with you, if we had acknowledged the annexation; but that is not the case. We do not look upon ourselves as British subjects, and the question of the tax is not a private question of

THE WAR OF INDEPENDENCE

Bezuidenhout's, but a question of principle which concerns the whole country."

In consequence of these events, I and the other leaders now held a committee meeting at Kaalfontein, at which the secretary of the former Transvaal Government was also present, and it was decided that the mass meeting at Paarde Kraal, which had been fixed for the 8th of January 1881, should take place instead as early as the 8th of December 1880, and that the people should then decide if a peaceful solution of the difficulties was possible. Two days before, the meeting was forbidden and those who were to take part in it were proclaimed rebels. Nevertheless, a mass of burghers met on the appointed day, and it was unanimously resolved that the Government of the Republic should resume office and summon the Volksraad. The business of government was entrusted to a triumvirate consisting of myself, as Vice-President, Piet Joubert, as Commandant General,[1] and Ex-President M. W. Pretorius. The triumvirate thereupon drew up a proclamation in which the good right of the Republic was borne out by historical facts and the restoration of the Government of the South African Republic made known to one and all.

The proclamation must now be printed, and

[1] Joubert was elected to this post on Kruger's motion, although he long resisted, declaring that he was no general and that he did not feel suited to this appointment.—*Note by the Editor of the German Edition.*

Commandant Piet Cronjé was sent for this purpose to Potchefstroom with about 400 men, while the Government left for Heidelberg, there temporarily to fix the seat of government. Heidelberg was easily occupied, as it contained no English garrison, and the landdrost handed over his office forthwith, under protest. In the meanwhile, Cronjé had arrived at Potchefstroom and taken measures to have the proclamation printed. Here the first shot was fired that opened the war. The English fired on a burgher watch posted in the street. A bullet struck Frans Robertse, of Wijsfontein Farm, in the Rustenburg District, and passed through his arm. The members of the newly-appointed Government sent one more petition to the representative of the British Government, the Governor of the Transvaal, and appealed to the "generosity of the noble British Nation" in order to recover their country in a friendly fashion. The answer was that the local troops were called out to suppress the "revolt."

I do not intend to give here a history of the War of Independence, which has been described in its smallest details. It is only necessary to say that, in view of their very small number—in all about 7,000 men—it was necessary for the Boers to go to work with the greatest circumspection. The plan was to cut off all the villages in which the English had a garrison and to send the rest of the burghers to the

THE WAR OF INDEPENDENCE

Natal frontier, there to arrest the approaching reinforcements of the enemy. Another difficulty was the scarcity of ammunition. At the beginning of the war the Boers had only about 15 rounds per man, so that they had to do precisely as they did in the later stages of the last war, first capture ammunition from the enemy and then fight him with his own ammunition. In these circumstances, our enterprise would have been madness, the more so as the Kaffirs had also been called out against us, if God had not strengthened our hearts, so that we went bravely to face greatly superior numbers.

Let us linger for a moment on only one fight in this war, the Battle of Bronkhorstspruit, and that for certain reasons. This was an engagement with the 94th Regiment, which was on its way from Lydenburg to Pretoria. The Boer commanders, who had received news of its approach, sent Commandant Frans Joubert, with about 150 men, to meet it. When the two forces came into touch, Joubert sent a message to the British commander, Colonel Anstruther, asking him to return to Lydenburg, in which case no fighting need take place. The man who carried the message was a burgher, called Paul de Beer, who spoke English well. Anstruther's answer was brief:

"I am on my way to Pretoria and I am going to Pretoria."

Joubert and his men, therefore, had no choice but to attack the English. The field of battle was a bare hill, on which stood a few hawthorn-trees. The English took up their position in a sunk road, while the burghers had to charge across open ground. The fight lasted only a few minutes. About 230 of the English were dead or wounded; the rest surrendered. Colonel Anstruther, who himself was mortally wounded, sent for Commandant Joubert, told him that he was beaten in fair fight, and asked him to accept his sword as a present. He died a few minutes later. It would not have been worth while to enter into these details, notwithstanding the earlier lying accusations that the English had been treacherously attacked on this occasion, if Field-Marshal Earl Roberts of Waterford, Kandahar and Pretoria had not rescued this contemptible calumny from oblivion. When, in the course of the last war, he arrived at Bronkhorstspruit, he telegraphed to England that he was now at the spot where a British force had been decimated by treachery in 1881. But this only shows what a regular genuine Englishman Lord Roberts is.

The war was continued throughout the territory of the Republic under the able command of the late General Joubert, who was then in the full vigor of his years and displayed his military capacity in a brilliant fashion that aroused general amazement.

THE WAR OF INDEPENDENCE

Under Joubert stood other capable men, such as General Smit and General Piet Cronjé, who distinguished himself in the last war by his heroic resistance at Paarde Kraal. The campaign reached its climax in the Battle of Majuba Hill, on the 27th of February 1881.

During the war, I remained for the most part with the Government at Heidelberg, but I also made several journeys to the commandos, for instance to Potchefstroom, in the Drakensberg, and to Standerton, to exhort and encourage the burghers in those places. I also went to Rustenburg to address the burghers who were besieging the British garrison. Here I learnt that Magato's Kaffirs, who lived near Rustenburg, had assumed a threatening attitude, and I at once proceeded thither, accompanied by seven men, including my son, Piet Kruger. On arriving at Magato's town, I found the Kaffirs gathered to the number of thousands under arms in their huts, clearly with no good intention. I went straight to Magato's hut and addressed him in these words:

"Why did you supply the English in their camp at Rustenburg with provisions, although I had told you to observe a strictly neutral attitude in this war, which is a war between white men?"

Magato replied:

"I received a message from the English saying

that they had already taken Heidelberg and were on the way here, and that, if I did not obey their orders, they would come to punish me."

I retorted:

"If you won't listen to me, I shall have to bring you before the court-martial," and caught him by the hand.

While I was speaking to the chief in these threatening terms, the Kaffirs stormed into the hut from every side, armed with axes, assegais and rifles. But one of my men, Piet van der Walt, placed himself with his rifle beside Magato, and threatened to shoot him down if the least harm came to me. When Magato saw that his life was at stake, he ordered his captains to disperse the Kaffirs. The captains had to beat back the crowd with cudgels and knobkerries before they succeeded in separating them. When the riot had subsided, I said to Magato:

"Call in your Kaffirs again; I want to give them my orders."

Magato at first refused, saying that I could tell him, Magato, what I wanted. But I said:

"No, I will speak to your people myself."

Thereupon the Kaffirs were summoned, and approached unarmed and timidly. I spoke to them, rebuked them for their bad conduct and warned them to keep quiet in the future, as "Kaffirs had nothing to do with this war." After that, I resumed

THE WAR OF INDEPENDENCE

my conversation with Magato, told him how reprehensible his conduct was, and eventually persuaded him to promise that he would remain neutral and neither assist nor oppose the English or the Boers. As I had to go back to Heidelberg, I asked Magato for a couple of horses. Magato beckoned me into his hut and, when we were alone, said:

"I cannot give you any horses, for, if I did, the English would know it to-morrow. But repeat your request in the presence of my Kaffirs; then I will refuse, and then you must say, 'Very well, then I will take them by force, if you will not give them to me.' Then I shall say in my heart, 'It is good,' but I shall refuse with my mouth."

I did so, and took two excellent horses for my return journey to Heidelberg.

About this time, a messenger came to ask me to come to the Natal frontier, as the English had requested an armistice in order to negotiate for peace. I at once hastened to proceed to the appointed spot. It was a very difficult journey. Thanks to the heavy rains, the roads were hardly practicable, and a circuitous route had to be followed in order to avoid the places occupied by the English. The armistice was to come to an end on the 14th of March; but it was impossible for me to reach my destination, Laing's Nek, in Natal, by that date. In the meanwhile, General Joubert, in view of the delay of the journey, obtained a four days' prolongation of the armistice. Together with my companions, Pretorius, Maré and Dr. Jorissen, I was enthusiastically received by the burghers. Soon after, a conference was held between the representatives of the Boers on the one hand and Sir Evelyn Wood, for the British Government, on the other. It took place halfway between the two camps. During the armistice, Sir Evelyn had received instructions from the British Colonial Secretary which were to form the basis of the negotiations. These were:

(1) Amnesty for all the Boer leaders.

(2) The Boers to be entitled to empower persons to negotiate a peace.

(3) The appointment of a royal commission to investigate all military questions and to hand over the country.

(4) Self-government under British suzerainty.

(5) A British resident to be appointed at Pretoria.

(6) The foreign policy of the South African Republic to be placed under British control.

The late President Brand of the Orange Free State was to be present at the negotiations in order to facilitate a settlement. The composition of the so-called royal commission gave rise to many difficulties. The British Government wished it to consist exclusively of British subjects, with the excep-

THE WAR OF INDEPENDENCE

tion of President Brand, who was to sit on behalf of both parties. The Boer leaders, on the other hand, desired a mixed commission, consisting of representatives of both parties. Moreover, the British Government wished to keep back for themselves a portion of the Republic, namely, the Utrecht and Wakkerstroom districts. But this I and the other leaders refused to hear of in any case. After long arguments, Sir Evelyn Wood asked:

"Suppose we do not yield on this point, will you go on fighting?"

I replied:

"That is not a fair question. If we do not yield, will you go on fighting?"

Sir Evelyn Wood answered, "Yes;" whereupon I took up my hat, rose and said:

"Then we need not discuss matters further."

Thereupon Sir Evelyn took me by the arm, and said:

"No, come back, you must not be so hasty."

General Smit went so far as to say:

"The best thing would be to let the sword decide."

Another difficulty was the question of the withdrawal of Her Majesty's troops from the Republic and the provisioning of the English garrisons in the villages during the negotiations. It looked for one moment as though the negotiations would fall through, and that was the moment at which Dr.

Jorissen, by my order, drew up his so-called third proclamation.[1] I caused this third proclamation to be read out to President Brand, who had by that time arrived and who made every effort to induce me to refrain from publishing that document and to continue the negotiations. This was done, at O'Neill's house. It was a very difficult matter to agree on the different points. Sir Evelyn Wood did his very utmost to get off with verbal assurances; and, as the armistice had to be prolonged in order to continue the negotiations, he seized the opportunity, while I was engaged in conversation with General Joubert and Dr. Jorissen, to charge an orderly to take the news of the prolongation of the armistice to the camp. But I noticed this and asked:

"Where is the man going?"

As soon as I heard the nature of his mission, I said to one of Wood's aides-de-camp:

" Stop that man!"

I then went in to the tent and said to General Wood that I asked him, as an honest man, first to sign the agreement containing the points discussed between us. The document lay on the table, but Sir Evelyn refused to sign. It was not until I cried, " Burghers, saddle!" that Wood, who now saw that further evasion was impossible, gave in and signed.

[1] The text of this proclamation will be found in Dr. Jorissen's *Transvaalsche Herinneringen*, 1897.—*Note by the Editor of the German Edition.*

THE WAR OF INDEPENDENCE

The orderly was then allowed to go off with the news of the prolongation of the armistice.

When the provisional peace protocol was signed, the English officers tried to disparage the Boer victory and to make us confess that we had suffered fearful losses and could, therefore, not have continued our resistance:

"How many did you have killed on the Nek?" one of them asked Joubert, confidently.

"I myself had one," answered Joubert, "and one wounded."

The officer laughed and maintained that he had seen more of our men killed with his own eyes:

"Very well," said Joubert, very angrily. "Do you go and dig one of them up and bring him here; and I promise you I'll eat him, skin and all."

A chaplain from Newcastle, on the other hand, expressed to me his regard for the Boers and his admiration of their courage. The officers standing near were meantime saying that the English had fought very bravely and shot down many Boers, until their ammunition gave out; then, of course, they had to give up the fight:

"Our fellows would let themselves be shot before handing over a cartridge."

I made no reply, but again turned to the chaplain and said:

"When you see Her Majesty, mind you tell her

that she must give her soldiers a special reward for the care with which they guarded their ammunition supply; we found it on the hill, quite safely packed on the donkeys!"

Wood himself put similar questions. He asked, among other things:

"What were the 200 men for whom you were sending to the Biggarsberg?"

"We heard that you were marching there with 12,000."

"And you sent your 200?"

"Yes, we had no more to send; but I have seen that they would have been enough."

By this agreement, which was signed by myself and Joubert in the name of the people of the South African Republic, the following objects were secured: absolutely free autonomy under British suzerainty, with the appointment of a British Resident at Pretoria, and the return of British property seized during the war. The point that nearly led to the breaking-off of the negotiations, namely, the question of the loss of territory, was left to the decision of the royal commission. Sir Evelyn Wood bound himself not to occupy the positions on Laing's Nek, if the Boers abandoned them, nor to send troops or ammunition to the Transvaal. Moreover, the royal commission was to settle all undecided matters within six months, to confirm the treaty of peace and to restore the country to the Boers. This com-

THE WAR OF INDEPENDENCE

mission, which met shortly after, consisted of Sir Hercules Robinson, the newly-appointed High Commissioner; Sir Henry de Villiers, Chief Justice of Cape Colony; and Sir Evelyn Wood. They effected a draft treaty, which is known by the name of the Pretoria Convention of 1881. Long and violent discussions took place in the Volksraad, which was summoned to approve this convention. Five months earlier, in an extraordinary session, I had praised England's magnanimity, expressed my full confidence in the commission and pointed to a reconciliation with England as the basis of a happy national existence, in order to appease the burghers. But I, too, now found myself obliged to protest against certain articles of the convention, and complained by telegram, but in vain, to Gladstone that several clauses of the treaty contained the opposite of what had actually been arranged by word of mouth. Eventually the treaty was only accepted with the reservation that we were yielding to force and that we trusted that, in view of this forced acceptance, the British Government would see their way to alter the convention and to remove the points which made it unacceptable to the Volksraad, notably the imposition of the suzerainty and the unjust curtailments of territory.

One of the points which offended the burghers was that, instead of being called the "South African Republic," the Republic kept the name of the

THE MEMOIRS OF PAUL KRUGER

"Transvaal State." The country only recovered the title of South African Republic by the London Convention of 1884. But, in the meanwhile, in my official correspondence with the British Resident, I was always accustomed to speak of the South African Republic. One fine day the latter came to me to complain about this, saying that the name of the country was the Transvaal State, and not the South African Republic.

"How do you prove that?" said I.

"Why," answered Hudson, "by the convention, which clearly says, 'Transvaal State.'"

"Very well," I rejoined. "If I sell you a farm and, in the deed of sale, I say, 'I, Paul Kruger, hereinafter called the Vendor, and so on,' then, in what follows, I am no longer 'Paul Kruger,' but the 'Vendor.' Even so in this case. In the convention, just as in drawing up a deed, the Republic is referred to as the 'Transvaal State;' but that does not make it its real name, but only its specification. Its real name is and remains the 'South African Republic.'"

Hudson laughed and said:

"Well, call it as you please, only do not mind if I keep to the name of the Transvaal State."

On the 8th of August, after the Volksraad had met, the country was restored in due form and the dear *Vierkleur* was once more solemnly hoisted.

CHAPTER IX

PAUL KRUGER'S FIRST PRESIDENCY:
1883-1888

CHAPTER IX

PAUL KRUGER'S FIRST PRESIDENCY:
1883–1888

The election—The war with the Kaffirs in the Lydenburg District—Kaffir disturbances on the south-western frontiers of the Republic—Boer volunteers, in spite of the President's proclamation, enlist under the chiefs Moshette and Mankoroane, for their war against other Kaffir chiefs, and found the republics of Stellaland and Goshenland on the territory awarded them for their services—The chiefs Montsioa and Moshette place themselves under the protection of the Transvaal—England protests against this arrangement—Negotiations regarding the western borders between Kruger, Sir Charles Warren and Cecil Rhodes—Kruger's third visit to London—Sir Hercules Robinson—Repeal of the suzerainty by the London Convention of 1884—Visits to the European Governments—Dr. Leyds—Internal situation of the Republic in 1885—The Delagoa Bay Railway—Unsatisfactory condition of the finances—Disturbances on the western frontiers—Discovery of the gold-fields—The population of the gold-fields, the "Uitlanders"—Negotiations with the Free State for a closer alliance—Incorporation of the "New Republic."

IN 1882 the Raad, on Joubert's motion, unanimously resolved to elect a State President. Joubert and I were asked to stand. We both accepted, but each of us recommended the other's candidature to the people. In my answer to the invitation to stand, I explicitly stated the principles on which

THE MEMOIRS OF PAUL KRUGER

I intended to govern, should I be elected. God's Word should be my rule of conduct in politics and the foundation upon which the state must be established. The promotion of agriculture; the opening up of fresh resources of the country and their exploitation through the creation of new industries; railway extension towards the sea; restrictions on immigration (I apprehended the least danger from an invasion from Holland), in order to prevent the Boer nationality from being stifled; a friendly attitude towards England and a closer alliance of the South African states; the maintenance of the authority of the Government towards the natives and the friendly treatment of obedient native races in their appointed districts; the furtherance of all efforts which would bring the life of the people under the influence of the Gospel, " and above all," the advancement of instruction for the young:—these were the questions which I considered of vital importance to the Republic. I obtained two-thirds of the votes at the election, and was consequently elected State President for the next five years.

About the time when a presidential election was decided on, the Republic became involved in a war with Mapoch in Secucuniland, in the east of the Republic.

Since the restoration of the Republic, Secucuni had been her loyal friend. Mapoch was now sheltering Mampur, Secucuni's murderer and refused to give him up. War consequently became inevitable. It lasted for nine months, and in order to bring it to a successful termination, it at length became necessary to place 4,000 burghers in the field. I myself visited the several commandos during the siege to point out to them the necessity of making every effort to bring the war to a quick and successful conclusion. With the commandos was a foreigner named Nelmapius, who blew up the caves of the Kaffirs, in which they had entrenched themselves, with dynamite. The war did not come to an end until July 1883. Mapoch gave up Mampur. Mampur was hanged and Mapoch condemned to imprisonment for life. But he was liberated shortly before the commencement of the late war and settled with some of his dependents in the neighborhood of Pretoria. The Republic gained in importance through this war, for even her enemies had to acknowledge that she was strong enough to enforce law and order and need not throw herself upon the protection of any foreign power, through inherent weakness.

About the same time complications occurred on the south-western border. Two Kaffir chiefs, Moshette and Montsioa, were at war with each other. Later, Mankoroane came to Montsioa's assistance, and Massouw to Moshette's. Mankoroane was always very friendly with the English, and tried to induce volunteers to join him. Massouw and Moshette followed his example, promising each volunteer three thousand *morgen* of land. This was, of course, a very tempting offer. Applicants came not only from the Transvaal but also from the Orange Free State and even from Cape Colony. The Government of the Transvaal issued a proclamation which forbade the burghers to join the Kaffirs. But some of them refused to obey the proclamation, renounced their burgher rights and reported themselves to the Kaffir captains. Later, the Government sent General Joubert to the western frontier to demand once more the return of those burghers who had ignored the proclamation. The Royal Commission of 1881 had deprived the Republic of the power of direct interference in the quarrels of the Kaffir chiefs. The volunteers firmly refused to return. Meanwhile, the chief Calveyn had also rebelled, in the Marico district, but submitted immediately upon General Joubert's threatening him with a commando. Massouw and Moshette, with the assistance of their volunteers, completely defeated their respective opponents. The volunteers were not all Boers. There were a good many Englishmen amongst them. These men chose the land which had been promised them and, joined by other emigrants, founded the two small republics of Stellaland and Goshenland. The administrator of the first was G. T. van Niekerk and its capital

KRUGER'S FIRST PRESIDENCY

Vryburg. Of the second Rooigrond was the capital and Gey van Pittius the administrator. Both republics, however, were in a constant ferment and continually quarreling, and had even to fight against the afore-mentioned Kaffir chiefs. One party in the republics desired incorporation with Cape Colony, while the other applied to the South African Republic. Cape Colony sent Cecil Rhodes north to settle things. The Transvaal sent General Joubert, who was at the same time " Commissioner for the Western Border," for the same purpose. The latter informed the Rooigronders that the Government of the Transvaal could do nothing for them, as the London Convention—we were now in 1884—had excluded them from the sphere of influence of the Republic. Joubert was obliged to make this statement, because the British agent in Pretoria had accused the Government of the Transvaal of secret dealings with the Rooigronders, and the Republic might otherwise have become involved in difficulties with England. Shortly afterwards, Pastor du Toit, the Director of Education, succeeded General Joubert as Commissioner of the Western Border. At the same time, a letter from Montsioa was published in which the latter asked to be allowed to become a subject of the South African Republic, in order to obtain protection, as he was " almost exterminated." A proclamation was now issued, subject to the conditions of the convention of 1884, which gave the Republic the right to enter into contracts with the Kaffir chiefs in the east and west of the Republic, on the condition that such contracts were approved of by England. This proclamation placed the chiefs Moshette and Montsioa, with their subjects and their rights, under the protection of the South African Republic, in order to put an end to further bloodshed. The decree closed with these words:

> This proclamation is issued provisionally, subject to the conditions and having regard to article 4 of the London Convention.[1]

These words left open the door to an eventual recall of the proclamation, and showed, at the same time, that the Government had applied to the British Government for their consent to the annexation. The British Government, however, had not the least intention of granting this, but sent Sir Charles Warren with a strong force to South Africa to put a stop to the disturbances on the western border, and Sir Hercules Robinson telegraphed to Pretoria that the Republic must recall their proclamation, as England

[1] Du Toit had meantime hoisted the flag of the Republic over the "proclaimed" territory. This act gave rise to lively disputes at the time. But, as soon as Kruger heard of it, he called du Toit's attention to this, and asked him how he came to do it. Du Toit answered that he had not hoisted the flag as a sign that he was taking possession, but only to attract attention to the proclamation, and that he had hauled it down since. The proclamation was not, as has since been stated, the result of an intrigue or of an unreflected act, but of a resolution which President Kruger to this day defends as lawful.—*Note by the Editor of the German Edition.*

KRUGER'S FIRST PRESIDENCY

had already declared the said districts to be under her sphere of influence. Thereupon the Republic recalled the proclamation, not being aware at the time that England was Montsioa's suzerain. I went with Dr. Leyds, the State Attorney, to the western frontier in order personally to enforce law and order, and warned the inhabitants of Goshenland to keep the peace.

Shortly after, a meeting took place at Fourteen Streams between Warren, Rhodes and myself. This conference had no result except an agreement that each side should nominate commissioners to mark off the frontier line as fixed by the convention, and that President Brand of the Orange Free State should arbitrate in case of disagreements. Rhodes pretended to be on my side in the business. On the other hand, he tried to abuse Joubert, until I pointed out to him that he was attacking an absent man. The Commissioners now finally fixed the western frontier. I myself had proposed to settle the business once and for all, by ordering the mounted commando, together with the police and a few burghers who had accompanied me, to ride round the frontier. The ground marked by the horses' hoofs would make a capital "frontier line." Warren, however, refused his consent to this proposal, giving as excuse his fears lest it might lead to a hand-to-hand fight between his force and the burghers.

THE MEMOIRS OF PAUL KRUGER

I have anticipated the events of nearly two years, for the above incidents occurred after my return from my third journey to England. This journey was the result of a resolution of the Volksraad of 1883, which had decided to send a deputation to England to endeavor to have the convention of 1881 replaced by one more in harmony with the wishes of the people. The attempt to settle the western frontier question satisfactorily was necessarily bound up with it. The deputation consisted of myself, General Smit and Dr. du Toit, at that time Director of Education. Dr. Jorissen preceded the deputation, and had sent home a report from England to the effect that she was willing to receive us and to enter into a discussion on matters submitted to her.

Dr. du Toit had been the editor of the *Patriot* at Paarl, Cape Colony, and had warmly defended the Afrikander interest during the war. Shortly after the declaration of peace, he came to the South African Republic and was appointed Director of Education. The same sitting which agreed to the dispatch of a deputation to England deprived Dr. Jorissen of his position as State Attorney through the instrumentality of Chief Justice Kotzé, with du Toit's assistance. His dismissal made room for du Toit as a member of the deputation. It was not only a discourteous proceeding, but, in the highest sense, unjust, taking into consideration the important services which Dr. Jorissen had rendered his country. I protested in vain. It was contended against me that the secretary of such legation must have special qualifications which Dr. Jorissen did not possess.

Our commission started on its journey to England in August 1883, traveled by Kimberley, Paarl, and Cape Town, meeting everywhere with a hearty reception, and landed at its destination on the 28th of September. The lengthy negotiations with Lord Derby, the Colonial Secretary of that day, commenced at once. We were soon informed that the British Government was prepared to grant us the same independence, as regarded internal politics, as that enjoyed by the Orange Free State. This concession was not obtained by us in return for any concession nor by means of any diplomacy on our part. We regarded it as a question of right. We pointed out that, on the ground of the Convention of 1852, the Republic had a right to her independence, which had been unjustly taken from her and which had not been restored to her in 1881 in the way in which we had been virtually promised that it would be. Besides this point, modifications regarding the western frontier were discussed, and our deputation succeeded in securing for the Republic a considerable tract of land to which we laid claim and which had been unjustly taken from us in 1881. During the negotiations Sir Hercules Robinson and

I had the misfortune to come into collision. I was pointing out and insisting that certain farms, among others Polfontein and Rietfontein, should come within the boundaries of the Republic, especially as they had formerly belonged to us. When I made this statement, Sir Hercules Robinson, who was present at the negotiations, whispered to Lord Derby:

"It's a lie."

I jumped up, quite prepared to fall upon Sir Hercules. Lord Derby and the other gentlemen present interfered, and Lord Derby said:

"Gentlemen, you are not going to fight?"

I answered that Sir Hercules had insulted me, and that I did not intend to put up with it. I accepted his apology, however, and his assurance that "no offence was meant."

Despite this incident, Sir Hercules and I afterwards became very good friends and remained so until his death. He was the only High Commissioner with whom I exchanged private and confidential letters. He was an honorable man and a gentleman in the best sense of the word.

The Convention of 1884 was shortly afterwards signed and the Republic regained her complete independence. There was, however, one article which curtailed her rights, namely, the well-known article 4. But the hateful suzerainty was repealed. The asser-

KRUGER'S FIRST PRESIDENCY

tion made by Mr. Chamberlain at a later date that the British suzerainty was still in force is false, as will be proved.

After the Convention of 27 February 1884 had been signed, the deputation started for the Continent, hoping to raise a loan, especially in Holland, for the construction of a railway to Delagoa Bay. We were received on every hand with the greatest heartiness and enthusiasm. Banquets were given in our honor and all seemed glad to make the personal acquaintance of their kinsmen from South Africa; but the principal thing, namely, the money to build the railway, we failed to obtain. Our deputation went from Holland, by Brussels, Paris, and Madrid, to Lisbon: we were received most cordially on our road by the French President and the King of Spain. The Portuguese declared themselves ready to build the Delagoa Railway, or at least to commence without delay that part of the line which would run through Portuguese territory. We could not arrange for Portugal to take over the whole line, so that it might all be under one management. After our return to Holland, we granted the concession to build on Transvaal territory to a few private persons, who laid the foundation of the future Netherlands South African Railway Company. From there we returned through Germany, where we were most cordially received by Bismarck and the Emperor William I,[1] to South Africa. In the next session of the Volksraad, I was able to state that our independence had been obtained—that henceforward the Republic took her place as an equal with other independent powers, and that the suzerainty had ceased to exist. It never occurred to England to contradict this statement. I brought back with me from Holland Dr. W. J. Leyds as State Attorney. The important part which Dr. Leyds was to play in subsequent events is known to all. His name will always remain associated with the history of the Republic.

The Delagoa Railway concession came up for discussion during the session of the Volksraad of 1884. Petitions protesting against the scheme had meanwhile accumulated. I defended my plan with all my might. I pointed out the importance of possessing a railway of our own. The duties imposed by Cape Colony were excessive and prevented our finding a market there for our products. Besides, I assured the Raad that the expenditure would not necessitate the levying of fresh taxation, and that it would be the very means for the exploitation of the new

---

[1] It was on this occasion that Prince Bismarck stumbled on the stairs of the Royal Palace in Berlin, and the Emperor William jestingly said: "Prince, you are growing old."

Bismarck replied:

"Yes, Majesty, that's usually the case, that the horse grows old before his rider."

The story of Kruger's stay with a large landed proprietor, of which many versions exist in Germany, is an invention. President Kruger states that he paid no such visit.—*Note by the Editor of the German Edition.*

KRUGER'S FIRST PRESIDENCY

resources which were about to be opened up and added to those already existing in the country. The Volksraad agreed to the concession.

The election of a new commandant general took place at the same time. General Joubert was almost unanimously re-elected.

The year 1885 witnessed another war on the western frontier. Massouw, whom the Frontier Commission had declared entirely independent, had voluntarily enrolled himself as a vassal of the Transvaal, but now refused to pay his taxes and assumed a very threatening attitude. General Joubert was obliged to march against him with a commando and artillery. The well-known general Piet Cronjé stormed Massouw's entrenchments with his accustomed daring and took possession of his town after a short battle, in which the Kaffir chief was killed. The Boers lost 14 killed and about 30 wounded. Among the killed was Schweizer, the commandant of the artillery. The losses of the Korannas were very heavy, and the whole tribe broke up.

It was a most unfortunate time for the Republic. The finances were in a sad condition. The credit with the Standard Bank had become exhausted, and they refused to advance more money. I had enough to do to encourage the burghers during my circular journeys and to impress upon them not to lose courage; for help, I said, would surely come. It did, but in a very different way from that which I had anticipated. The rich gold-fields of the Witwatersrand were discovered and brought about a complete revolution in the financial aspect of the affairs of the Republic. The history of the Republic entered upon a new phase with this discovery. Can we possibly look upon it as fortunate? As I have already said, gold and the embittered feelings which were the outcome of the first annexation are the causes of the present misery in South Africa. It will presently be seen that, of the two causes, the gold-fields assumed the greater importance. It is quite certain that, had no gold been found in the Transvaal, there would have been no war. No matter how great the influx of Englishmen, no matter how varied and manifold their complaints, the British Government would not have lifted a finger in their defence, had it not been tempted by the wealth of the country. The question of the franchise, which in reality caused no hardships to foreigners, was made use of by intriguers to further their plans. The words uttered by the late General Joubert, when a burgher came gleefully to tell him that a new gold-reef had been discovered, were prophetic:

"Instead of rejoicing," he said, "you would do better to weep; for this gold will cause our country to be soaked in blood."

The quartz-reefs of the Witwatersrand, which

KRUGER'S FIRST PRESIDENCY

resources which were about to be opened up and added to those already existing in the country. The Volksraad agreed to the concession.

The election of a new commandant general took place at the same time. General Joubert was almost unanimously re-elected.

The year 1885 witnessed another war on the western frontier. Massouw, whom the Frontier Commission had declared entirely independent, had voluntarily enrolled himself as a vassal of the Transvaal, but now refused to pay his taxes and assumed a very threatening attitude. General Joubert was obliged to march against him with a commando and artillery. The well-known general Piet Cronjé stormed Massouw's entrenchments with his accustomed daring and took possession of his town after a short battle, in which the Kaffir chief was killed. The Boers lost 14 killed and about 30 wounded. Among the killed was Schweizer, the commandant of the artillery. The losses of the Korannas were very heavy, and the whole tribe broke up.

It was a most unfortunate time for the Republic. The finances were in a sad condition. The credit with the Standard Bank had become exhausted, and they refused to advance more money. I had enough to do to encourage the burghers during my circular journeys and to impress upon them not to lose courage; for help, I said, would surely come. It did, but in a very different way from that which I had anticipated. The rich gold-fields of the Witwatersrand were discovered and brought about a complete revolution in the financial aspect of the affairs of the Republic. The history of the Republic entered upon a new phase with this discovery. Can we possibly look upon it as fortunate? As I have already said, gold and the embittered feelings which were the outcome of the first annexation are the causes of the present misery in South Africa. It will presently be seen that, of the two causes, the gold-fields assumed the greater importance. It is quite certain that, had no gold been found in the Transvaal, there would have been no war. No matter how great the influx of Englishmen, no matter how varied and manifold their complaints, the British Government would not have lifted a finger in their defence, had it not been tempted by the wealth of the country. The question of the franchise, which in reality caused no hardships to foreigners, was made use of by intriguers to further their plans. The words uttered by the late General Joubert, when a burgher came gleefully to tell him that a new gold-reef had been discovered, were prophetic:

"Instead of rejoicing," he said, "you would do better to weep; for this gold will cause our country to be soaked in blood."

The quartz-reefs of the Witwatersrand, which

were discovered in the year 1886, yielded a great wealth of gold, and so it became necessary for the Government to proclaim these districts as public gold-fields which would in consequence come under the influence of the mining laws. This happened in the middle of the year 1886 with regard to several farms, for example, Turffontein, Doornfontein, and others. Miners, speculators, and adventurers now arrived at the gold-fields from every part of the world. It does not need to be specially pointed out that among these thousands were many suspicious characters; but, on the other hand, it must also be acknowledged that the bulk of the population of the Witwatersrand consisted of law-abiding people, who looked for no political quarrels, but had come merely with the object of making their fortunes. Other gold-fields were discovered: those of Krugersdorp in the west, Heidelberg and Nigel in the east and, later, Malmanie and Klerksdorp. The increase in the population and the working of the mines brought increased prosperity in their train. The Boer found a market for his products and the treasury benefited by licenses and other sources of income. The first *bewaarplaatsen* of the Witwatersrand were sold, or, rather, leased during the same year: that is, the gold district was surveyed and parceled out into fields, claims or stations of 100 by 50 or 50 by 50 feet, and leased for 99 years against the payment of monthly taxes. At the expiration of the 99 years, they returned to the State. The big town of Johannesburg had its origin in this parceling-out of the gold-fields, and in time its trade became the most important of South Africa; consequently both Natal and Cape Colony were anxious to have access to it by rail. But I refused to listen to this, so long as the Delagoa Railway was unfinished. I feared that the independent trade of the Republic would be injured if other railway connections were opened up with Johannesburg. That my fears were well-grounded was fully proved, later, in the quarrel concerning the drifts, which very nearly involved the Republic in trouble with England.

In order to assist the new population as much as possible in their difficulties, a new committee was established, known as the "Delvers" or Mining Committee, for the purpose of settling differences among the gold-diggers and negotiating between them and the Government. Cecil Rhodes was for a long time a member of this Delvers Committee. In 1887, I visited Johannesburg in order to acquaint myself personally with the existing conditions. My reception was a friendly one; but I was presented with an address containing nothing but complaints against the Government. I replied that, in the first place, if grievances existed, they would be a matter for the decision of the Delvers Committee, and I

KRUGER'S FIRST PRESIDENCY

hoped that, in this way, a friendly settlement would be arrived at, and that I should not be compelled to have recourse to force. Much exception has been taken to my attitude, and perhaps I should have been wiser had I shown more consideration for the feelings of the foreigners. But we must not forget the elements of which the population was composed, nor the fact that a population of the same class at Kimberley had caused a rebellion, which obliged the British Government to send a considerable force to hold it in check; nor, lastly, that a former accusation of inherent weakness had cost the Republic dear. I was determined, therefore, to do all in my power to avoid a renewal of that accusation. In other respects, the complaints of foreigners always met with the friendliest consideration; for instance, when they complained that the taxation of their bewaarplaatsen was too heavy, it was soon afterwards considerably reduced.

The first conference held with a view to a closer alliance between the Orange Free State and the South African Republic took place in 1887. But it led to nothing, partly because I insisted that the Orange Free State should not permit a railway to be built through her territory which would connect the South African Republic with any of the British colonies in South Africa. I was opposed to a closer connection with the British South African states so long as the independence of the Transvaal was not guaranteed by the possession of a railway of her own, and I feared that the construction of the only possible self-supporting railway for which the Government had made itself liable would be delayed, or the railway rendered unproductive if other lines were started in the meantime. The second reason why the conference failed was that I demanded an offensive and defensive alliance in case the independence of either was threatened. President Brand could not see his way to accept this proposal. I need hardly say that the press of Cape Colony was exceedingly indignant with me on account of my attitude with regard to the railway question. But I went my own way, knowing that my first duty concerned the interest of my country.

The incorporation of the "New Republic" with the South African Republic took place during the same year, and it was afterwards formed into the Vryheid district. This republic owed its existence to a quarrel between two Zulu chiefs, Dinizulu, the son of Cetewayo, and Usibepu, who were at war with one another in 1884. Dinizulu had received assistance from a number of Boers, subjects both of the South African Republic and Natal, but without the authority of the Government. Dinizulu defeated Usibepu, and showed his gratitude by giving the Boers who had helped him a piece of land, on which a new

KRUGER'S FIRST PRESIDENCY

republic came into existence. Lucas Meyer, who, as a member of the Executive Raad, took part in the campaigns of the late war, was elected president of this republic. But, in 1887, it was incorporated with the South African Republic, at the request of the inhabitants, and received the same right as the other four great districts to send four members to the Volksraad of the South African Republic.

The period of five years for which I had been elected President had meanwhile nearly expired, and it became necessary, in 1887, to give notice, through the Volksraad, of the election of a new president to manage the affairs of the country from 1888.

KRUGER'S FIRST PRESIDENCY

republic came into existence. Lucas Meyer, who, as a member of the Executive Raad, took part in the campaigns of the late war, was elected president of this republic. But, in 1887, it was incorporated with the South African Republic, at the request of the inhabitants, and received the same right as the other four great districts to send four members to the Volksraad of the South African Republic.

The period of five years for which I had been elected President had meanwhile nearly expired, and it became necessary, in 1887, to give notice, through the Volksraad, of the election of a new president to manage the affairs of the country from 1888.

CHAPTER X

PAUL KRUGER'S SECOND PRESIDENCY:
1888–1893

CHAPTER X

PAUL KRUGER'S SECOND PRESIDENCY: 1888-1893

Dr. Leyds appointed State Secretary—Cecil Rhodes causes trouble on the northern frontiers of the Republic: the Chartered Company, Lobengula, Khama—Treaty of alliance between the Orange Free State and the South African Republic —Arrangements in favor of the Uitlanders: the Law Courts at Johannesburg; the Second Volksraad—Paul Kruger's " hatred of the Uitlanders "—The Swaziland Agreement— British perfidy—The Adendorff trek—Religious differences —Kruger the " autocrat "—The educational question—New elections.

FOR the new elections writs were issued in my name and Joubert's. Both of us accepted the candidature, but I was re-elected by a large majority and, in May 1888, was sworn in as State President for the second time. In the session of the Volksraad of that year, instead of the former Secretary to the Government, E. Bok, Dr. Leyds was now elected State Secretary, and the former, on my motion, was appointed Secretary to the Executive Raad, a post which was created for this purpose.

In the first year of my new presidency, an event occurred which might easily have led to the most serious complications. Cecil Rhodes had at that time begun to realize his imperialistic dreams, that is, his efforts to extend the British authority towards the north of Africa. At that time, Matabeleland and Mashonaland, to the north of the Transvaal, were governed by the Zulu Chief Lobengula, the son of Moselikatse, who had been driven out by the earlier settlers. But Moselikatse, the once so hated and cruel enemy of the Boers, had in later years entered into friendly relations with the Republic, and this friendship was continued under his son. Lobengula was even on very good terms with the Boers and often came into contact with the burghers of the Republic, who hunted in his territories. In 1887, he sent one of his principal indunas to Pretoria with the request that the South African Republic would appoint a consul in his domains. This wish was granted, and Piet Grobler, who was well acquainted with the Matabele Kaffirs, was sent to represent the Republic. Before he started, I drafted a treaty by which Lobengula placed his country under the protection of the Republic. Grobler took this document with him and, on his arrival at Bulawayo, read it to Lobengula, who fully agreed to the treaty, but asked for a few days' delay, to summon his indunas and hear their opinion before signing.

Grobler thought he would make use of this delay to meet his wife, who was on her way to join him,

KRUGER'S SECOND PRESIDENCY

and who was at that time on the Crocodile River. On the road, he came upon an armed detachment of Khama's Kaffirs, who were at war with Lobengula. A patrol of these blacks were the first to approach him: he rode straight up to them, to ask what they wanted, but they all took to flight. Grobler caught one of them and told him to go and fetch the captain or leader of the detachment, so that he might hear what their object was. He himself went on a few hundred yards from his wagons to meet the main body, which immediately opened fire upon him. While running back to his wagon, he was hit in the leg and fell. A young Kaffir girl called Lottering ran up and placed herself between the Kaffirs and the wounded man, so as to cover him with her own body. Grobler's companions, consisting of five or six men, now opened fire and soon drove the enemy to flight. Grobler was carried to his wagon and was able to resume his journey towards the Crocodile River, but died of his wounds a few days after his arrival.

There is no doubt whatever that this murder was due to the instigation of Cecil Rhodes and his clique. It was Rhodes's object to obtain possession of the South African interior, and he was afraid lest his plans should be frustrated by Grobler's appointment. A long correspondence ensued between the Government of the South African Republic and the

British High Commissioner concerning this incident, for Khama was under British protection. In order to avoid an open conflict, the Government of the Republic was obliged to content itself with an arrangement by which Khama was to pay Grobler's widow a pension of £200 a year.

In order to explain Rhodes's connection with this matter and with the whole further history of my own struggles and those of the Republic, I must here refer to the origin of the Chartered Company and the aims and efforts of the Rhodes party. Cecil Rhodes is the man who bore by far the most prominent part in the disaster that struck the country. In spite of the high eulogiums passed upon him by his friends, he was one of the most unscrupulous characters that have ever existed. The Jesuitical maxim that " the end justifies the means " formed his only political creed. This man was the curse of South Africa. He had made his fortune by diamond speculations at Kimberley, and the amalgamation of the Kimberley diamond-mines put him in possession of enormous influence in the financial world. Later, he became a member of the Cape Parliament and, in 1890, rose to be prime minister of Cape Colony. But, long before this, he had turned his attention to Central South Africa; for it was due to him that Goshenland and Stellaland became incorporated with Cape Colony. He looked upon these domains

KRUGER'S SECOND PRESIDENCY

as a thoroughfare, a kind of Suez Canal, to Central South Africa.[1]

As early as 1888, he induced Sir Hercules Robinson, the High Commissioner of that time, to enter into a treaty with Lobengula, the chief of the Matabele. Later, he managed to turn this to his advantage when, through the payment of a large sum of money, supplemented by a quantity of fire-arms, he succeeded in obtaining a concession from Lobengula for himself. This concession merely gave him the right to search for gold or other metals in the country; but he used it to obtain a firm footing in Matabeleland, with the intention of preventing the extension of the South African Republic in this direction. He soon saw that he would not be able to carry out his plans without protection from England. So he went to England to obtain a charter giving him the right to certain monopolies and independent action. He procured it without much difficulty, for he found

---

[1] In the early days of Kruger's presidency, Rhodes tried to win him as an ally. On his way from Beira to Cape Town, he called on Kruger at Pretoria and said:

"We must work together. I know the Republic wants a seaport: you must have Delagoa Bay."

Kruger replied:

"How can we work together there? The harbor belongs to the Portuguese, and they won't hand it over."

"Then we must simply take it," said Rhodes.

"I can't take away other people's property," said Kruger. "If the Portuguese won't sell the harbor, I would n't take it even if you gave it me; for ill-gotten goods are accursed."

Rhodes then ceased his endeavors to gain Kruger over.—*Note by the Editor of the German edition.*

bribery a useful ally when fine speeches were insufficient for his purpose, and he was not the man to spare money if some object was to be attained. It is certain that a number of influential persons in England received shares in his Chartered Company. He even tried to win over the Irish faction in Parliament, which was not at all in harmony with his plans, by a present of £10,000. Who knows how many more large sums he spent with the same object! This will never be revealed. Rhodes was capital incarnate. No matter how base, no matter how contemptible, be it lying, bribery or treachery, all and every means were welcome to him, if they led to the attainment of his objects.

Rhodes obtained his charter, although one might well ask what rights England possessed over this district to enable her to grant a charter; and a company was formed with a capital of one million sterling. Soon afterwards, in 1890, Rhodes fitted out an expedition to take possession of " his " territory. The protest of the Matabele king was ignored. Rhodes took possession of Mashonaland, and built several forts: Fort Charter, Fort Salisbury and Fort Victoria. It soon became evident, however, that Mashonaland was of little value, either agriculturally or as a mining district. Under the impression that Matabeleland possessed valuable gold-fields, he set about to annex it. In order to do so, he must involve

KRUGER'S SECOND PRESIDENCY

Lobengula in a war, and he succeeded but too well. It is affirmed in Africa that it was Rhodes, through his administrator, who informed Lobengula that the Mashonas had stolen cattle, and that it was his duty to punish the raiders. Lobengula at once dispatched a band of his people, as was the custom in such cases, to revenge the robbery. Rhodes used this fact as an excuse to demand Lobengula's punishment, on account of the massacre of the Mashonas. Whether there be truth in this statement or not, one thing is certain: Rhodes had his way and his war. A force under Dr. Jameson quickly dispersed the Matabele; the Maxim guns cut them down by hundreds. It is said that Lobengula died near the Zambesi during his flight. What must have been the thoughts of the black potentate, during those last few hours of his life, when they dwelt on the arts of a so-called Christian nation? Such thoughts never influenced a man like Rhodes. He forthwith explored Matabeleland in all directions in search of gold, but with poor results. So he deliberately made up his mind to possess himself of the rich gold-fields of the South African Republic, the highroad to which was the possession of South Africa itself. History knows the successful issue of this base design.

In 1888, President Brand of the Orange Free State died, after having been President for twenty-five years. In his stead was elected Francis William Reitz, who afterwards became State Secretary of the South African Republic: a man esteemed by all who know him; one of those men of whom we often read in books, but whom we seldom meet in real life; a man of superior and noble character, whose one aim in life is to serve his country: in a word, a man whom it is a privilege to know. Shortly after his inauguration as State President, in 1889, a second conference took place between the Governments of the two Republics, with the object of establishing a closer alliance between the two states. The conference met at Potchefstroom and had a very different result from the first. The two Republics bound themselves to come to each other's assistance in case the independence of either should be wantonly threatened from without. A commercial treaty was also concluded, establishing mutual free trade, with the exception of the products and other goods on which the South African Republic was bound to levy import duties in order to protect the monopolies which she had granted. An arrangement touching the railways, which I had proposed at the first conference, was now accepted.

In 1888, I again visited Johannesburg, where I met with a very friendly reception. In the addresses that were presented to me, I was asked to establish a municipality and to increase the number of judicial officers. This last request I at once

KRUGER'S SECOND PRESIDENCY

granted by appointing Dr. Jorissen as a special judge for Johannesburg (the other demands were fulfilled later). After granting this request, I never ceased thinking how I could meet the wishes of the new population for representation, without injuring the Republic or prejudicing the interests of the older burghers. For, although all the complaints of the Uitlanders always met with a friendly hearing from the Executive Raad, which had received full powers from the Volksraad to legislate for the population of the gold-fields, and although as much was granted as possible, nevertheless it was evident to me that some means must be found to give the Uitlanders a voice in the representation of the country. I believed that I had discovered this means in the institution of a Second Volksraad, and it was my own idea, for which I made myself alone responsible, that to this body might be entrusted the discussion of all questions, such as, for instance, the gold laws, telegraphs, etc., which were mainly of interest to the new arrivals.

In this manner I endeavored to open the way to the new population for the legal presentation and remedy of their grievances. Hitherto they had been prevented by the conditions necessary for obtaining the franchise. The constitution prescribed that a foreigner must have been registered for five years on the field cornets' lists before he could be naturalized. My proposal for a Second Volksraad involved this alteration in the law, that only two years' registration would be necessary for purposes of naturalization and that the naturalized person would then have the right to vote for members of the Second Volksraad and for all officials holding elective posts, with the exception of the State President, the Commandant General and the members of the First Volksraad. Any person enjoying this right for two years, therefore, in four years in all after his registration on the field cornets' lists as an inhabitant of the Republic, would become entitled to be himself elected a member of the Second Volksraad. Ten years later, he was to receive full burgher rights, that is to say, the same civic rights as those possessed by the old burghers.

This proposal met with lively opposition, as some members of the Volksraad looked upon it as a piece of class legislation, as, in a certain measure, it undoubtedly was, while others were of the opinion that it gave too many rights to the foreigners. The matter was adjourned in order that the opinion of the people might be taken. The burghers, however, approved of the proposal, which was a proof of their confidence in their President; for I feel sure that such a proposal would never have been carried if it had been moved by any other than myself. In re-

KRUGER'S SECOND PRESIDENCY

granted by appointing Dr. Jorissen as a special judge for Johannesburg (the other demands were fulfilled later). After granting this request, I never ceased thinking how I could meet the wishes of the new population for representation, without injuring the Republic or prejudicing the interests of the older burghers. For, although all the complaints of the Uitlanders always met with a friendly hearing from the Executive Raad, which had received full powers from the Volksraad to legislate for the population of the gold-fields, and although as much was granted as possible, nevertheless it was evident to me that some means must be found to give the Uitlanders a voice in the representation of the country. I believed that I had discovered this means in the institution of a Second Volksraad, and it was my own idea, for which I made myself alone responsible, that to this body might be entrusted the discussion of all questions, such as, for instance, the gold laws, telegraphs, etc., which were mainly of interest to the new arrivals.

In this manner I endeavored to open the way to the new population for the legal presentation and remedy of their grievances. Hitherto they had been prevented by the conditions necessary for obtaining the franchise. The constitution prescribed that a foreigner must have been registered for five years on the field cornets' lists before he could be naturalized. My proposal for a Second Volksraad involved this alteration in the law, that only two years' registration would be necessary for purposes of naturalization and that the naturalized person would then have the right to vote for members of the Second Volksraad and for all officials holding elective posts, with the exception of the State President, the Commandant General and the members of the First Volksraad. Any person enjoying this right for two years, therefore, in four years in all after his registration on the field cornets' lists as an inhabitant of the Republic, would become entitled to be himself elected a member of the Second Volksraad. Ten years later, he was to receive full burgher rights, that is to say, the same civic rights as those possessed by the old burghers.

This proposal met with lively opposition, as some members of the Volksraad looked upon it as a piece of class legislation, as, in a certain measure, it undoubtedly was, while others were of the opinion that it gave too many rights to the foreigners. The matter was adjourned in order that the opinion of the people might be taken. The burghers, however, approved of the proposal, which was a proof of their confidence in their President; for I feel sure that such a proposal would never have been carried if it had been moved by any other than myself. In re-

KRUGER'S SECOND PRESIDENCY

sponse to the public wish, the law was now passed, by a large majority, at the next annual session of the Raad.

The Uitlanders contended in the English press, and Mr. Chamberlain made the contention his own, that the Second Volksraad was of no practical use. It is only necessary to say that, notwithstanding that the laws and resolutions of the Second Volksraad had to be submitted to the ratification of the First Volksraad, the latter body only once rejected a decision of the Second Volksraad, and that was in the matter of the dispute about the bewaarplaatsen, when the Second Volksraad wished to grant the mining rights of an estate, without more ado, to a tenant who had leased only the surface rights.

It must not be forgotten either that these alterations of the constitution in favor of the Uitlanders were introduced by myself and accepted by the Volksraad in spite of the fact that, only a little earlier, an incident had occurred at Johannesburg of a character very insulting to me and to the burghers. I was going to Norval's Point, on the Orange River, to meet the High Commissioner in the matter of the Swaziland question. On the road, I stopped at Johannesburg, where, as usual, a deputation came to lay its grievances before me. It was quite impossible for me to concede all the wishes of these people on the spot. One of the deputation threw the reproach in my face that I treated the new population with contempt. I angrily answered:

"I have no contempt for the new population, but only for men like yourself."

In the evening, a riot took place in front of Mr. van Brandis's house, where I was staying: the flag of the Republic was pulled down and torn to pieces. It is easy to see that this provoked the old population almost beyond endurance, but I quieted them by saying that the inhabitants in general were loyal burghers and that the scandal must be laid to the charge of a few rioters. When I met the High Commissioner at Norval's Point, he spoke to me of the riot at Johannesburg, and I said:

"Yes, Sir Henry; you see, those people remind me of a baboon I once had, which was so fond of me that he would not let any one touch me. But one day we were sitting round the fire, and unfortunately the beast's tail got caught in the fire. He now flew at me furiously, thinking that I was the cause of his accident. The Johannesburgers are just like that. They have burnt their fingers in speculations and now they want to revenge themselves on Paul Kruger."

A fresh occasion for provoking foreign hatred against me presented itself at the time of the septennial commemoration of the Declaration of Inde-

KRUGER'S SECOND PRESIDENCY

pendence at Paarde Kraal. I made a long speech to some thousands of people in which I set forth how I viewed the history of my people in the light of God's Word. I began by addressing my hearers:

"People of the Lord, you old people of the country, you foreigners, you new-comers, yes, even you thieves and murderers!"

The Uitlanders, who were always on the watch to invent grievances against the President and the Government, were furious at this address, and declared that I had called them thieves and murderers, which was, of course, an absolute lie. I merely wished to say that I called upon everybody, even thieves and murderers, if there were any such in the meeting, to humble themselves before God and to acknowledge the wonders in God's dealings with the people of the Republic. If any insult was conveyed in these words, it applied just as much to the old as to the new population, as any sensible person, who took the trouble to follow my train of thought, would have perceived for himself.

The Swaziland question, in connection with which I had gone to meet Sir Henry Loch, had given the Republic great trouble. Swaziland formerly belonged to the Republic, but was taken from it by the Royal Commission of 1881. Except on the east, it is bounded on every side by the South African Republic. Some of the burghers had obtained certain concessions from the Swazi king, Umbandine. Other persons, mostly adventurers, demanded similar concessions, and were so great a nuisance and annoyance to the King that he asked the British Government to send him an adviser. No time was lost in complying with his request, as this would bring Swaziland within the sphere of British influence. Offy Shepstone, son of the Sir Theophilus Shepstone who annexed the Republic in 1877, was appointed adviser to Umbandine by the High Commissioner. But the confusion in the land grew worse and worse, till at last the real government of the country was handed over to a kind of committee consisting of Boers and Englishmen. It was obvious that such a condition of things could not last, and Sir Hercules Robinson did not appear at all averse to the annexation of the country by the Republic. Needless to say that this arrangement did not suit the Jingoes and "humanitarians" in England; so the British Government decided to dispatch Sir Francis de Winton as a special envoy to look into the affairs of Swaziland.

General Joubert had an interview, on behalf of the South African Republic, with Sir Francis de Winton, at which he explained the reason why the Transvaal Government desired to incorporate Swaziland with the Republic. After the British Government had received de Winton's report, they pendence at Paarde Kraal. I made a long speech to some thousands of people in which I set forth how I viewed the history of my people in the light of God's Word. I began by addressing my hearers:

"People of the Lord, you old people of the country, you foreigners, you new-comers, yes, even you thieves and murderers!"

The Uitlanders, who were always on the watch to invent grievances against the President and the Government, were furious at this address, and declared that I had called them thieves and murderers, which was, of course, an absolute lie. I merely wished to say that I called upon everybody, even thieves and murderers, if there were any such in the meeting, to humble themselves before God and to acknowledge the wonders in God's dealings with the people of the Republic. If any insult was conveyed in these words, it applied just as much to the old as to the new population, as any sensible person, who took the trouble to follow my train of thought, would have perceived for himself.

The Swaziland question, in connection with which I had gone to meet Sir Henry Loch, had given the Republic great trouble. Swaziland formerly belonged to the Republic, but was taken from it by the Royal Commission of 1881. Except on the east, it is bounded on every side by the South African Republic. Some of the burghers had obtained certain concessions from the Swazi king, Umbandine. Other persons, mostly adventurers, demanded similar concessions, and were so great a nuisance and annoyance to the King that he asked the British Government to send him an adviser. No time was lost in complying with his request, as this would bring Swaziland within the sphere of British influence. Offy Shepstone, son of the Sir Theophilus Shepstone who annexed the Republic in 1877, was appointed adviser to Umbandine by the High Commissioner. But the confusion in the land grew worse and worse, till at last the real government of the country was handed over to a kind of committee consisting of Boers and Englishmen. It was obvious that such a condition of things could not last, and Sir Hercules Robinson did not appear at all averse to the annexation of the country by the Republic. Needless to say that this arrangement did not suit the Jingoes and "humanitarians" in England; so the British Government decided to dispatch Sir Francis de Winton as a special envoy to look into the affairs of Swaziland.

General Joubert had an interview, on behalf of the South African Republic, with Sir Francis de Winton, at which he explained the reason why the Transvaal Government desired to incorporate Swaziland with the Republic. After the British Government had received de Winton's report, they commissioned Sir Henry Loch, the new Governor of Cape Colony, to communicate with me. We met in conference at Blignautspont; and Rhodes was also present at the meeting. I did all I could to induce the British Government to agree to the incorporation of Swaziland, as well as of Sambaanland and Umbigesaland, with which the Republic had already come to an understanding. Sir Henry Loch did all in his power to obtain the consent of the Republic to a scheme for a railway which Natal desired to build as far as Johannesburg in order to bring about a general South African customs-union. I would not listen to the proposal of a general customs-union; not because I was opposed to the scheme, but because my first condition was always my demand for a port: port first, customs-union after. I agreed to the railway scheme, not on any special grounds, but because I desired to meet Natal in the matter. But I declined to treat this railway scheme, as a condition in entirely different questions; and with regard to the tariff question, it was necessary that I should first put myself in communication with the Portuguese Government, as there already existed an understanding between myself and them on the subject. In fact, the Portuguese Government had only determined to build the Delagoa Bay Railway on condition that no new line to Johannesburg should be built that would be shorter than the Delagoa Line. The outcome of the conference was that the High Commissioner agreed to draft a deed which he was to submit to me. At the same time he expressed the wish that Dr. Leyds, who was present at the negotiations, should remain behind and be present also at the drafting of the document in order to explain it, should it be necessary to throw additional light upon any particular point for my benefit. He was then to sign a declaration that he had been present at the drafting of the deed. Thereupon the conference broke up.

Shortly afterwards Sir Henry Loch sent me his draft proposals, containing the following main points:

Swaziland to be governed in common; the Republic to receive permission to build a railway as far as Kosi Bay. A strip of land, three miles broad, was ceded to her for this purpose. But the British Government retained the protectorate over this district and over Kosi Bay as well: a condition which made the acceptance of the offer by the Republic impossible from the commencement;

The Transvaal, besides, to receive permission to annex a small piece of land, the so-called Little Free State, situated between the Republic and Swaziland.

Sir Henry Loch insisted that this was the understanding at which he had arrived with me at Blignautspont, and that Dr. Leyds, after the closing of the conference, had expressed himself satisfied with the conditions and had signed them in proof of his agreement. Both Dr. Leyds and I disputed this assertion, and I refused to accept the conditions of the draft. Loch threatened that, unless it was accepted, the British Government would avail themselves of their right, under the London Convention, to send an armed force into Swaziland.

Shortly after, Jan Hofmeyer came to Pretoria, in order to mediate, and, with his assistance, the first Swaziland Convention was agreed upon. Needless to say that the Republic received very little benefit indeed: nay, she lost; for she was prevented from making any treaty in future with the natives in the north and north-west. Further, she had to agree not to put any difficulties in the way of a railway connection with Natal and—here we again see Cecil Rhodes's hand—to assist the Chartered Company to the best of her ability in the north. This last condition, as we shall see later, gave rise to great difficulties.

The Volksraad accepted the agreement, but expressed its regret very freely at the absence of mutual accommodation which the Republic had encountered on the part of England. The unsatisfactory state of things resulting from this agreement lasted until 1893, when a second Swaziland Convention was concluded.

Two events occurred during my second presidency which called forth great opposition against myself. The first of these was the Adendorff trek; the second a conference on church matters. The Adendorff trek had its origin in a concession which a certain Adendorff and Mr. B. Foster, jun., had obtained in Banjailand and which they vainly endeavored to sell to Cecil Rhodes. Rhodes declared that the concession was illegal, whereupon its owners resolved to trek to the territory which had been leased to them. The High Commissioner and Rhodes both opposed this trek, as they considered that it endangered the interests of the Chartered Company, and they asked me, in accordance with the Swaziland Convention, to forbid the trekkers to carry out their project. I immediately published a declaration against the trek and issued a proclamation in which the burghers throughout the country were strictly forbidden to take part in it. Any one disobeying the proclamation was threatened with the utmost rigors of the law. A section of the burghers openly protested against this proclamation, and, although I knew that it was likely to cost me some of my popularity, I was in honor bound to observe the decisions of the Swaziland Convention, little though they appealed to me. How dear this attitude cost me was shown at the next presidential election; for, although my opponents brought up many other grievances against me, the fact that I had prevented the Adendorff trek was one of the chief reasons that caused a number of burghers to vote for my opponents. This question afterwards came up for discussion in the Volksraad, and, in the debate that followed, many influential members spoke against the proclamation, including the late General Joubert and Mr. Schalk Burger, who became Acting President of the Republic during the late war, after my departure for Europe. Eventually, however, the Volksraad accepted the proclamation and nothing came of the whole movement, this being due, to a great extent, to my endeavors to see the burghers personally, whenever I could, and persuade them from joining the trek.

At the same time that the Republic had to encounter these difficulties in external politics, quarrels arose in regard to church matters.

After the war of 1881, the burghers felt the necessity of consolidation in ecclesiastical matters, and the result was a union between the *Hervormde* and the *Nederduitsch-Gereformeerde* Churches. The third evangelical church community, the *Christelijk-Gereformeerde*, or so-called Dopper Church, of which I was a member, had hesitated to join the union, and was therefore not directly mixed up in these quarrels. Shortly after the union, fresh differences of opinion arose, and several burghers, whose leader was Christian Joubert, wished to have no more to do with the union and decided to remain in the *Hervormde* Church. Others followed later on, and their leader was A. D. W. Wolmarans, who was at that time in Europe as a delegate. Difficult questions naturally arose regarding the right of ownership to church property, for the members who separated from the *Hervormde* Church laid claims to its property, as did those who remained faithful to the union. It is not surprising that this situation gave rise to bitter disputes and many quarrels.

In order to put a stop to these bickerings, I sent a circular note to the pastors and elders of the different parties, inviting them to a conference at which an attempt would be made to remove these difficulties. It took place, in 1891, in the House of the Second Volksraad, I myself presiding. All parties were represented. In my opening speech, I asked them to look upon me, not as the State President, but as a brother and fellow-Christian, anxious to do my share to put an end to the unhappy state of things by removing the cause of quarrel. I tried hard to restore the union, thinking that, by doing so, I should succeed in healing the breach. But it soon became obvious that my attempts were doomed to failure, and I accordingly passed on to the ques-

KRUGER'S SECOND PRESIDENCY

tion of the right of property. But here, too, all my efforts to reconcile their differences proved fruitless. The conference closed without any satisfactory solution of the vexed question having been arrived at.

Although I really instituted this conference with the best intentions, it was nevertheless employed as a weapon against me by my enemies. I was reproached at the next presidential election with being an autocrat and with wishing to interfere in everything, even in church matters.

This new presidential election was due in the following year. This time, there were three candidates in the field: myself, Joubert and Chief Justice Kotzé; and it proved the most violent electoral struggle through which the Republic ever passed. I was accused by the Opposition of being autocratic, of squandering the national money, of giving away all rights and privileges in the form of concessions and of awarding all the offices of state to the Hollanders. Reproaches upon reproaches were also hurled against the Opposition. It is far from pleasant to carry back one's thoughts to that time, when the two chief men in the Republic were painted so black that, if only the tenth part of the accusations flung at us had been based upon truth, neither of us would have been worthy to enjoy the confidence of the people for another hour.

CHAPTER XI

PAUL KRUGER'S THIRD PRESIDENCY: 1893-1898

CHAPTER XI

PAUL KRUGER'S THIRD PRESIDENCY: 1893-1898

The Transvaal National Union—The second Swaziland Agreement—Difficulties with the Kaffir tribes in the Blue Mountains—The English immigrants refuse to perform military service—Sir Henry Loch at Pretoria—The President insulted—Annexation of Sambaanland and Umbigesaland by England—Solemn opening of the Delagoa Bay Railway and tariff war with Cape Colony—The Jameson Raid—Mr. Chamberlain's policy of provocation—The report of the Mining Commission—The struggle between the Government and the Supreme Court—Sir Alfred Milner—New elections—The Queen of England a *"kwaaie vrouw"*—Closer alliance with the Orange Free State.

THE result of the new election was:

    Kruger . . . . 7,854 votes
    Joubert . . . . 7,009 ,,
    Chief Justice Kotzé . . .   81 ,,

Joubert's party was dissatisfied with the result and entered a protest against my election. When the Volksraad met, on the 1st of May, a committee of six, consisting of three of Joubert's followers and three of mine, was appointed to hold a scrutiny. A resolution was passed, at the same time, by which I was to remain in office until the committee had given its decision, although my term of office nominally expired on the 5th of May. The majority of the committee were of opinion that the election had been legally conducted. Nevertheless the minority handed in their own report recommending a new election. The Volksraad, on the other hand, accepted the report of the majority by 18 votes to 3, with the result that, on the 12th of May 1893, I was installed as State President for the third time. After being sworn in, I once more addressed the people, this time from the balcony of the new Government Buildings, while the public stood crowded in large numbers in the Church Square in front. I exhorted the burghers to remain unanimous, spoke a word of greeting to the women of the country and, lastly and particularly, admonished the children, with whom the future lay, to continue true to their mother tongue.[1] Combined

---

[1] This admonition was uttered especially in connection with the educational reforms which had been introduced in the previous year and which were based upon the principle that the Dutch language was to be employed as the educational medium.

The portion of Kruger's speech to which he refers, ran as follows:

"Dear children, you are the ones upon whom the State President keeps his eye, for I see our future Church and State in your hands, for when all the old people are gone, you will be the Church and State; but, if you depart from the truth and stray, then you will lose your inheritance. Stand firm by God's Word, in which your parents have brought you up. Love that Word. I shall endeavor with all my might to assist churches and schools, to let you receive a Christian education, so that you may both religiously and socially become useful members of Church and State, and I trust that the teachers and ministers will also do their best. It is a great privilege that your Government has ordered a Christian education, and you are greatly privileged in being able to enjoy a Christian education, and not you alone, for the object is to extend it so that every one may have the opportunity of receiving it and turning it

KRUGER'S THIRD PRESIDENCY

efforts on the part of the burghers were especially needed that year, as the country had been visited by

to account. . . . It is also a great privilege for you that the Government and Volksraad have accepted our language as the State language. Keep to that, keep to the language in which your forefathers, whom God led out of the wilderness, struggled and prayed to God, and which became ever dearer and dearer to them: the language in which the Bible comes to you, and in which your forefathers read the Bible, and which contains the religion of your forefathers. And, therefore, if you become indifferent to your language, you also become indifferent to your forefathers and indifferent to the Bible and indifferent to your religion; and then you will soon stray away entirely and you will rob posterity of your Dutch Bible and of your religion, which God confirmed to your forefathers with wonders and miracles. Stand firm then, so that you shall not be trusted in vain, and keep to your language, your Bible and your religion. It is a good thing to learn foreign languages, especially the language of your neighbors with whom you have most to do; but let any foreign language be a second language to you. Pray to God that you may stand firm on this point and not stray, so that the Lord may remain amongst you, and then posterity will honor you for your loyalty."

It was just the two points of view touched upon in this speech which President Burgers had neglected in the educational law which he had drafted in 1874, and, with the aid of his eloquence, had induced the Volksraad to pass. He was opposed to the religious convictions of the nation. He had abolished the religious basis upon which the schools were founded. And therefore his law, wherever he himself was not able to plead for it with the power of his rhetoric, remained a dead letter.

After the War of Independence, one of the first cares of the regency, at whose head Kruger stood as Vice-President, was to obtain an educational law that should satisfy the real needs and wishes of the nation. Kruger thought he had found the man who possessed the necessary experience and who shared the convictions of the Boers in Dr. du Toit, and appointed him Superintendent of Education. He drafted a law which was passed by the Volksraad in 1882, but, although his intention was good, the execution was faulty. Du Toit was more of a politician than a schoolman, and he resigned his office in 1889. The development of the gold-fields and the influx of emigrants at that time made such demands upon the powers and attention of the Government that it was unable to devote as much care to the schools as it would have wished. And so the post of Director of Education remained vacant for some time. After this, when a new holder of this post was looked for, the division of the people into different Church parties determined them not again to appoint heavy floods. The rivers rose higher than had been known within human memory and did enormous damage.

In the year preceding the election of 1893, which an ecclesiastic. Professor Mansvelt, the Professor of Modern Languages at Stellenbosch, was therefore approached. He at first refused, but, when again called upon and after a personal interview with the President, accepted, at the end of 1891. After he had satisfied himself by a long journey of inspection as to the condition of the schools throughout the country, he drafted a new law with the assistance of a committee appointed by the Volksraad for that purpose. The law was first submitted to the people and afterwards passed unanimously by the Volksraad.

In the main points, the outlines of the law of 1882 were preserved, but in certain respects the new law was a great improvement and advance upon the old. President Kruger took part personally in all the deliberations; most of the sittings were even held in his house. He had originally entertained misgivings as to three points in particular. The increased state grants caused him to fear lest private initiative should be relaxed and the duty incumbent upon Christian parents transferred to the state. He had seen in his own church how the heavy burdens which it owed towards the state church had strengthened its readiness to perform acts of self-sacrifice. But he was at last obliged to admit that the perception of the necessity for supplying the best possible education to the children of a people that was called upon to hold its own in the inheritance of its fathers against a great European influx was not yet sufficiently general to allow him to act in accordance with his idealistic views. Moreover, model schools were required, and higher schools for the training of civil servants out of the children of the country, and this necessitated financial sacrifices that could not be borne by private individuals. And so now, as again later, the President accepted the position, without in any way surrendering his principle.

He also entertained misgivings regarding the demand of a general proof of the possession of a certain degree of qualification among the teachers, for he thought that this showed ingratitude towards the old teachers, who had given their services almost gratuitously to the land and people in bad times and who would now have to be dismissed. This objection was settled by a compromise, by which this class of teachers was allowed to continue in the " Outer " or " Boer Schools," at least if they were able to satisfy modest requirements.

The third point against which President Kruger at first raised an objection was the subsidy to the higher girls' schools. He feared that this would result in changes and revolutions in the life of the people,

KRUGER'S THIRD PRESIDENCY

placed me for the third time at the head of the state, an association had been formed at Johannesburg which exercised a most disastrous influence upon the

which had always considered that a woman's place was at home. But he gave way to his advisers, and, afterwards, it was he himself who recommended to the so-called Progressives the admission of clever girls into the State Gymnasium. And in 1894 he personally opened the State Girls' School at Pretoria with prayers and an address. The people was converted to these reforms at the same time as its President.

Determined to make education as general as possible, he was at once prepared to agree to the proposals that in districts with a mixed population, State subsidies should also be allowed, under certain conditions, to those schools in which education was not given in Dutch. A law of his own proposing was passed, with this object, on the 1st of June 1892, and a few English schools and the flourishing German school developed under his protection at Johannesburg. And when the President saw that the English population made too little use of the advantages granted them and the political Opposition established an educational commission with an educational fund of £100,000 for the maintenance of schools conducted in an anti-national spirit, despite his objection, on principle, to state schools, he gave his consent to the erection of Uitlander schools at the cost of the state, to which the mixed inhabitants of the gold-fields could send their children either gratuitously or on payment of very small fees. The only duty prescribed to these schools was to give opportunities for instruction in the language of the country; and at the expiration of two years, there were twelve of these schools, with 49 teachers and 1,499 children, each of whom cost the state £20 a year. In this way the English enjoyed advantages superior to those of the whole population. The fact, moreover, that the President would never give up his principle that the Dutch language should be maintained as the one and only educational medium merely shows that he saw, as did others, the necessity of the preservation of the national tongue for the independent development and consolidation of a nation, especially such a nation as that of the Boers, which had to hold its ground in the midst of an overwhelming foreign population.

Education made such great strides in the course of the next eight years that, at the Paris Exhibition of 1900, the commission received two *grands prix:* a distinction which is all the more deserved when one thinks of the many obstacles with which education in the South African Republic had to grapple, such as a scattered population, Kaffir wars, dearth of laborers, continuous droughts, the rinderpest and so on.—*Note by the Editor of the German Edition.*

fate of the Transvaal. This was the so-called "Transvaal National Union," which made it its business to keep the Johannesburg population in a state of constant ferment and to manufacture complaints against the Government. Every method of agitation was put into force by these gentry for the furtherance of their intrigues. Apparently they were agitating for the franchise; but their real object was a very different one, as will be seen. That Rhodes's influence was here, too, paramount was proved by later events.

The seditious spirit which actuated the National Union stood clearly and distinctly revealed at the very first opportunity; and this came during the Kaffir War in the Blue Mountains. The Republic, at that time, had to contend against constant difficulties with the Kaffir tribes in the North. To-day it was this one, to-morrow that other, that assumed an insolent attitude towards the Government. At last, one of their chiefs, by name Malapoch, who lived in the Blue Mountains, behaved so outrageously that the Government was compelled to send a commando against him. His audacity had gone so far as to order a number of his subjects, who lived in the plains round about the Blue Mountains, to be murdered, because they had paid taxes to the Government of the Republic in accordance with their lawful obligations.

KRUGER'S THIRD PRESIDENCY

General Joubert collected the young men of Pretoria for an expedition against Malapoch. These young men of course included many subjects of foreign Powers, but all obeyed the field-cornet's summons with the greatest alacrity, with the exception of the English.

These, as "British subjects," thought themselves much too grand to fight for the despised Boers. The English clergy did all they could to stir up the minds of these young men by public addresses. At last, the field-cornet found himself compelled, in compliance with Article 5 of the Regulations of War, to arrest the recalcitrants. These lodged a complaint with the Chief Justice, and demanded that the field-cornet be ordered to leave them alone. The court, however, decided that they were obliged to serve, and so these fine young gentlemen were sent under a burgher escort to the commando. Meanwhile, the so-called National Union had not been idle, but made every possible attempt to harass the Government. The insolence of these people would be incomprehensible, if it had not afterwards appeared who were behind them. The British Government took official notice of the occurrence and sent Sir Henry Loch to Pretoria to discuss the question with the Government of the Republic.

In the meantime, the Volksraad had passed a resolution by which any person not yet enjoying full burgher rights might be released from military service on the payment of a certain sum of money. Shortly afterwards, Sir Henry Loch came to Pretoria. On his arrival, the English behaved in the most disorderly fashion and, as soon as the Governor and I were seated in the carriage, the Jingoes took out the horses and drew us to the Transvaal Hotel, singing the usual English satirical ditties as they did so. One of the ring-leaders jumped on the box waving a great Union Jack. On arriving in front of the Transvaal Hotel, they stopped the carriage and read an address to Sir Henry Loch. A number of Transvaal burghers, seeing what was going on, drew the carriage, in which I had remained seated alone, to the Government Buildings. I need not say that this incident made a very bad impression on the minds of the burghers and added new fuel to the already existing dislike of the English. The Volksraad was sitting at the time and passed a resolution asking the Government for an explanation why no measures were taken to prevent an exhibition so offensive to the people of the Republic. Soon after, a number of burghers assembled in the town, having come up determined to prevent a repetition of these insults.

Meantime, the so-called National Union continued their work. They invited Sir Henry Loch to visit Johannesburg; for they were fully aware that it would be much easier to provoke a riot there than

KRUGER'S THIRD PRESIDENCY

at Pretoria. What they were working for was intervention from England. I was fully alive to the difficulties which must of necessity arise from Sir Henry Loch's visit to Johannesburg, and advised him most earnestly not to go. I even went so far as to say to him, in private conversation, that the responsibility, should he accept the invitation, must rest entirely with him. He thereupon abandoned his proposed visit to Johannesburg. His whole public attitude was, in fact, perfectly correct. But how did he act in secret? When the National Union discovered that the visit to Johannesburg was not to take place, they sent some of their members, including Tudhope and Leonard, to Pretoria, with an address to Sir Henry Loch. The address contained the most insulting accusations against the Government and the Volksraad. But this caused no surprise to those who knew its source. In public, Sir Henry Loch advised the deputation to carry their complaints quietly before the Volksraad. In secret, he asked them how many rifles and how much ammunition they had at Johannesburg, and how long they could hold out against the Government, until he was able to come to their assistance with English troops from outside.

How typically English was this conduct on the part of a high-placed British official! It is characteristic of the entire English policy in South Africa.

THE MEMOIRS OF PAUL KRUGER

Lies, treachery, intrigues and secret instigations against the Government of the Republic: these have always been distinguishing marks of English politics, which found their final goal in this present cruel war. If, encouraged by the question, which amounted almost to a suggestion, the Johannesburgers did not rise there and then, this is owing only to the fact that they were without rifles and ammunition. But it is not difficult to trace the consequences of this advice in the events which, soon afterwards, ensued.

I have been obliged to anticipate, in order to give a connected picture of the nature and aims of the National Union; but events of great importance in foreign politics had taken place in the meantime. In 1893, the second Swaziland Convention was concluded. In this connection, a conference was held at Colesberg between the High Commissioner and myself: it led to no result, but was followed by a second conference at Pretoria. Here came Sir Henry Loch, with his wife, his two daughters and a numerous staff, and was given a brilliant reception. Judging by the festivities held in Sir Henry's honor, an uninitiated observer would have thought that a solemn welcome was being offered to a true friend and ally of the Republic. The arrangement which was soon made was not of a nature to give rise to much rejoicing; but it was the best we could obtain. The chief points were:

KRUGER'S THIRD PRESIDENCY

The Republic received the right to conclude a treaty with the Queen of the Swazis by which the suzerainty and right of administration passed to the Republic, while the internal affairs of the Kaffirs were left to the Queen and her council, so that Swaziland could not be considered to form a part of the Republic.

All the white male inhabitants of the country were to obtain full burgher rights in the Republic, provided that they applied for them within six months.

The Dutch and English languages were to enjoy equal rights in the law-courts.

The South African Republic confirmed her renunciation, already conceded in the first Swaziland Convention, of her claims on certain districts in the north and north-west of the country.

This arrangement was not to become valid until the Swazi queen and her council gave their consent.

A strong opposition now sprang up among the Swazis against our taking possession of their country, as we were to do in accordance with the convention. This opposition was provoked and strengthened by all sorts of English Jingoes and adventurers, including a certain Hulett, who had come from Natal. The latter persuaded the Swazis to send a deputation to England, to protest against the transfer of their country into the hands of the Republic. The deputation achieved no result. Since, however, nothing but feuds and quarrels arose in Swaziland and since, under existing conditions, it was impossible for the South African Republic to suppress them, an unbearable situation arose and a new meeting accordingly took place between Sir Henry Loch and myself at Volksrust, in 1894, at which a new, or third, Swaziland Convention was concluded, giving the Republic the right to take over Swaziland, without, however, making it an integral portion of this country. But for this restriction, Swaziland now practically formed part of the Republic. This convention was accepted by the Volksraad in an extraordinary session, in 1895, and thus this troublesome matter was settled.

We had hardly time to breathe after these difficulties about the native territories, when England suddenly annexed Sambaanland and Umbigesaland. The Republic had long had treaties of friendship with both these countries and, during the time of the Swaziland negotiations, it had always been taken for granted that the Republic would later, as soon as the Swaziland question was settled, put forward her claims over the two countries and treat with England for their annexation. Nevertheless, as soon as the Volksraad had ratified the Swaziland Convention, in 1895, England suddenly annexed the territories in question, although she had no more claim upon them than upon the moon. The object of this proceeding can only have been to vex and harass the Republic; for, by acting as she did, England cut off the Transvaal's last outlet to the sea, an outlet which England did not require. It goes without saying that the Republic protested against the annexation; but England did not trouble herself about that.

In 1895, one of my fondest wishes was at last effected. The railway to Delagoa Bay was solemnly opened at Pretoria. After many difficulties, the line had at last been completed, thanks to the industry of the Netherlands South African Railway Company. All the governments of South Africa were represented at the inauguration, and the Volksraad voted £20,000 to enable the burghers who cared to avail themselves of this privilege to travel to Delagoa Bay and inspect the whole work. Thousands of burghers were thus enabled to become acquainted with the new enterprise and to appreciate its value.

This railway changed the whole internal situation in the Transvaal. Until that time, the Cape Railway had enjoyed a monopoly, so to speak, of the Johannesburg traffic. This was now altered. In order to facilitate friendly competition and to secure an adequate proportion of the profits on the railway traffic to the largest city in the Republic, the Government proposed that the profits on the joint goods and passenger traffic should be divided in equal shares between the three States whose railway-lines ran to

Pretoria. These three were Cape Colony, Natal, and the Transvaal. Cecil Rhodes, who was then for the second time Premier of Cape Colony, and his advisers thought differently. They asked for 50 per cent. for Cape Colony, leaving the remaining 50 per cent. to be divided between Natal and the Transvaal. The Government of the Republic would not hear of this proposal, and a tariff war ensued.

The Cape Government lowered their tariff as far as Vereeniging, the frontier station between the Orange Free State and the Transvaal (the Free State railways were at that time still under the control of the Cape Government). The South African Railway, on the other hand, raised its tariff on its own portion of the line, running from Vereeniging to Johannesburg, in order to neutralize the reduction in prices on the other portion. The Cape Government now thought out a new plan. In order to avoid sending their goods over the expensive stretch of line, they had them unloaded at Viljoensdrift, in order to convey them thence to Johannesburg in ox-wagons. Now the customs laws of the Republic contained a clause by virtue of which the President was enabled to proclaim certain places on the frontiers as " import ports "; while no goods could be imported except at places thus proclaimed. When, therefore, the Cape Government caused their goods to be carried in ox-wagons, the Government of the Republic (whose interests coincided with those of the Netherlands South African Railway Company, as they had guaranteed the latter's profits) determined to close the existing "import ports," really fords, or "drifts," to goods from over the seas. The Government proclamation was directed only against goods from over the seas, so as not to injure the home trade of the Orange Free State and Cape Colony.

What did Rhodes and his Government now do? They asserted that the London Convention had been violated. This Convention contained a clause according to which no article coming from any portion of the British Empire could be excluded, unless the importation of that same article from any other country was also forbidden. The Republic, therefore, had violated the Convention, inasmuch as she had favored Cape Colony, a British possession, and the Orange Free State, her sister state, above the countries over the seas. She must now either withdraw her decision, or else resort to the odious measure of forbidding the entire importation. Rhodes addressed his complaint to the British Government. A general election had recently taken place in England, and the same Government was in power that held office at the time of the late war. Mr. Chamberlain was a member of this Government and was, of course, at once prepared to send the Republic an ultimatum. He stipulated, however, that, if the ultimatum led to a war, Cape Colony should bear half the cost, raise a force of auxiliaries and lend her railway for the free carriage of troops. To the shame be it spoken of the Afrikanders who had seats in the Ministry, they agreed to this suggestion forthwith. The Republic received her ultimatum and was, of course, obliged to give way and to undertake not to close the drifts again.

The most striking event during my third presidency was Dr. Jameson's filibustering expedition, an enterprise of which the responsibility does not rest with Dr. Jameson. It is true that Mr. Chamberlain, at the time of the raid, declared that he knew nothing of the whole conspiracy. Later, however, it was shown that the British Government, or at least the Colonial Secretary, was fully informed of Cecil Rhodes's plans and intrigues, which resulted in Jameson's disgraceful raid. Rhodes had long entertained the project of making himself master of the Republic in one way or another; and he devoted his money, his influence and his position as Premier of Cape Colony to this object. The National Union, of which I have already spoken, was employed by him to keep men's minds at Johannesburg in a constant state of ferment, and it soon became his chief tool in the conspiracy against the existence of the country. Through his instrumentality, arms and ammunition were secretly smuggled into Johannesburg and con-

KRUGER'S THIRD PRESIDENCY

cealed in the Simmer-and-Jack Mine, in which he was the largest shareholder. Rhodes was aware that Johannesburg alone was not able to start a revolution with any chance of success. He had therefore to try to obtain a place of his own, on the frontiers of the Republic, where he could collect troops in support of a rising. With this object, with the aid of his factotum, Dr. Rutherfoord Harris, and a lady journalist called Flora Shaw, he opened negotiations with the British Government in order to extend the territory of the Chartered Company, so as to include the necessary strategic positions. The telegrams exchanged between the above-named persons during the negotiations with the British Government show that Mr. Chamberlain knew all about the matter. One of Miss Shaw's telegrams to Rhodes ended with the words:

Chamberlain sound in case of interference European Powers, but have special reasons to believe wishes you must do it immediately.

Add to this the following telegram from Rhodes to Miss Flora Shaw:

Inform Chamberlain that I shall get through all right, if he supports me, but he must not send cables like he sent to the High Commissioner in South Africa. To-day the crux is I shall win and South Africa will belong to England.

And again:

Unless you can make Chamberlain instruct the High Commissioner to proceed at once to Johannesburg, the whole posi-

THE MEMOIRS OF PAUL KRUGER

tion is lost. High Commissioner would receive splendid reception and still turn position to England's advantage, but must be instructed by cable immediately. The instructions must be specific, as he is weak and will take no responsibility.

It must be remembered, moreover, that the British Government laid only a portion of the telegrams before the so-called Select Parliamentary Committee on British South African Affairs, and probably kept back those which were most compromising. Why should this be done when an inquiry is instituted to discover the truth? Is it not the natural conclusion that Chamberlain was equally guilty with Rhodes? However, no one can seriously deny that the above-mentioned published telegrams clearly prove Mr. Chamberlain's complicity in the plot.

As soon as Rhodes was sure of obtaining the desired strip of land from the British Government, he at once began to take measures to collect the troops of the South African Police at that point and to equip them with horses and materials of war so that they might be ready to invade the Republic as soon as things at Johannesburg were ripe for the attack. Meanwhile, he had entered into correspondence with the leaders of the National Union and sent his brother, Colonel Rhodes, to Johannesburg to work in his interest and represent him. Colonel Rhodes had his unlimited authority to spend as much money as he considered necessary. Mr. Lionel Phillips, one of the conspirators, had gone to Cape Town, presumably to discuss the details with Rhodes in person. He returned suddenly, on the pretext of opening the new buildings of the Chamber of Mines, of which he was chairman. The buildings, however, were not even finished, and the opening was only an excuse to give Mr. Phillips the opportunity of making a political speech. It took place at the end of November, and Phillips delivered a speech full of violent attacks upon the Government. Some time earlier, one or two members of the National Union had gone to Cape Town to discuss the execution of the plan. In accordance with what was then arranged, Dr. Jameson came to Johannesburg at the end of November to concert the necessary measures with the leaders of the Union. On this occasion, he asked them to give him a letter in which they appealed to him for his assistance and which he could use at any time as an excuse for an invasion. The letter contained the statement that a collision was imminent between the Uitlanders and the Government and that the women and children and private property at Johannesburg were in danger. This letter, which was signed by Mr. Charles Leonard, Colonel Frank Rhodes, Messrs. Lionel Phillips, J. Hays Hammond and Farrar, was left undated, so that Jameson might be able to make use of it at any time. In the meanwhile, the inhabitants of Johannesburg were incited in every possible manner by the Rhodes press in order artfully to prepare the way for an outbreak. Towards the end of December 1895, Leonard, as chairman of the National Union, issued a long manifesto raising a series of accusations against the Government. Everything that could serve to excite men's minds against the Republic was dragged in. Of course, the franchise question was one of the main grievances, although Lionel Phillips, who was also a leading member of the Union, had not long before written to his partner in London, a German Jew called Beit, who was closely connected with Rhodes, that " we do not care a fig for the franchise."

Just when the ferment at Johannesburg was at its height, I returned to Pretoria from my usual annual tour of the districts, and it was then that, in reply to an address in which the burghers pressed for the punishment of the rebellious element, I used the words:

" You must give the tortoise time to put out its head before you can catch hold of it."

An attempt has been made to prove from these words that I knew of the preparations for the Jameson Raid, and that by the tortoise I meant Jameson. But this statement is quite unfounded. Neither I nor any of the Transvaal authorities at that time thought such a deed possible, much less expected it.

KRUGER'S THIRD PRESIDENCY

It is true that horses, provisions and fodder were being bought up by the English even in the Republic; but the English stated that the assembling of the police on the western frontier of the South African Republic was intended for an expedition against the Kaffirs, particularly against the Chief Linchwé. And the burghers, therefore, entertained so little suspicion that they themselves assisted in the purchase of the military stores and in conveying the goods to all the places which afterwards represented roadside stations for Jameson's ride from Kimberley to near Krugersdorp. I myself had, but a short while before, offered the British High Commissioner, Sir Hercules Robinson, the assistance of the Republic for the protection of the women and children against the Matabele, who were giving trouble to the English, and Sir Hercules had replied thanking me for my offer, but saying that our assistance would not be needed for the present. If I had had the smallest inkling of Jameson's plan, I should assuredly not have allowed him to push so far into the Republic. In the days when the troops were being collected for the Jameson Raid, General Joubert, the Commander-in-chief of the Boer forces, was not even at Pretoria, but on his farm in the Wakkerstroom district, and he did not return to Pretoria until a couple of days before the raid.

What I meant by the tortoise was the National

THE MEMOIRS OF PAUL KRUGER

Union, which was continually abusing the Government and threatening to resort to force in order to obtain the removal of its grievances. I intended to convey that we must allow the movement quietly to take its course, until it revealed its true character and showed itself so undoubtedly guilty that the Government could punish the leading members, the real rebels, for high treason. Had those men been arrested earlier, they could still have tried to deny their misconduct and we should then, perhaps, have been unable to convince the world of their guilt.

Towards the end of December 1895, the state of affairs at Johannesburg was such that thousands left the town and fled for safety to the coast, while the National Union, which henceforth adopted the name of the Reform Committee, raised corps of volunteers to whom it distributed arms and ammunition. In order to avoid a collision and prevent bloodshed, the Government resolved to confine the police to barracks. We did not look upon the rebellion as serious, since it did not originate with the people, but was artificially manufactured from above by intriguers. The whole thing would have presented a farcical spectacle, if the results had been less serious. The only man among the so-called Reformers who understood his business was Colonel Rhodes. All the others were theatrical revolutionaries.[1]

[1] It has been related that the President kept his horse saddled in his stable and his rifle loaded by his bed-side during the time of the Jameson

KRUGER'S THIRD PRESIDENCY

I received different deputations from Johannesburg which made it clear that a large number of the inhabitants did not wish to have anything to do with the insurrection. I promised one of these deputations that I would meet the Uitlanders in the matter of certain grievances and propose a general grant of the franchise, and I also issued a proclamation in which I declared that the rioters formed only a small proportion of the population of Johannesburg, and expressed my confidence that the law-abiding inhabitants would support the Government in its endeavors to maintain law and order.

This injunction was issued on the 30th of December 1895. On the same day, however, General Joubert received a telegram from Mr. Marais, Commissioner of Mines at Ottoshoop, informing him that a commando of 800 of the Chartered Company's troops, with Maxims and guns, had gone past, at half-past five that morning, in the direction of Johannesburg, and that the telegraph wire between Malmanie, Zeerust, and Lichtenburg had been cut.

General Joubert immediately dispatched telegrams to the different commandants, and first to those of Rustenburg, Krugersdorp, and Potchefstroom, acquainting them with these reports and charging them

---

Raid. Not a word of this is true, except in so far that some friends advised him to leave Pretoria because of the danger of an attack, whereupon he replied:

"If it comes to that, I shall take my horse and my gun and join my commando."—*Note by the Editor of the German Edition.*

at once to summon the burghers and stop the invaders. Meanwhile, the Government had appointed a committee at Johannesburg to maintain order. It is certainly due to the tact displayed by this committee that no bloodshed occurred. The Reformers now resolved to send a deputation to Pretoria to confer with the Government. They were received, on behalf of the Government, by General Kock and Judges Kotzé and Ameshoff, and demanded that Dr. Jameson should be allowed to enter Johannesburg, in which case they would make themselves responsible for his peaceful departure from the town and his return across the frontier. In the meanwhile, the High Commissioner, Sir Hercules Robinson, who had succeeded Sir Henry Loch at the end of 1895, offered his friendly mediation and proposed to come to Pretoria in order to prevent bloodshed. An answer was, therefore, given to the deputation to the effect that, pending the arrival of the High Commissioner, the Government would take no measures against Johannesburg, provided the town conducted itself quietly.

Meantime, Dr. Jameson had advanced with the greatest rapidity in the direction of Johannesburg. The High Commissioner issued a proclamation calling upon Dr. Jameson and all his companions to withdraw across the frontier (this proclamation was shortly followed by Cecil Rhodes's resignation of the premiership of Cape Colony). The proclamation, together with a letter from Sir Jacobus De Wet, the British Agent at Pretoria, was carried to Dr. Jameson by Ben Bouwer, a Transvaal burgher. Dr. Jameson, however, took not the slightest notice of it. Lieutenant Eloff, of the Krugersdorp police, who rode out to meet him and to charge him to turn back, was taken prisoner by his orders. A number of Transvaal burghers, however, under Commandants Malan, Potgieter and Cronjé had outstripped Jameson and taken up their stand on the hills near Krugersdorp. Jameson at once turned the fire of his guns on the burghers' positions; but, as soon as his troops attempted a charge, they were driven back with loss. When Dr. Jameson saw that he could not get through, he faced about to the right, in order to try to turn the Boer position. He was stopped, however, during the night by Field-cornet D. Fouché, and the next morning, when he moved still further to the right, he came up against Cronjé's burghers, at Doornkop, who compelled him to surrender after a short engagement.

It has been stated that Dr. Jameson surrendered on condition that his life and the lives of his men should be spared. Commandant Cronjé had, in fact, in a note to Sir John Willoughby, the officer in command of Jameson's troops, informed him that he would spare their lives on the understanding that they surrendered with all that they had with them and paid the expenses entailed upon the South African Republic. But, while Commandant Cronjé was still in conversation with Dr. Jameson, Commandant Malan, of Rustenburg, approached, asked what was being done and, when he heard the conditions, said to Cronjé:

"We cannot make conditions of any kind; that is a matter for the Government at Pretoria."

Cronjé agreed, and thereupon Commandant Malan caused Dr. Jameson to be informed, in English, that he must clearly understand that what Cronjé had said was that the prisoners' lives were only guaranteed as far as Pretoria, where they would be handed over to the Commandant General.

"At this moment," he continued, "we cannot make any final conditions; those must be left to the Government."

Jameson thereupon bowed and said:

"I accept your conditions."

It was not till that moment that the surrender was completed and Dr. Jameson and his men disarmed and taken to Pretoria.

In the meantime, the High Commissioner had arrived and at once had an interview with myself and my advisers. After expressing his regret at what had happened, he immediately began to speak of the grievances of the Uitlanders and of other necessary

KRUGER'S THIRD PRESIDENCY

reforms. I cut him short at once, however, by pointing out to him that this was not the time to speak of those matters, and that the only questions that could now be discussed were those of the measures to be taken in order to avoid further bloodshed,[1] and how Johannesburg should be made give up its arms. The High Commissioner asked:

"On what conditions is Johannesburg to give up its arms?"

I replied:

"Unconditionally."

And, when the High Commissioner continued to hesitate and to raise difficulties against my demand, I added:

"I will give Johannesburg twenty-four hours in which to surrender unconditionally. Otherwise, I shall compel the town to do so by force."

Sir Hercules could obtain no concession. I continued inexorable, and the interview ended.

The burghers and their commandants were in a condition of extreme excitement. It is easily understood that, after being plagued and provoked for so

---

[1] Sir Hercules had asked whether he might come to help to bring about a peaceful settlement of the Jameson business, and he received a reply saying:

"Yes, come, you can perhaps prevent bloodshed."

He took this to mean that he might do something to prevent the insurgents from being shot; but when he was told that he could advise the Johannesburgers to surrender and thus prevent bloodshed, he was no longer so assiduous with his offer.—*Note by the Editor of the German Edition.*

many years by the National Union, they were not in the mood to allow Jameson and the Johannesburg fire-brands to go unpunished. The following will serve as an instance of the spirit that prevailed among the burghers:

A commandant and some 400 burghers, who were on their way to stop Jameson, when the latter had not yet surrendered, passed through Pretoria and took the opportunity of calling on me to bid me good-day. I went out to thank the burghers, when the commandant addressed me in these words:

"President, we have come to greet you, and at the same time to inform you that, when we have captured Jameson, we intend to march straight on to Johannesburg and to shoot down that den with all the rebels in it. They have provoked us long enough."

I replied:

"No, brother, you must not speak like that. Remember, there are thousands of innocent and loyal people at Johannesburg, and the others have been for the most part misled. We must not be revengeful; what would be the result of such a step?"

The commandant answered:

"No, President, you speak in vain. What is the use of clemency? It is only because we have shown the rebels clemency too long that they have now gone

KRUGER'S THIRD PRESIDENCY

so far. My burghers and I are determined to put an end to this sedition for good and all."

I thereupon lost my temper, or, at least, pretended to do so, and said:

"Very well, if you will not listen to me, you can depose me from the presidency and govern the country after your own fashion."

The commandant now calmed down and said:

"No, President, I did not mean that; we are quite willing to listen to you, but we have been terribly provoked."

I too answered more calmly:

"Well, if you will listen to me, do what I say and leave the rest to me."

At the meeting of commandants which, together with the Executive Raad, was to decide Jameson's fate, I had a hard battle to fight. My intention, which had already been approved by the Executive Raad, was to hand over Jameson and his companions to the British Government, in order that the criminals might be punished by their own Government according to their own laws. But the commandants would not hear of this, and it was only after Messrs. Fischer and Kleynveld, of the Orange Free State,[1] had also advised them to follow my

[1] Mr. Fischer is the gentleman who was afterwards dispatched as one of the delegates to Europe. He and Mr. Kleynveld had been sent by the Orange Free State to see if it was necessary for that state to come to the assistance of the Republic in accordance with her obligations.—*Note by the Editor of the German Edition.*

wishes that I succeeded in obtaining their consent to leave this matter to the Government.

When the High Commissioner saw that I insisted on the unconditional surrender of Johannesburg, he instructed Sir Jacobus De Wet to telegraph to that effect to the Reform Committee. It is hardly necessary to say that they complied before the twenty-four hours had expired, for, with the exception of Colonel Rhodes and perhaps one or two more, there was not one among the conspirators but would have taken to his heels as soon as the first shot was fired. They had wooed and organized rebellion only in the hope that England would pull the chestnuts out of the fire for them. They did not think of endangering their lives for the sake of a matter for which one of their principal members had declared, but a little while before, that he " did not care a fig."

Meanwhile the Government had informed the High Commissioner that it intended to hand over Jameson and his men to the British Government so that they might be brought to justice in England. Mr. Chamberlain telegraphed to me to thank me, in the name of Her Majesty, for my magnanimous act. Subsequent events have shown the depth of this gratitude and the way in which England has rewarded my magnanimity.

Johannesburg gave up its arms, but in much smaller quantities than was expected. Only some

KRUGER'S THIRD PRESIDENCY

1800 rifles and three damaged Maxims were handed in. Soon after, Dr. Jameson and his followers were delivered to the Governor of Natal, who sent them to England. The rank and file were at once set at liberty by the British Government. Jameson and a few of the other officers received short terms of imprisonment and were released before the expiration of their sentence.

On the 9th of January, the Reformers were arrested in their homes, or at their clubs, and taken to Pretoria. On the 10th, I issued a proclamation to the inhabitants of Johannesburg in which I declared that I only looked upon a small number of crafty men within and without Johannesburg as the conspirators, and pointed out that the plot might have led to fearful disasters. I promised to confer a municipality upon Johannesburg, and ended by appealing to the inhabitants to enable me to appear before the Volksraad with the motto, " Forgive and forget."

It is not necessary to enter into details concerning the trial of the conspirators. The Government applied to the Orange Free State to allow Judge Gregorowski to preside over the trial. The object of this request, which was readily granted, was to obtain a judge who was outside the quarrel and who could not be regarded as in any way prejudiced against the Reformers. Most of them escaped with imprisonment or fines: only the four leaders, Messrs. Lionel Phillips, Farrar, Hammond, and Colonel Rhodes, were condemned to death; but this sentence was commuted by the Executive Raad to a fine of £25,000 apiece. Thus ended the first act of the drama of which the last act has just been finished on the blood-stained plains of South Africa.

Before closing this chapter, mention should be made of the great calamity with which Johannesburg was afflicted, on the 19th of February, 1896, by the explosion of a number of trucks loaded with dynamite. A portion of the suburbs of Jorisburg and Braamfontein was destroyed, very many persons were killed and wounded, and hundreds were rendered homeless. The Uitlanders showed their sympathy with the victims by subscribing a sum of about £70,000 within two days. To this the Government added a gift of £25,000. I repaired without delay to Johannesburg, visited the wounded in the hospital and praised the sympathy displayed in this matter by the Uitlanders, which it cheered my heart to see. I reminded them of the words of the Gospel: " Blessed are the merciful, for they shall obtain mercy."

And so the attempt upon the independence of the Republic failed. But now Mr. Chamberlain was to set to work to try whether he could not be more successful. With his assistance, Jameson's Raid was to be replaced by a gigantic British Raid.

His first step was to invite me to come to England to confer on Transvaal matters, while he began by declaring that he was not prepared to discuss Article 4 of the London Convention, the only article which still in any way restricted the foreign relations of the South African Republic. One would really think, to judge from this invitation, that it was the Republic and not England that had to make amends.

At the same time, Mr. Chamberlain sent off another dispatch, in which he proposed that a sort of Home Rule should be granted to Johannesburg, and he published this dispatch in the London official press before I had received it. When one reflects that it was the very question of Home Rule for Ireland that caused Mr. Chamberlain to withdraw from Gladstone's party and barter his Radicalism for his present Jingoism, one must stand astounded at the effrontery of his proposal, especially under the existing circumstances.

The Government of the South African Republic at first received only a short excerpt from the dispatch, embracing the principal points, whereas the whole text had already been published in the London official press, and to this it sent the reply, in brief, that it was undesirable and inadvisable to give previous publicity to views which the British Government thought fit to adopt towards the Republic, adding that the Republic could not permit any interference in her internal affairs. This reply was now also at once published in the *Staatscourant* of the South African Republic. Shortly after its receipt, Mr. Chamberlain dispatched a telegram in which he said that, if his proposal was not acceptable to the parties concerned, he would not insist upon it. Thereupon I telegraphed the conditions upon which I would be willing to come to England. The chief point was the substitution of a treaty of peace, commerce, and amity for the London Convention. Into this Mr. Chamberlain refused to enter. He continued to speak of admitted grievances which must be removed, as that was a matter of the highest importance to England as the paramount power in South Africa, stating, furthermore, that, even if the London Convention was replaced by another, Article 4 of that Convention must, in any case, be included in the new agreement. Where, then, would have been the sense of undertaking that troublesome journey? And what would have been the use of substituting a new convention for the old one, if the only article by which the independence of the Republic was in any way restricted was to be included? Mr. Chamberlain, seeing that he could not induce me to visit England without giving some guarantee that my journey would not be futile, withdrew his invitation.

Meanwhile, it had become evident to the Government that it must prepare for possible events, and consequently a commencement was made in the purchase of ammunition, rifles, and guns. This was the more necessary inasmuch as, at the time of the Jameson Raid, the Republic was practically defenceless. The burghers, at that time, had none but Martini-Henry rifles and many did not possess a rifle at all. There was not sufficient ammunition to wage war for a fortnight. It must be added that, by the law of the land, every burgher was bound to be armed; and, when it appeared, on the occasion of the Jameson Raid, how sadly this duty had been neglected, the Government took the necessary measures, but no more, for the proper arming of the burghers, in order that they might be ready to protect themselves against further filibustering raids.

Still greater supplies of ammunition, rifles and guns were ordered after the investigation of the so-called South African Committee had taken place in London, because matters then came to light which showed that Mr. Chamberlain was not so innocent of the Raid as he represented. This is proved by the telegrams which I have already quoted and which were laid before the committee, and still more by those which were deliberately kept back, while, shortly after the investigation, Mr. Chamberlain declared in the House of Commons that Rhodes was a man of honor, and that there existed nothing which affected Rhodes's personal position as such. It was impossible to avoid drawing the conclusion that Mr. Chamberlain was Rhodes's accomplice, and that he now publicly defended Rhodes because he feared lest the latter should make statements which would be anything but pleasant hearing for the Colonial Secretary. This, at least, was the view taken of the matter in the Republic; and it was confirmed in this view by the fact that Dr. Jameson was released from prison on account of illness and recovered his health immediately afterwards.

In view of these facts, can the Government of the South African Republic be blamed for making preparations, so that it might not fall a prey to England without striking a blow? Nay, more; was it not her bounden duty to take care, as she did, that the country was placed on a defensive footing? Yet this is the action which was constantly thrown in my face, by way of reproach, by the English ministers and the English press, and which they afterwards quoted in order to justify their unjust war.

Shortly after the closing of the South African Committee, Mr. Chamberlain began his uninterrupted series of dispatches, which continued until the war broke out, and which had no other object than to embitter the British people against the Republic and to make them believe that it was constantly sinning against England and systematically violating the London Convention. Thus, for instance, in the early part of 1897, he sent a dispatch in which he declared that the Republic had broken the London Convention by the following acts: by joining the Geneva Convention; by the Press Law; the Immigration Law; the conclusion of an extradition treaty with Portugal, etc. He based his contentions particularly on the oft-quoted Article 4 of the Convention,[1] which lays down that no treaty shall be in force until the same has been approved by the British Government.

Mr. Chamberlain now contended that the intention of this article was that, as soon as a treaty was drawn up (and therefore before its completion), a copy must be delivered to Her Majesty's Government, whereas the Government of the South African Republic maintained that this was not to be done until after the treaty was finally settled, and based its contention upon the words, "Upon its completion," which occur in the article. The Government,

[1] This article 4 reads as follows :

"The South African Republic will conclude no treaty or engagement with any State or nation other than the Orange Free State, nor with any native tribe to the eastward or westward of the Republic, until the same has been approved by Her Majesty the Queen.

"Such approval shall be considered to have been granted if Her Majesty's Government shall not, within six months after receiving a copy of such treaty (which shall be delivered to them immediately upon its completion), have notified that the conclusion of such treaty is in conflict with the interests of Great Britain or of any of Her Majesty's possessions in South Africa."—*Note by the Editor of the German Edition.*

therefore, in its reply, laid stress upon the fact that it did not agree with Mr. Chamberlain's opinion, and suggested that, in view of the difference that existed as to this point, it would be best to submit the matter to an impartial arbitrator. To this Mr. Chamberlain replied that England was the suzerain of the South African Republic and, in this quality, could not consent to refer a difference to arbitration.

It is unnecessary to say that this reply of Mr. Chamberlain's was in the highest degree vexatious to the Government of the Republic. For what other purpose than to obtain the abolition of the suzerainty had we made the journey to London in 1883 and endeavored to secure a new convention? And, since the Convention of 1884, no one had entertained the very slightest doubt but that the suzerainty was annulled. Even Sir Hercules Robinson, who was himself one of the authors of the Convention of 1884, declared in an interview with a journalist [1] that there was no question but that the suzerainty had been abolished by the Convention of 1884. In his greatly-praised reply of the 16th of April, 1898, Dr. Leyds irrefutably established this fact. He was able, moreover to quote a dispatch of Lord Derby's, of the 15th of February, 1884, in which the then Secretary for the Colonies enclosed a draft of a new convention

[1] Mr. Frank Harris, at that time editor of the *Saturday Review*. Note by the Editor of the German Edition.

intended to replace the Convention of Pretoria. This draft commences with a reprint of the preamble of the Convention of 1881, followed by that of the Convention of 1884 and headed by the following note:

"The words and paragraphs bracketed or printed in italics are proposed to be inserted, those within a black line are proposed to be omitted."

And now the whole preamble of 1881 is contained within a black line; moreover, the words " subject to the suzerainty of Her Majesty, her Heirs and Successors " had been struck out by Lord Derby. It was especially important to prove that the preamble of the Convention of 1881, in which the suzerainty was mentioned, had lapsed, because Mr. Chamberlain contended that this preamble still existed and continued in force. In addition to what has been shown above, that this preamble was contained within brackets and had therefore lapsed, we should, had Mr. Chamberlain's contention been correct, have had two conflicting preambles to one and the same convention. Which would have been absurd.

Now any reasonable person would have thought that Mr. Chamberlain would see that he was wrong; but no: he simply continued to maintain that the suzerainty existed. It will be universally admitted that it is impossible to come to a logical understanding with a man like that; and we must blame the well-known English insolence, where a small nation is concerned, which alone can have permitted Mr. Chamberlain to keep up his nonsensical argument.

The correspondence between the Government and Mr. Chamberlain was interrupted and accompanied by two important events in the internal life of the Republic: the negotiations concerning the work of the Industrial Commission and the conflict between the judicial and state authorities.

The Industrial or Mining Commission was appointed to investigate the complaints of the mining industry. That there were certain burdens which pressed too heavily upon that industry and which must be decreased was an undoubted fact, and was shown in the report of the committee; but the principal reason why some mines gave no profit and others less profit than the shareholders would have liked to see was to be found in over-capitalization, in the floating of companies on worthless properties, in the reconstruction of companies whose profits went to the financial houses, and in the speculative fever which drove up shares to such a height that it became impossible for the purchaser to rely on receiving a good dividend. The great financial houses had everything in their hands and caused prices to rise or fall as they pleased; and the public was the victim of their manœuvres.

The commission, which held its sittings at Johannesburg and heard a crowd of witnesses, made a series of suggestions in its report as to how the demands of the industry could be met. The principal suggestions were:

A reduction of the import-duty on food-stuffs.

An agreement with the other States of South Africa to facilitate the engagement and cheapen the transport of colored laborers.

The appointment of a committee to enquire into the possibility of abolishing the dynamite monopoly. Meantime, it was recommended that the Government should itself import dynamite and sell it to the mines at cost price, with the addition of an import duty of twenty shillings.

A reduction in the railway tariff equal to a decrease of £500,000 in the gross profits of the company.

These were the principal suggestions; a few others of lesser importance may be passed over. The Government submitted the report to the Volksraad, which appointed a committee to examine the report and make suggestions. After long debates on the opinion of the Volksraad committee, it was at last moved and carried that the railway company should reduce its charges to the extent of reducing its takings by £200,000 and that the Government should endeavor to find means for a cheaper supply of dynamite to the mines. The Government succeeded in reducing the freights, especially for coal and foodstuffs, and in diminishing the price of dynamite by five shillings a case. Moreover, an arrangement was concluded with Portugal by which large contingents of Kaffir laborers were obtained from Portuguese territory. Mr. Chamberlain afterwards accused the Government of disregarding the suggestions of its own Industrial Commission.

I have mentioned the conflict between the judicial and state authorities, in other words, between the Government and the Volksraad on the one side and a section of the Supreme Court on the other. The dispute arose as follows. It was a generally accepted principle that the resolutions of the Volksraad were valid in law, even if they conflicted with the constitution. The Supreme Court, particularly Judge Kotzé, with whom the conflict now arose, had, in former law-suits, as for instance in the "Doms" case, accepted and acknowledged this principle. Suddenly, in a subsequent case, it refused to do so. Certain tracts of land in the Krugersdorp district had been "proclaimed" as gold-fields, and, on the day when this proclamation was to come into effect, thousands of people assembled, each intending, as the law originally provided, to peg out his claims or bewaarplaatsen for himself. They who first pegged out those bewaarplaatsen, to the extent to which each was entitled in law, became their owners, subject, of course, to the payment of the legal dues. The Government had been informed that there was a danger of disorders arising out of this manner of dividing the land, owing to the great rush to the new gold-fields. They accordingly determined, so as not to give England a fresh opportunity for an undeserved attack, to ask the Volksraad to pass a resolution to the effect that the " proclaimed " places should not, as the gold-law prescribed, be pegged out, but drawn by lot. In this way, each applicant stood the same chance of success, and all disorder would be avoided. A certain Brown, however, took no notice of this resolution, but, on the day when the proclamation (which had meantime been withdrawn) was to take effect, pegged out a large number of claims and tendered the legal dues, which were refused. When Brown's case was brought before the Supreme Court, which was sitting, Chief Justice Kotzé went back upon his former decisions and declared that the Volksraad had no right to pass resolutions which violated the principles of the constitution.

This decision would have upset the whole country, for a number of rules concerning the gold-fields, the franchise and so on depended on resolutions of the Volksraad. It was therefore impossible for the Government to acquiesce in this decision, which would have caused unspeakable confusion. In a country whose conditions undergo such rapid alterations as is naturally the case in a gold-producing country, and which harbors so many speculators and schemers as were constantly flowing into the South African Republic, it was absolutely necessary that, at any given moment, certain interests could be protected and dangers averted from the State by decrees of the Volksraad. To give an instance: in November, 1896, the revised gold-law, which had been passed in the former session, was to come into operation. It contained one clause, however, which was not quite clear and which, unless the point in doubt was elucidated by force of law, might seriously injure the mining industry and deliver its rights into the hands of speculators. What happened? The mining industry naturally went to the Government and called attention to the danger. Dr. Leyds thereupon attended a sitting of the Volksraad, explained the position and obtained a decree which removed the danger. Every one looked upon this as the natural course. Now, suddenly, a different view was taken; and it was this that caused the conflict.

Sir Henry de Villiers, the Chief Justice of Cape Colony, who, by the way, shared the opinion of the Government, brought about an adjustment: the judge promised to respect the decrees of the Volksraad and I, on my side, promised to move the revision of the constitution in the Volksraad. Not long before, a law had been passed by which every judicial

KRUGER'S THIRD PRESIDENCY

functionary, on taking his oath of office, was to promise not to assume the right of *toetsing*,[1] that is to say, of testing the laws as to their validness. In February, 1898, however, Chief Justice Kotzé wrote to me saying that I had not effected the revision of the constitution which I had promised him, that he therefore considered himself to be released from his own promise and that he intended in future to test the validness of all the resolutions of the Volksraad by the constitution. This was too much: I had had no opportunity of introducing a bill for the revision of the constitution, seeing that the Volksraad did not meet till May. I now gave the Chief Justice his dismissal. The English press ranted and raged, and Mr. Chamberlain afterwards turned this incident into an " Uitlander grievance."

Meanwhile Mr. Chamberlain had found the man he wanted for his dealings with the South African Republic. In 1897, Sir Alfred Milner was appointed Governor of Cape Colony and High Commissioner for South Africa. Sir Alfred had formerly served his country in Egypt, and, if he learned anything there, it was to look upon the fellahs as creatures of an inferior species. The ideas which he had imbibed in Egypt he brought with him to South Africa, so

[1] Testing, or criticising. In my translation of President Kruger's speech, printed in the Appendix, in which he ascribes the invention of this right to the Devil, I have ventured to employ the phrase, "the right of criticism," throughout.—*Translator's Note*.

much so that he forgot that the Afrikander is a different creature from the Egyptian fellah. There is no doubt that Mr. Chamberlain appointed Sir Alfred Milner only with a view of driving matters in South Africa to extremes. The appointment was received by the Jingoes with loud jubilation. The aim and principle of his policy are to be found in the words which he spoke to a distinguished Afrikander:

"The power of Afrikanderdom must be broken."

This tool of Mr. Chamberlain's has fulfilled his mission faithfully, and to-day enjoys the satisfaction of having turned South Africa into a wilderness and robbed thousands of innocent people of their lives. Lord Milner is the typical Jingo, autocratic beyond endurance and filled with contempt for all that is not English.

When this man assumed office, my term as President had expired and new elections were about to be held. This time three candidates presented themselves: myself, Joubert, and Schalk Burger, a member of the Executive Raad and Chairman of the Industrial Commission of 1897. This was the first election which, according to the new law, was held by ballot.

Meanwhile, new elections had also taken place in the Free State, as President Reitz was obliged, owing to long illness, to resign his office. Judge M. T. Steyn was elected President in his place. To give

KRUGER'S THIRD PRESIDENCY

a portrait here of this man would be superfluous. His heroism, his resolution and his patriotism are known to all the world; and, write what one may, it will always remain an impossible task to give a description of the feelings of attachment, respect and love that fill the hearts of all true Afrikanders for President Steyn. He will certainly be handed down in the memory of his people to the furthest generation as one of the greatest and noblest men that have seen the light in South Africa.

Some time after President Steyn's election, a new conference was held at Bloemfontein with the object of bringing about a closer alliance between the two Republics. The impulse towards this closer alliance was felt on both sides and was due, above all, to the Jameson Raid. I and some of my councilors went to Bloemfontein with this object; and it was during our stay there, on the occasion of a dinner that was given us, that I made a jest in the course of my speech by saying that Queen Victoria was a "*kwaaie vrouw.*" Now, although every one who knows the Afrikander Taal understands that, by this, I meant to convey only that Queen Victoria was a lady with whom one must be careful what one does, the Jingo press tried to make it appear as though I had grossly insulted the Queen, whereas the opposite, of course, was true.[1]

[1] The reader may take it that to call a woman a *kwaaie vrouw* in the Taal, or *kwade vrouw* in European Dutch, is equivalent to saying that

THE MEMOIRS OF PAUL KRUGER

The conference between the two Governments was eminently successful. It was resolved that burghers of both States should be treated on an equal footing, so that, for instance, the rights which a Transvaaler enjoyed in the Free State were also granted to a Free Stater in the Transvaal, only the franchise being left untouched. Furthermore, a political alliance was concluded, which created a council of delegates, or federal council, which was to sit every year, alternately at Pretoria and Bloemfontein, and make recommendations on matters that might lead to federation as well as suggestions for the assimilation of the laws of the two Republics. The Volksraad of each State approved this treaty, and the only modification introduced was to resolve that a burgher of either Republic should receive burgher rights in the sister state so soon as he had taken the oath prescribed.

she is "a bad woman to deal with, to quarrel with, or to trifle with." The epithet, in short, can be used in Dutch in an objective as well as in a subjective sense.—*Translator's Note.*

CHAPTER XII

PAUL KRUGER'S FOURTH PRESIDENCY

CHAPTER XII

PAUL KRUGER'S FOURTH PRESIDENCY

The Bunu Question—Sir Alfred Milner—F. W. Reitz—J. C. Smuts—The agitation of the South African League—The Edgar Case—The crisis: the suffrage, the suzerainty—The ultimatum—The war—President Kruger during the war—On the way to Europe—On foreign soil—Homeless—Conclusion.

THE result of the new election came as a surprise to friends and enemies alike; for, although my re-election was certain, no one suspected that I would obtain such an overwhelming majority. The official figures were:

Kruger	12,858 votes
Schalk Burger	3,750 "
Joubert	2,001 "

On the 12th of May 1898, I took the oath for the fourth time as State President. On this occasion I made a speech which took almost three hours to deliver, and in which I set forth my religious and political views on the actual situation and on the problems confronting the State.[1]

[1] This speech, by far the longest speech that President Kruger ever delivered, is really a series of addresses to the First and Second Volksraad, the Executive Raad, the representatives of the Orange Free State, the *corps diplomatique*, the burghers, the naturalized foreigners, the new immigrants, the judges, the clergy, the schoolmasters and mistresses and the children. It will be found in the Appendix.—*Note by the Editor of the German Edition.*

THE MEMOIRS OF PAUL KRUGER

During the session of the Volksraad of 1898, Dr. Leyds was almost unanimously re-elected State Secretary, but was shortly afterwards appointed Envoy Extraordinary of the Republic in Europe. As his successor, Abraham Fischer was elected, one of the ablest and most sagacious statesmen in South Africa, and at that time a member of the Executive Raad of the Orange Free State. He refused, however, to accept the proffered appointment, whereupon Mr. F. W. Reitz, who had recently been promoted to a judgeship in the South African Republic, was elected State Secretary, a happy choice, for Mr. Reitz is looked upon by friend and foe alike as one of the most honest men that have ever played a part in politics. Moreover, he possessed an abundant knowledge of affairs, thanks to his long political career.

At the same time, J. C. Smuts, a representative of the younger generation of Afrikanders, was appointed State Attorney. Smuts is one of the cleverest lawyers in South Africa and a man of versatile attainments besides. He is personally a very simple man, and, to meet him, one would not suspect that he possesses so firm a will and so determined a character as he does. Although scarcely 30 years of age and without the slightest previous experience of military affairs, he developed, in the later phases of the war, into a most brilliant general, so that he added

KRUGER'S FOURTH PRESIDENCY

to his position as State Attorney that of an assistant commandant general of the South African Republic. Smuts will yet play a great part in the history of South Africa.

Shortly after the swearing-in of Messrs. Reitz and Smuts, the Bunu question became urgent, and Sir Alfred Milner received his first chance to provoke and thwart the Republic.

The Bunu question was briefly as follows: according to the old custom, the Swazi king had the right to put any of his subjects to death whenever he pleased. This condition was naturally altered from the moment when the Republic took over the administration of Swaziland. In the early part of 1898, Bunu murdered one of his indunas, named Umbaba, in addition to some others. It was stated by eye-witnesses that Bunu had killed Umbaba with his own hand. When Bunu was summoned by the State Attorney to appear before the court at Bremersdorp, he at first refused to come, and, when eventually he did come, arrived accompanied by an armed suite, and adopted a threatening attitude towards Krogh, the Special Commissioner for Swaziland. Krogh was consequently obliged to let the matter drop, and Bunu returned to his town.

The Government had no choice but to send an armed force to Swaziland, in order to protect life and property and to compel Bunu, if necessary by force, to appear before the court. Meanwhile, the High Commissioner deemed it necessary to interfere in the matter, probably with no other object than to cause the Republic needless annoyance. Perhaps, also, he thought that the Bunu question would give him the occasion to involve the Republic in war with England. He contended, namely, that the Government had not the right to summon Bunu before the Swaziland court, notwithstanding that the Swaziland Convention contained an article stipulating that criminal cases occurring in Swaziland should be tried by the Supreme Court at Bremersdorp. When Bunu saw that the Government of the Republic was in earnest, he fled to Zululand and placed himself under the protection of the British Government. In order to avoid getting into difficulties for Bunu's sake, the Government was obliged to conclude an agreement with the High Commissioner which determined that Bunu should be allowed to return, and that he should only be punished with a fine. At the same time, a clause was added to the Swaziland Convention, distinctly deciding which cases should, in future, be within the competence of the Supreme Court of that country.

Already at that time, and shortly after the settlement of the Bunu question, the English in and outside South Africa were adopting a defiant attitude towards the Government of the Republic. At Johannesburg, a branch of the South African

KRUGER'S FOURTH PRESIDENCY

League had been established, at the undoubted instigation of Cecil Rhodes. This league did its utmost to involve the Republic in difficulties with England. No methods were too base or too mean to attain that end. When the Government arrested some colored persons, British subjects, because they were without the passes which they were obliged to carry by the Pass Law, a great hubbub was raised and the League leaders called a meeting in the Amphitheater at Johannesburg to protest against the action of the Republic. The burghers' blood boiled at the attitude of this Rhodes institution: they attended the meeting in large numbers, with the result that a brawl arose and the demonstrators were dispersed with sticks by the burghers. That this brought grist to the mill of the Jingoes, that it was probably just what they desired, is easily understood.

Shortly after, another incident occurred which caused yet more excitement and which was represented by the English press in a shamefully distorted fashion. Even Mr. Chamberlain did not blush to make use of these misrepresentations, although it would have been easy for him to learn the whole truth. What was the question? On the night of the 18th of December 1898, a certain Foster, a British subject, was attacked by another British subject called Edgar, and so maltreated that he was left lying for dead. He was taken to the hospital and died a few days later in consequence of the blows which Edgar had given him. Immediately after the perpetration of his crime, Edgar fled to his room and soon a few police came upon the scene, attracted by the screams of the bystanders. Among the police was one named Jones, a son of a former coachman to the Queen of England, who had, however, in his quality as a policeman, become a burgher of the Republic. This Jones, thinking that Foster was dead, followed Edgar to his apartment to arrest him for murder. As Edgar was caught in the very act, the police had the right, according to the laws, not only of the Republic, but of the whole of South Africa and of England herself, to enter his house, if necessary by force, and arrest the culprit. As Edgar had locked the door and refused to open it, Jones broke it open and, while doing so, was struck a violent blow by Edgar with a bar of iron. Thereupon Jones shot Edgar dead. Although every one will admit that the policeman only did his duty, he was nevertheless prosecuted by the State Attorney for manslaughter, in order to remove any ground for complaint on the part of England. He was, however, as was to be expected, acquitted by the court. But how did Mr. Chamberlain represent this matter? As follows: that policemen broke into a man's house at night without a warrant on the mere statement of one person, which subsequently turned out to be untrue, that the man had committed a crime, and killed him there and then, because, according to their own account, he hit one of them with a stick! Can malevolence go further than this? And ought not a minister to be ashamed thus to violate the truth in an official dispatch?

We now come to the period immediately preceding the serious crisis. In the meantime, the English and the English press, both in South Africa and England, were agitating and vociferating against the Republic. An election had taken place, in the previous year, in Cape Colony, in which the Afrikander party had gained the victory, a fact which drove Rhodes and all his Jingo clique to fury. Sir Alfred Milner, instead of confining himself to his *rôle* of Governor, showed himself in his true colors and openly espoused the side of the Jingoes in Cape Colony. It was evident to all that a crisis was at hand which, if not carefully treated, could end only in catastrophe. But where there are two parties, it avails nothing that one is yielding and compliant, when the other at all costs pushes matters to extremes and, as in this case, to a war. That the Government of the South African Republic, in the negotiations that preceded the war, was yielding and compliant is shown by the manner in which the correspondence with England was conducted at this time.

The question of the franchise was that which Sir

THE MEMOIRS OF PAUL KRUGER

Alfred Milner and Mr. Chamberlain employed as a pretext to force a war upon the Republic. Before, therefore, discussing the negotiations concerning the franchise question, it is well to mention the fact that, as early as the beginning of 1899, I had held meetings of the burghers at Rustenburg and Heidelberg in order to obtain their support for my proposal to reduce the period required for securing the full franchise from fourteen years to nine years. From there I went to Johannesburg and there declared at a public meeting that I hoped later to reduce the period of nine years' residence to a still shorter period. This fact deserves special mention, because it was probably that which startled Mr. Chamberlain and Sir Alfred Milner and impelled them to hurry on the crisis. Firmly determined as they were to force a war upon the Republic, these two men saw that they must lose no time, since I myself had begun to introduce reforms which might presently deprive them of their pretext for going to war. Sir Alfred Milner was in England at that time, and doubtless turned his stay to account to arrange with Chamberlain how they must set to work to carry out their imperialist programme. By the time he returned, the whole thing was settled and arranged.

The League at Johannesburg began by drawing up a petition to the Queen in which they enumerated a mass of grievances which, as British subjects, they claimed to have against the Republic, and ended by asking for the intervention of the British Government. Mr. Fraser, the acting British Agent, refused to receive the petition. For this he was rapped over the knuckles by the Colonial Secretary, who was just seeking an opportunity to meddle with the internal affairs of the Republic, with the result that, on a later occasion, Mr. Conyngham Greene, the real representative of the British Crown at Pretoria, who had also been to England with Sir Alfred Milner, knew better what was expected of him. In the meantime, Sir Alfred Milner had declared that an anti-British movement existed among the Afrikander population throughout South Africa. This, *nota bene*, after he had cabled to England in 1897, on the occasion of the Queen's Jubilee, that the Afrikanders in Cape Colony were very loyal to England.

A second petition was drawn up by the League and signed by 21,684 British subjects. The signatures were collected by every kind of fraud. The Government of the Republic obtained many sworn declarations which stated that individuals had signed as many names as came into their heads. In the same way, the names of deceased and absent persons were placed on the lists. This is easily understood, when one realizes that the persons who went round with the lists were paid according to the number of names which they obtained. A few days later the Government at Pretoria received a petition with nearly 23,000 signatures in which the signers, Uitlanders of every nationality, declared that they were satisfied with the administration of the country. But it was not Mr. Chamberlain's object to receive a genuine petition, so long as he could obtain a weapon with which to attack the Republic, and this weapon was afforded him by the aforesaid petition, which was speedily dispatched to him by the British Agent, Mr. Greene.

Meanwhile, at the commencement of May, Sir Alfred Milner had sent a cablegram to England which would have done credit to a sensation-mongering journalist. In this dispatch, he declared that Her Majesty's Government must give some striking proof of its intention not to be ousted from its position in South Africa, that thousands of British subjects were kept permanently in the position of helots and that the case for intervention was overwhelming. Mr. Chamberlain thereupon sent a dispatch, dated 10 May 1899, in which he acknowledged the receipt of the petition to the Queen, recapitulated all the grievances of the Uitlanders and ended by suggesting to Sir Alfred Milner that a conference should take place between him and myself at Bloemfontein at which the question would be discussed. In the meantime, prompted by a sincere desire to put an end to the prevailing disquiet, President Steyn, be-

KRUGER'S FOURTH PRESIDENCY

fore the receipt of this dispatch, had made the same proposal to both myself and Sir Alfred Milner. We both accepted the invitation and the well-known Bloemfontein Conference met on the 31st of May 1899, and lasted several days. With me were Schalk Burger and A. D. Wolmarans, members of the Executive Raad, and J. C. Smuts, the State Attorney. Mr. Abraham Fischer, a member of the Executive Raad of the Orange Free State, kindly offered to act as interpreter.

The conference came to nothing. Sir Alfred Milner showed from the commencement that he had not the least desire to come to an agreement. He demanded:

1. Franchise after five years' residence.
2. An alteration in the oath of naturalization.
3. Increased representation of the new burghers in the Volksraad.

After several days' discussion, I offered:

1. Naturalization after two years' residence. Full franchise after five years more (or seven years in all, instead of fourteen, as the law then stood).
2. Increased representation of the Uitlanders in the Volksraad.
3. An oath of naturalization similar to that in the Orange Free State.

I demanded, however, that the franchise should be made to depend on the possession of a certain amount of property and naturalization on the production of proof that the individual concerned possessed civic rights in his own country. I also asked that, as a compensation for the concessions which I was making, the British Government should accept the principle of arbitration in the case of differences between the two States. Sir Alfred Milner, however, declared that the concessions were quite insufficient.

During this conference, I pointed out to Sir Alfred that a quantity of the signatures appearing on the petitions to the Queen were spurious, whereupon the latter answered:

" Very well, we will investigate the matter."

He asked me whether the petition which had been addressed to the Government of the Republic did not also contain false signatures. I denied this positively, and said I was prepared at once to appoint a committee to inquire into the genuineness of both petitions. I said I was further prepared to grant the British Government the right of nominating Englishmen to act as members of this committee. Only the committee must not be appointed from England or acquire an official character, as this might make it appear as though the Republic were under British suzerainty. Hereupon Sir Alfred would hear no more, and said:

" Let us drop the subject."

KRUGER'S FOURTH PRESIDENCY

For the rest, he continued to insist upon what he called "his irreducible minimum." He declared that he had other grievances, which would remain, even if the franchise question was settled, and refused to produce them until the franchise question had been settled in his way.

The same evening, I sent to Sir Alfred asking him to meet me again the next morning for further deliberation; but Sir Alfred answered that he " considered this unnecessary and that the conference was ended."

As soon as I had returned to Pretoria, the State Secretary wrote a letter to the British Agent touching the proposed arbitration tribunal, towards which proposal Sir Alfred Milner had adopted an apparently friendly attitude. This letter was dated 9 June 1899, and in it the State Secretary made the following proposal to the British Government:

(1) All future differences between the two Governments arising out of varying interpretations of the London Convention shall, subject to what is set forth under paragraph 3, at the instance of this Government or of Her Majesty's Government, be referred to an arbitration tribunal, on the understanding, however, that no matters or differences of trifling importance shall be submitted to arbitration.

(2) The arbitration tribunal shall consist of an arbitrator to be nominated by this Government and an arbitrator to be nominated by Her Majesty's Government (as, for example, the Chief Justices respectively of the South African Republic and the Cape Colony or Natal). These two must agree respecting a third person, who shall act as President of the

arbitration tribunal, this person not to be a subject of one of the arbitrating parties; and failing agreement upon this point, the two Governments shall together name a President; the decision in every case to take place by a majority of votes.

(3) The Act of Submission shall in every case be drawn up jointly by the two Governments, so that each shall have the right to reserve and exclude points which appear to it to be too important to be submitted to arbitration, provided that thereby the principle itself of arbitration be not frustrated.

(4) The arbitration tribunal shall itself decide the place of its sittings, and shall deal as it thinks fit with the condemnation of parties in the costs, unless special arrangement has been made concerning these points in the Act of Submission.

(5) The regulations of procedure of this arbitration tribunal can be similar to those agreed to by the Institute of International Law in the Hague in 1875, in so far as they do not conflict with the foregoing provisions, and in so far as they are not amended by both parties in the Act of Submission.

(6) In order to obtain a test of the suitability of such tribunal, this Government has no objection to its being agreed that this reference of Conventional differences shall provisionally take place for a period of five years.

The letter ended by expressing an earnest hope that Her Majesty's Government would accept the proposal, which would put an end to the permanent feeling of anxiety from which South Africa was suffering.

The proposals were made in the manner set forth above, with the special purpose of meeting the views of the British Government, as that Government objected to an arbitration court composed of foreigners

KRUGER'S FOURTH PRESIDENCY

and, in any case, declined to submit all questions to arbitration.

Meanwhile, of my own initiative, I introduced a draft law into the Volksraad which fixed:

1. A seven years' residence for obtaining the franchise.

2. The immediate grant of the franchise to all who had lived nine years in the country, while only five years' residence should be necessary for those who had been in the country for two years.

3. All adult sons of foreigners, born in the Republic, to receive the franchise immediately on attaining their majority.

4. An increase in the representation of the goldfields in each Raad by four members.

The bill was passed on the 19th of July. In the meanwhile, the Intelligence Department of the War Office in England had already issued "military notes" indicating how war should be waged against the Republic. At the same time (although this was not yet known), Lord Wolseley had laid his plans before the British Government for the conquest and seizure of the two Republics.

On the 26th of June, the British Agent replied to the arbitration proposals as set forth in Mr. Reitz's letter. In this answer he stated that Sir Alfred Milner could not recommend the acceptance of the proposal to the British Government, as he considered that the question of finding a remedy for the grievances of the Uitlanders should first be disposed of. Furthermore, he intimated that the scheme drawn up by Mr. Reitz was not acceptable to Her Majesty's Government, seeing that, to make no mention of other objections, the president of the court, according to that scheme, could not be a subject of either of the arbitrating parties.

At the beginning of July, the leaders of the Afrikander party, Messrs. Hofmeyer and Herholdt, went from Cape Town to Bloemfontein and thence to Pretoria to persuade the Government still further to simplify the new Franchise Law in such a way as to make the seven years' clause retrospective: so that every one who had spent seven years or more in the Republic could obtain the franchise at once; those who had been six years in the country would have to wait one year more in order to obtain the franchise; those ones who had spent three years in the country must wait four years more, and so on. Their suggestions found a ready hearing among the members of the Government and the Volksraad, who were inclined to make even more concessions for dear peace' sake.

On the 18th of July, probably after having been informed by Messrs. Hofmeyer and Herholdt of the result of their mission, the Cape Ministry issued a note in which they expressed the conviction that there

KRUGER'S FOURTH PRESIDENCY

existed not the least occasion for intervention on the part of England in the internal affairs of the Republic.

On the 20th of July, the so-called Uitlanders' Council telegraphed to England that they were not satisfied with the Franchise Law which had just been passed (the law of the 19th of July).

On the 27th of July, Mr. Chamberlain sent a dispatch in which he recapitulated the events since the conference, persisted in his contentions that not only the letter but the spirit of the London Convention of 1884 had been constantly violated by the Government of the Republic, and ended by maintaining his contention that the preamble to the Convention of 1881 (respecting the Suzerainty) still held good. He rejected the proposed arbitration court, although he suggested that certain questions might be submitted to some judicial authority.

On the 1st of August, Mr. Chamberlain telegraphed to the High Commissioner proposing that England and the Republic should appoint a joint commission to revise the Franchise Law which had been passed, and to enquire whether this law would afford a sufficient representation to the Uitlanders and, if this were not the case, to see what additions or alterations might be necessary to attain this object. This proposal of Mr. Chamberlain's was a direct violation of the London Convention of 1884, for it is hardly possible to imagine a clearer case of interference with the internal affairs of the Republic.

The State Secretary, accordingly, replied on the 12th of August, calling Mr. Chamberlain's attention to the fact that, according to the Convention of 1884, the British Government was not to meddle in the internal affairs of the Republic, and expressed the hope that, in making his proposal, Mr. Chamberlain did not mean to encroach upon the rights of the Republic. The State Secretary further gave expression to the opinion that the object which Mr. Chamberlain had in view in the appointment of a joint commission could be as easily attained by asking questions and obtaining information about the measure. He also observed to Mr. Chamberlain that a judgment could only be formed as to whether a law answered its purpose or not, if it had been in operation for some time.

On the 15th of August, the State Attorney, Mr. J. C. Smuts, had an interview with the British Agent, in which he asked him whether Her Majesty's Government would consider the seven years' retrospective franchise, with an increase of seats for the Uitlanders in the Volksraad, to be sufficient and, in that case, waive the joint commission. Mr. Greene answered that he did not know whether Her Majesty's Government would consent to abandon their demand, but that the position was very critical; that Her

KRUGER'S FOURTH PRESIDENCY

Majesty's Government had made promises to the Uitlanders, and that they would, therefore, be obliged to insist on their demands and, if necessary, to employ force. He added that the only chance for the South African Republic was to comply without delay with the demands put forward by Sir Alfred Milner at Bloemfontein.

On the 19th of August, the State Secretary wrote to the British Agent making the following alternative proposal to Her Majesty's Government:

(1) The Government are willing to recommend to the Volksraad and the people a five years' retrospective franchise as proposed by His Excellency the High Commissioner on June 1st, 1899.

(2) The Government are further willing to recommend to the Volksraad that eight new seats in the First Volksraad, and, if necessary, also in the Second Volksraad, be given to the population of the Witwatersrand, thus, with the two sitting members for the gold-fields, giving to the population thereof ten representatives in a Raad of twenty-six, and in future the representation of the gold-fields of this Republic shall not fall below the proportion of one-fourth of the total.

(3) The new burghers shall equally with the old burghers be entitled to vote at the election for State President and Commandant General.

(4) This Government will always be prepared to take into consideration such friendly suggestions regarding the details of the franchise law as Her Majesty's Government, through the British Agent, may wish to convey to it.

(5) In putting forward the above proposals to the Government of the South African Republic assumes—

(a) That Her British Majesty's Government will agree that the present intervention shall not form a precedent for future similar action, and that, in the future, no interference in the internal affairs of the Republic will take place.

(*b*) That Her Majesty's Government will not further insist on the assertion of the Suzerainty, the controversy on this subject being allowed tacitly to drop.

(*c*) That arbitration from which foreign element, other than Orange Free State, is to be excluded, will be conceded as soon as the franchise scheme has become law.

(6) Immediately on Her British Majesty's Government accepting this proposal for a settlement, the Government will ask the Volksraad to adjourn for the purpose of consulting the people about it, and the whole scheme might become law, say, within a few weeks.

(7) In the meantime the form and scope of the proposed tribunal are also to be discussed and provisionally agreed upon, while the franchise scheme is being referred to the people, so that no time may be lost in putting an end to the present state of affairs.

The State Secretary ended by saying " that the Government trusts that Her Majesty's Government will clearly understand that in the opinion of this Government, the existing franchise law of this Republic is both fair and liberal to the new population, and that the consideration that induces them to go further, as they do in the above proposals, is their strong desire to get the controversies between the two Governments settled; and, further, to put an end to the present strained relations between the two Governments, and the incalculable harm and loss it has already occasioned in South Africa, and to prevent a racial war, from the effects of which South

KRUGER'S FOURTH PRESIDENCY

Africa may not recover for many generations, perhaps never at all; and, therefore, this Government, having regard to all these circumstances, would highly appreciate it, if Her Majesty's Government, seeing the necessity of preventing the present crisis from developing still further, and the urgency of an early termination of the present state of affairs, would expedite the acceptance or refusal of the settlement here offered."

On the 21st of August, the State Secretary again wrote to the British Agent to explain and complete his letter of the 19th of August. In this second letter, he makes it clear that the proposals regarding the question of franchise and representation in the dispatch of the 19th of August must be regarded as expressly conditional on Her Majesty's Government consenting to the points set forth in paragraph 5 of the dispatch, viz.:

(*a*) In the future no interference in the internal affairs of the South African Republic.

(*b*) No further insistence on the assertion of the existence of the suzerainty.

(*c*) The acceptance of arbitration for the settlement of questions in dispute.

These proposals were made after the State Attorney had had a new interview with Mr. Greene, the result of which was to convince him that the British Government would be prepared to take those proposals into consideration. This would cause the proposal for a joint commission to lapse.

On the 25th of August the so-called Uitlanders' Council and the South African League declared that the franchise reforms were still insufficient, and demanded further "reforms," such as the disarming of the Boers and the demolition of the forts.

On the 26th of August, Mr. Chamberlain made a speech on the occasion of a garden-party at his place at Highbury, in which, among other things, he said:

> Mr. Kruger dribbles out reforms like water from a squeezed sponge, and he either accompanies his offers with conditions which he knows to be impossible, or he refuses to allow us to make a satisfactory investigation of the nature of these reforms. . . . The sands are running down in the glass. . . . The knot must be loosened . . . or else we shall have to find other ways of untying it.

On the 30th of August, he sent a dispatch in which he stated, among other things, that Her Majesty's Government assumed that the adoption in principle of the franchise proposals would not be hampered by any conditions which would impair their effect; that Her Majesty's Government were unable to appreciate the objections entertained by the Government of the South African Republic to a joint commission of inquiry; that Her Majesty's Government, however, would appoint a commission on their side to institute an inquiry into the law and to make the nec-

KRUGER'S FOURTH PRESIDENCY

essary suggestions to the Government of the Republic, and trusted that different conditions, as to previous registration, qualification and behavior, would be omitted from the proposed new law. With regard to the conditions of the Government of the South African Republic, Mr. Chamberlain said, as regards intervention, Her Majesty's Government hoped that the fulfilment of the promises made and the just treatment of the Uitlanders in future would render unnecessary any further interference on their behalf, but that Her Majesty's Government could not debar themselves from their rights under the conventions. (*N.B.*—The convention of 1881 had lapsed, as is known.) With regard to the suzerainty, Mr. Chamberlain referred the Government to a former dispatch, in which he maintained that the suzerainty still existed. With regard to the proposed tribunal of arbitration, he agreed to a discussion of the form and scope of such a tribunal, from which, however, foreigners and foreign influence were to be excluded. He moreover proposed that a further conference should take place between myself and the High Commissioner at Cape Town, and ended by reminding the Government of the South African Republic that there were other matters of difference which could not be settled by the grant of political representation to the Uitlanders and which were not proper subjects for reference to arbitration.

THE MEMOIRS OF PAUL KRUGER

Mr. Chamberlain afterwards declared that, in this dispatch, he accepted the proposals of the Government of the South African Republic as set forth above. He is probably the only man in the world who read his dispatch in this light: every impartial judge will think the opposite.

On the 31st of August, Sir Alfred Milner telegraphed to Mr. Chamberlain:

> The purport of all the representations made to me is to urge prompt and decided action; not to deprecate further interference on the part of Her Majesty's Government. British South Africa is prepared for extreme measures. . . . I fear seriously that there will be a strong reaction of feeling against the policy of Her Majesty's Government if matters drag.

In reply to Mr. Chamberlain's dispatch of the 30th of August, the State Secretary, on the 2d of September, wrote to the British Agent at Pretoria that the Government of the South African Republic had heard with the deepest regret that Her Majesty's Government had not seen their way to accept the proposals which were set forth in the notes of the 19th and 21st of August, under the conditions attached thereto, the more so as the Government had supposed from semi-official discussions that it might infer that its proposal would have been acceptable to Her Majesty's Government. In consequence, the Government of the South African Republic considered that its proposal had lapsed. With regard to the unilateral inquiry, the Government was willing, if it should appear that the existing franchise law might be made more effective, to lay proposals before the Volksraad. It appeared, however, to it that the findings of a unilateral commission, especially when made before the working of the law had been properly tested, would probably be of little value. Passing to the remarks made by Mr. Chamberlain in connection with the conditions attached to the proposals in the note of the 19th of August, the State Secretary observes:

(*a*) That this Government has never, with reference to the question of intervention, either asked or intended that Her Majesty's Government should abandon any right it may have, as a matter of fact by virtue of either the Convention of London of 1884 or of general international law, to take action here for the protection of British subjects.

(*b*) That with regard to the alleged existence of suzerainty, the denial of its existence by this Government according to its view has already been so clearly explained in its dispatch of 16th of April, 1898, that it would be superfluous to repeat the facts, arguments and consequences mentioned therein: it merely wishes to observe that it adheres to its contentions stated in that dispatch.

With reference to a tribunal of arbitration the Government was pleased to see that Her Majesty's Government were prepared to enter into negotiations with regard to the form and scope of such tribunal. It was however not clear to it:

(a) If Her Majesty's Government consents that burghers of the Orange Free State may also be appointed as members of such tribunal.

(b) What subjects shall be submitted to the decision of such court.

(c) What are the subjects Her Majesty's Government thinks cannot be laid before such court. Her Majesty's Government states that there are such points, but does not specify them.

The object contemplated by the Government of the South African Republic, *i.e.*, the securing of a final regulation of all points at issue, would, it opined, be altogether frustrated by these limitations. With reference to the recommendation of a conference to be held, the Government would await further communications from Her Majesty's Government. The State Secretary went on to remark that the proposal made by his Government with reference to the franchise and representation of the Uitlanders was extremely liberal, and, as a matter of fact, went further than the propositions of the High Commissioner put forward at the Bloemfontein Conference; that the conditions attached by his Government did not demand from the side of Her Majesty's Government any abandonment of existing rights under the Convention of London of 1884; that the Government of the South African Republic could never have expected that the answer of Her Majesty's Government to its proposal would be unfavorable; that it continued to cherish the hope that a solution of existing differences might be arrived at; and, in order to attain this peaceful solution, the State Secretary ended his letter by accepting the joint commission formerly proposed by Mr. Chamberlain.

On the 12th of September, Mr. Greene, on behalf of the British Government, answered Mr. Reitz's dispatch of the 2d of September, and said that Her Majesty's Government could not now consent to go back to its former proposal of a joint commission; that Her Majesty's Government were still prepared to accept the proposals, provided that the inquiry which Her Majesty's Government had proposed, whether joint or unilateral, showed that the scheme would not be encumbered by conditions which would nullify its intentions. His Government assumed that the new members of the Volksraad would be permitted to use their own language. He ended his letter by pressing for an immediate reply, and stating that, if the reply was negative or inconclusive, Her Majesty's Government reserved to itself the right to reconsider the situation *de novo* and to formulate its own proposals for a final settlement.

To this the State Secretary replied, on the 15th of September, that his Government learned with deep regret that Her Majesty's Government withdrew its invitation and substituted in its place an entirely new proposal; that the proposal contained in the notes of the Government of the 19th and 21st of

THE MEMOIRS OF PAUL KRUGER

August was induced by suggestions given by the British Agent to the State Attorney, and these were accepted by his Government in good faith, and on express request, as equivalent to an assurance that the proposal would be acceptable to the British Government; that his Government could not disguise from itself that, in making the proposal contained in its note of the 19th of August, it probably ran the danger not only of its being disclaimed by the Volksraad and by the people, but also that its acceptance might affect the independence of the state by, as therein proposed, giving an immediate vote in the legislature of the state to a large number of inpouring foreigners; but it set against that the continuous threatening and undoubted danger to its highly prized independence arising from the claim of suzerainty made by Her Majesty's Government, from the interference of that Government in the internal affairs of the Republic and from the want of an automatically working method of regulating differences between Her Majesty's Government and the Government of the Republic, and was in consequence prepared to recommend to the Volksraad and to the people to run the danger attached to the offer made in order to avoid the certainty of the greater danger; inasmuch, however, as the conditions attached to the proposal, the acceptance of which constituted the only consideration for its offer, had been declared unacceptable, it could not understand on what grounds of justice it could be expected that it should be bound to grant the rest. As regards the point that the new members should speak their own language in the Volksraad, the Government could not enter into this and denied having made any such promise. The State Secretary ended his letter by expressing the hope that the British Government would abide by its own proposal for a joint commission and thus put an end to the present state of tension.

To this letter of the State Secretary the British Agent replied, on the 25th of September, that Her Majesty's Government had on more than one occasion repeated its assurances that it had no desire to interfere in any way with the independence of the South African Republic (*N.B.*—It was always doing so); that it had not asserted any rights of interference in the internal affairs of the Republic other than those which were derived from the conventions (*N.B.*—There was only one!); and ended by saying that it was useless to pursue further a discussion on the lines hitherto followed, and that Her Majesty's Government was now compelled to consider the situation afresh, and to formulate its own proposals for a final settlement of the issues which had been created in South Africa by the policy constantly followed for so many years by the Government of the South African Republic.

On the 17th of September, the State Secretary asked the High Commissioner for explanations regarding the concentration of troops on the frontiers of the South African Republic. The High Commissioner replied that those troops were there to defend British interests and in order to be prepared for " possibilities."

On the 22d of September, the mobilization of an army corps for South Africa was announced in England, and, on the 28th of September, it was announced that the greater part of that army corps would leave for South Africa without delay. The Government thereupon commandeered the greater part of the burghers to take up their position near the frontiers of the Republic, in order to be prepared for a sudden attack on the part of England.

On the 30th of September, the State Secretary informed the British Agent that he would be glad to know the decision of the British Government (*i.e.* with reference to the " own proposals " announced in the dispatch of 25 September). Mr. Chamberlain answered, on the 2d of October, that the dispatch of Her Majesty's Government was being prepared, but that it would not be ready for some days. It is clear that Mr. Chamberlain only desired to gain

KRUGER'S FOURTH PRESIDENCY

time, in order first to have sufficient troops in South Africa, before sending his promised dispatch, which was nothing else than an ultimatum.

Before the final steps were reached, President Steyn of the Orange Free State had intervened in order to make every effort, on his side, to avoid war. On the 19th of September, the High Commissioner telegraphed to President Steyn that a detachment of troops, ordinarily stationed at Cape Town, was being sent to assist in securing the line of communication between the Colony and the British territories lying to the north of it; and that, as this force, or a portion of it, might be stationed near the borders of the Orange Free State, he, the High Commissioner, thought it desirable to acquaint His Honor with this movement, and the reasons for it, in order to prevent any misconception. He added that Her Majesty's Government was still hopeful of a friendly settlement of the differences which had arisen between it and the South African Republic, but that, should this hope unfortunately be disappointed, the British Government looked to the Orange Free State to preserve strict neutrality.

President Steyn replied, on the same day, that he was unable to see that the differences justified the use of force as their only solution. Seeing the state of tension in South Africa, he noted with apprehension and regret the stationing of troops near the borders of the Orange Free State, since the burghers would consider this a menace to that state. If, therefore, unwished-for developments should arise, the responsibility would not rest with the Government of the Orange Free State. His Honor concluded his telegram by stating that he would view with deep regret any disturbance of those friendly relations which hitherto had existed between Great Britain and the Orange Free State.

On the 27th of September, the Volksraad of the Orange Free State adopted a resolution in which it declared that no cause for war existed, that such a war would be morally a war against the whole white population of South Africa, but that, come what might, the Orange Free State would honestly and faithfully observe its obligations arising from the political alliance with the South African Republic. At the same time the Government was instructed to do everything in its power to contribute by peaceful efforts towards the solution of the existing differences.

That same day, the 27th of September, President Steyn sent a dispatch to the High Commissioner in which he reminded him of the ties of blood and friendship by which the Orange Free State was bound both to Cape Colony and the South African Republic, and, in addition, of the close political alliance between the two Republics. He said that it was this strong feeling of amity towards both Great Britain and the South African Republic that led him to bring about the conference between the High Commissioner and myself; that it was largely due to the Orange Free State and other friends of peace that such radical reforms had been effected by the South African Republic in so short a time; that the Orange Free State ever kept in view the spirit in which it assumed that the British Government was willing to act, viz., " to adopt an attitude of friendly suggestion and not of dictation in the internal affairs of the Republic; " that, while the Government of the Republic, encouraged thereto by the advice of the Free State, was busy in meeting the wants of the Uitlanders, the British Government had departed from the basis of non-interference in the internal affairs of the Republic; that the request for the joint commission of inquiry emphasized that fact beyond any shadow of doubt; that, notwithstanding this, the Government of the Orange Free State advised the South African Republic to accept the invitation of the British Government, in the hope that an impartial investigation might inaugurate a renewal of the employment of friendly methods of negotiation; that great, therefore, was the disappointment of the Government of the Orange Free State when it transpired that the British Government now rejected its proposal and that the unfortunate tension seemed to be only increasing; that the Government of the Orange Free State was still prepared to tender its services to procure a peaceful solution of existing difficulties, but that it felt itself hampered now as in the past (*a*) by a want of knowledge as to the definite object and extent of the demands of the British Government, compliance with which that Government considered itself entitled to insist upon; and (*b*) by the fact that, notwithstanding the repeated assurances of the British Government that it did not wish to interfere in the internal affairs of the Republic nor to disturb its independence, that Government had pursued a policy which seemed to justify a contrary conclusion. As an instance in support of this contention, His Honor mentioned the enormous and ever-increasing military preparations on the part of the British Government, indicating a policy of force and coercion, notwithstanding the alleged friendly nature of the negotiations. His Honor, therefore, trusted that Her Majesty's Government might see its way clear to stop any further movements or increase of troops on or near the borders of both States, pending the arrival of the further dispatch intimated as about to be sent, and further to give an assurance to that effect; and added that his Government would be glad to be favored with the precise nature and scope of the concessions, the adoption of which Her Majesty's Government considered itself entitled to claim, or which it suggested as being necessary or sufficient to ensure a satisfactory and permanent solution of existing differences.

On the 2d of October, President Steyn informed the High Commissioner that, in view of the totally undefended state of the border, of the prevailing unrest, and of the continual increase and movement of troops on two sides of the Orange Free State, he had deemed it advisable to call up his burghers in order to satisfy them that due precautions had been taken to guard their borders, adding that he was still looking forward to a reply to his dispatch of the 27th of September.

The High Commissioner replied on the same day regretting that the President had called up the burghers and declaring that His Honor was aware that the South African Republic had placed a very considerable army on the borders of Natal.

The President replied, on the 3d of October, that the concentration of burghers on the Natal frontier by the South African Republic was only the natural result of the constant increase of British troops and their movement in the direction of the Transvaal border. He did not, however, anticipate any immediate aggressive action on the part of the South African Republic, unless further forward movements of British troops should indicate an intention of attack upon the Transvaal. He went on to press for an answer to his dispatch of the 27th of September.

The High Commissioner answered, on the same day, that all the movements of British troops had been necessitated by the natural alarm of the inhabitants in exposed districts and were not comparable in magnitude with the massing of armed forces on the borders of Natal by the Government of the South African Republic.

The President replied, also on the 3d of October, that he did not consider that the movements of British troops had been necessitated by the natural alarm of the inhabitants in exposed districts, nor in fact had he ever thought that there were any grounds justifying such movements. On the contrary, the ever-increasing military preparations, both in England and South Africa, had retarded and hampered the efforts that had been made to effect a fair settlement. He ascribed the failure to arrive at a solution of existing difficulties to the bitter and hostile tone of utterances, made both by responsible men and by the English press in South Africa and England, bristling with misrepresentations and menace to the Transvaal, accompanied by ever-increasing military preparations, not only in South Africa and in England, but throughout the British Empire, which were openly stated to be directed against the Transvaal. He wished to place on record his earnest conviction that on those in authority who introduced the military element, and who thereby inaugurated a policy of menace and forcible intervention, would rest the responsibility, should all efforts fail to secure peace and an honorable settlement. He could not but recognize the fact that, in view of the action of the British authorities already alluded to, the Transvaal Government could not be blamed for acting as it had done. He was the more confirmed in this view by the fact that while he was still without any reply to his telegraphic dispatch of the 27th of September, the reasonable request therein made that the increase and further movement of British troops should be stayed, which if acceded to would probably have prevented the calling out of the burghers both in the South African Republic and in this State, had not only been ignored but activity in military preparations and the dispatch of troops had been going on more persistently than ever. He was not in a position to judge whether the movement of British troops on the border of the South African Republic was comparable or not in magnitude with the recent massing of armed force by the South African Republic on the borders, but it must not be forgotten that on all sides, in the English press and elsewhere, the assertion constantly found expression that the British troops already in the country were more than a match for the undisciplined burgher force of the

Republic. Moreover, troops were being dispatched almost daily from England, which would justify a conviction in the minds of the burghers of the South African Republic that England had abandoned any idea of attempting to arrive at a solution of differences except by force.

On the 4th of October, the High Commissioner replied that there was, he thought, a conclusive reply to His Honor's accusation against the policy of Her Majesty's Government, but that no good purpose would be served by recrimination; that the present position was that burgher forces were assembled in very large numbers in immediate proximity to the frontier of Natal, while the British troops occupied certain defensive positions well within those borders. He would not despair of peace and felt sure that any reasonable proposal, from whatever quarter proceeding, would be favorably considered by Her Majesty's Government.

On the 5th of October, the President replied that he was prepared to make a proposal, but that he considered it would not be practicable to induce the Government of the South African Republic to make or entertain proposals or suggestions, unless the troops menacing their states were withdrawn farther from their borders, and an assurance were also given by Her Majesty's Government that all further dispatch and increase of troops would at once, and during negotiations, be stopped, and that those now on the water would either not be landed or at least would remain as far removed as might be from the scene of possible hostilities. The President urged upon His Excellency the urgent necessity of intimating to him without delay whether His Excellency saw his way clear to give effect to these his views and wishes; and if so he would take steps to obtain an assurance from the South African Republic to safeguard against any act of invasion or hostility against any portion of Her Majesty's territories. He would further support all reasonable proposals which would possess the element of finality and give the assurance of a lasting peace.

The High Commissioner replied, on the 6th of October 1899, that he regretted that the President should suggest, as a condition precedent to further negotiations, an assurance from Her Majesty's Government hampering its freedom of action with regard to the disposition of British troops in British territory. Such an assurance it was impossible for him to ask Her Majesty's Government to give. If, on the other hand, the President could obtain an assurance that, pending negotiations, no act of hostility would be committed, he was prepared to advise Her Majesty's Government to give an assurance to the like effect.

Steyn replied, on the same day, that he could not

be expected to ask the South African Republic to continue negotiations in the face of the fact that from all sides of Her Majesty's dominions troops were being poured into South Africa with the avowed object of coercing the South African Republic into accepting whatever terms Her Majesty's Government might decide to impose. The President added that he had no doubt that, in so far as Her Majesty's troops were intended for the defence of Her Majesty's possessions, the same purpose could be effected in another way, and he would be willing to assist in its being effected; but the point which he thought it fair to urge was that it would be taken by the South African Republic as virtually amounting to an act of hostility on the part of Her Majesty's Government to be continuously increasing their forces during the negotiations.

On the 7th of October, His Honor received a reply to his dispatch of the 27th of September, in which the British Government stated that it had repeatedly explained its views on the questions at issue between it and the Government of the South African Republic, and did not think its position open to misunderstanding; but, if the President of the Orange Free State desired elucidation of any special point, it was prepared to give it. As regards the military preparations, they had been necessitated by the policy of the South African Republic of converting that country into a permanent armed camp. In view of the rejection of its last proposals by the Government of the South African Republic, Her Majesty's Government was reconsidering the situation, having regard to the grave fact that both Republics had now placed themselves on a war footing.

On the same day, 7 October 1899, a royal proclamation appeared in England, summoning Parliament and calling out the reserves; at the same time an order was issued for the mobilization of an army corps for South Africa.

On the 9th of October, President Steyn sent a telegram to the High Commissioner demurring to the statement that the military preparations made by Her Majesty's Government had been necessitated by the action of the South African Republic. He again urged the withdrawal of forces on both sides, such withdrawal to include an undertaking by Her Majesty's Government to stop the further increase of troops.

I have now given the course of negotiations and described events precisely as they occurred. Any one who views these matters impartially must admit that the British Government, and particularly the High Commissioner and Mr. Chamberlain, did their utmost to cause the negotiations to fail and to bring on a war.

THE MEMOIRS OF PAUL KRUGER

The Government of the South African Republic clearly saw what the British Government wanted, that a collision was inevitable, and that the British Government was only waiting to send its ultimatum until sufficient troops had arrived in South Africa to overwhelm the Republic from every side. When it realized that a war was inevitable, that to make concessions availed nothing and that its only chance lay in compelling the British Government to display its real intentions before all the British troops were landed, the Government of the South African Republic had recourse to extreme measures, and, on the 9th of October, wrote a letter to the British Agent, the so-called " Ultimatum." In this document the Government once more set forth how England had not the slightest right to interfere in the internal affairs of the Republic; how the Republic had yet found occasion to discuss in a friendly fashion the franchise and the representation of the people with Her Majesty's Government; how on the part of Her Majesty's Government the friendly nature of those discussions had assumed a more and more threatening tone; how Her Majesty's Government had finally broken off all friendly correspondence on the subject; how the Republic was still waiting for the proposal which the British Government had promised to make for a final settlement; how, in view of the British military force on the frontiers,

KRUGER'S FOURTH PRESIDENCY

the Republic had been obliged, as a defensive measure, to send a portion of the burghers to protect the frontiers; how the unlawful intervention of Her Majesty's Government in the affairs of the Republic, in conflict with the London Convention of 1884, had caused an intolerable condition of affairs to arise to which the Government felt itself obliged, in the interest not only of the Republic but of all South Africa, to make an end as soon as possible, and therefore felt itself called upon and obliged to press earnestly and with emphasis for an immediate termination of this state of things, and to request Her Majesty's Government to give it the assurance:

(*a*) That all points of mutual difference shall be regulated by the friendly course of arbitration, or by whatever amicable way may be agreed upon by this Government with Her Majesty's Government.

(*b*) That the troops on the borders of this Republic shall be instantly withdrawn.

(*c*) That all reinforcements of troops which have arrived in South Africa since the 1st June 1899 shall be removed within a reasonable time, to be agreed upon with this Government, and with a mutual assurance and guarantee on the part of this Government that no attack upon, or hostilities against, any portion of the possessions of the British Government shall be made by the Republic during further negotiations, within a period of time to be subsequently agreed upon between the Governments, and this Government will, on compliance therewith, be prepared to withdraw the armed burghers of this Republic from the borders.

(*d*) That Her Majesty's troops which are now on the high seas shall not be landed in any port of South Africa.

THE MEMOIRS OF PAUL KRUGER

The dispatch ended by requesting Her Majesty's Government to return an answer before or upon Wednesday the 11th of October, not later than 5 o'clock p.m., adding that, in the event of no satisfactory answer being received within that interval, the Republic would with great regret be compelled to regard the action of Her Majesty's Government as a formal declaration of war and would not hold itself responsible for the consequences thereof, and that, in the event of any further movements of troops taking place within the above-mentioned time in the nearer directions of the borders of the Republic, the Government would be compelled to regard that also as a formal declaration of war.

On the 11th of October, Mr. Greene brought the reply of the British Government to the effect that the conditions demanded by the Government of the South African Republic were such as Her Majesty's Government deemed it impossible to discuss. At the same time he asked for his passports, in order to enable him to leave the country. And so, in spite of all the concessions, all the patience and indulgence of the Republic, the war broke out. The Volksraad, which was still sitting, adjourned when it became evident that hostilities were soon to begin; both our Volksraad and that of the Orange Free State unanimously declared themselves ready to risk their lives

KRUGER'S FOURTH PRESIDENCY

and property for their rights and for their liberty; and both repeated this vow in their last session during the turmoil of war.[1]

The course and the vicissitudes of the war do not come within the scope of these Memoirs, since I took no personal part in the fighting. I had a different work before me, which kept me employed day and night. All looked to me for advice, hints and consolation. Daily I sent off telegrams to all the commandos, encouraging, advising and exhorting the burghers. These labors fully occupied the mornings from eight to twelve and the evenings from two to four or five o'clock. Not till then did I leave the Government buildings. I went to bed at eight, only to get up again at eleven to go through the telegrams that had come to hand. I rose once more at two, to inspect any dispatches that had arrived in the meantime, and it was often four o'clock before I could seek my rest again. In the later stage of the war, when the federal troops were being driven back on every side, my sleep was interrupted regularly three times every night, and frequently as often as four times, in order that I might deal with the telegrams without delay. I was thankful for every success and did not

[1] Official reports of President Kruger's speech at the closing of the First and Second Volksraad and of the speeches of both Presidents at the last meetings of the Volksraads of the Transvaal and of the Orange Free State will be found in the Appendix.—*Note by the Editor of the German Edition.*

lose courage when reverses were announced, as many of my telegrams could show, had they not been scattered to the winds.

After the relief of Ladysmith, I went myself to Natal to exhort the burghers to keep courage. At Glencoe, where the burghers had once more taken up their position, I addressed them in a long speech, pointing out the urgency of keeping up the fight. General Joubert spoke to them to the same effect.

I had scarcely returned to Pretoria, when I went to Bloemfontein in order to proceed thence, by wagon, to Poplar Grove, on the Modder River, where I intended also to address and encourage the burghers. But I could not come so far, for I had only just reached General De Wet, when I was obliged to go back, as French, with his mounted troops, had effected a turning movement and I was in danger of being cut off. Heavy fighting took place on my arrival, for the English general in command knew of my presence, and I had only just time to retire: I had hardly crossed the Modder River, when French arrived with his cavalry. Here, however, De la Rey, who had just arrived with his staff, flung himself against him and held him in check until the laager and guns were safe. As I resumed my homeward course, the shells were flying all around me, and one fell just behind the cart in which I was seated. I was, therefore, obliged to return to Pretoria, but

KRUGER'S FOURTH PRESIDENCY

went straight on to Kroonstad, there to encourage the burghers and attend a general council of war. It was on this occasion that the deeply-lamented Colonel de Villebois-Mareuil received his promotion to General of the Foreign Legion.

Shortly after, I received a heavy blow through the death of General Joubert, who had worked together with me for so many years in building up the Republic. His death was profoundly mourned by the whole people, and there is no doubt that the decease of this upright lover of his country exercised a discouraging influence upon his fellow-burghers. Fortunately he had, before his death, appointed a successor in the present Commandant General Louis Botha, who has shown that the confidence placed in him by the dying general was well deserved.

Shortly before the capture of Bloemfontein, the two Governments resolved to send a deputation to Europe to endeavor to secure intervention. This deputation consisted of Mr. Abraham Fischer, a member of the Executive Raad of the Orange Free State, who had taken a prominent part in the negotiations during the crisis, and who now acted as a delegate for both states, with Mr. C. H. Wessels, President of the Volksraad of the Orange Free State, for his own state, and Mr. A. D. W. Wolmarans, a member of the Executive Raad of the South African Republic, for his state. All three were men in whom the Government and the people of both Republics placed the greatest confidence.

A short time before the surrender of Cronjé, the two Governments sent a dispatch to Lord Salisbury, in which they declared that the Republics were willing to make peace if their independence, the only thing for which they were fighting, were acknowledged. Lord Salisbury replied that he could not accept this proposal; for the Republics were not to be allowed to retain a shred of independence: and that after he had declared, only three months earlier, in a public speech, that England sought no goldfields and no territory.

Although the preceding days made heavy claims upon me, those that followed made even more strenuous demands. After the relief of Mafeking, when the British troops began to stream into the Republic from every side, it became daily more clear that, in my old age, I should have to leave my wife, my home and all that was dear to me, in order to seek a refuge in the east of the Republic, and there begin the struggle anew. The thought of this departure lay heavy upon my heart, the more so as my wife was so old and weak that I could not think of taking her with me. The doctor had declared that such a journey as this would mean death to her; and yet I felt sure that I should never see her again in this life. The day of our separation after a long and

KRUGER'S FOURTH PRESIDENCY

happy marriage came ever closer and closer, and an uncertain future, full of dangers and privations, faced me. It was with this knowledge that I opened the Volksraad at the beginning of May.[1] Many of the best-known figures in public life were already at rest in their graves, and their seats in the Volksraad stood empty.

Lord Roberts had at last pushed forward to Johannesburg, and, as we were informed that he intended, with a flying column, to cut the Delagoa Railway line to the east of Pretoria, it was resolved that I should leave Pretoria with the Government and transfer the seat of government to the east of the Republic. On the afternoon of my last day at Pretoria, 29 May, 1900, while my things were being packed, I received the American lad, Jimmy Smith, who brought me an address, in which thousands of school-boys in Philadelphia, the children of a city which was the first to declare its independence of Great Britain, " sent a message of sympathy to the leader of the people which was now engaged in defending its independence against the same nation." He also handed me a Transvaal flag which had been embroidered in America. I thanked the boy and the American gentlemen who had accompanied him, and, one hour later, when it was already dark, I drove

[1] For President Kruger's speeches delivered on this occasion, see the Appendix. They show that he had not lost confidence.—*Note by the Editor of the German Edition.*

with a few faithful friends to Eerste Fabrieken, the first station on the eastern line. From there I went by railway, over Middelburg, to Machadodorp, where the seat of government was provisionally established. I lived in my saloon-carriage, to which a telegraph apparatus had been fitted: my work was no less arduous than at Pretoria, and I was constantly sending telegrams to encourage the burghers in the fight.

The first days of June are among the darkest of my life. On the 5th of June, Lord Roberts occupied Pretoria, and many of the burghers, discouraged by recent events, listened to the tempting proclamations by which that general sought to seduce them from their allegiance and their duty to the land and people, laid down their arms and took the oath of neutrality. I warned and admonished them, for my faith in the future was still unshaken. On the 7th of June, I sent the following telegram to all the officers:

> Tell the burghers that it will avail them nothing to lay down their arms, as Lord Roberts has issued a proclamation that in future he will release no more burghers on their oaths, since he has found that the burghers continue to fight in spite of their oaths. He has moreover decided to take all male persons above twelve years of age prisoners, whether they be armed or not. If they are taken prisoners, they will be sent to St. Helena. Children also are therefore no longer safe. We have resolved to fight to the end. Be faithful and fight in the name of the Lord, for they who flee and leave their positions or run away from commando are fleeing straight to St. Helena.

KRUGER'S FOURTH PRESIDENCY

And in longer telegrams I set forth the religious grounds for my hopeful persistency.[1]

As Machadodorp is one of the coldest places in the Transvaal, and at that time I was suffering greatly from my eyes, I yielded to the pressure of the burghers and moved on to Waterval Onder, which lies on the Eland River, among high mountains, and enjoys a very mild climate in winter. Here I occupied a scantily-furnished little house, where I spent the happiest two months that I have known since my departure from Pretoria. The seat of government, however, remained at Machadodorp; and the State Secretary and the members of the Executive Raad also remained there, but came every morning by train to Waterval Onder to the sittings of the Executive Raad, in order to attend to the current business. From here, too, were issued the decrees and requisitions, the provisos for furlough, the enactments against dilatory burghers and officials, and the orders for the reorganization of the army, and the necessary measures were taken to frustrate the proclamations of the enemy and their consequences. Towards the end of August, President Steyn and his escort arrived at Waterval Onder to discuss the position in the country.

It was at about the same time that Lord Roberts, acting in conjunction with General Sir Redvers Bul-

[1] Some of these telegrams will be found in the Appendix.

ler, delivered his decisive attack on Botha's positions at Dalmanutha. The result is well known. After the burghers had fought for eight days like lions and defeated every attempt of the enemy to break through, Buller at last succeeded in capturing a weak post occupied by 79 men of the Johannesburg police and in thus forcing his way into our men's positions. Botha had about 4,000 men and had to defend a line that extended for over 30 miles. Roberts attacked him with over 50,000 men and a mass of heavy guns. The result of this battle made it clear to the Commandant General and the other officers that it was not possible for that small force of burghers to repel the enemy or to continue to fight him in the way they had done hitherto, and that it was better to send the President away, so as to leave the commandos freer in their movements. We moved on to Nelspruit, a station on the Delagoa Railway, about half-way between Waterval Onder and the Portuguese frontier. The removal of all the baggage, wagons, carts, horses, mules and so forth gave great difficulty, but the excellent manner in which the Netherlands South African Railway Company had so far satisfied every demand made upon it was now repeated. On arriving at the spot which had been selected as the seat of government, we received Lord Roberts's proclamation annexing the South African Republic. I at once issued a counter-proclamation:

KRUGER'S FOURTH PRESIDENCY

Whereas, in the month of October 1899, an unjust war was forced upon the people of the South African Republic and the Orange Free State by Great Britain, and those two small Republics have for ten months maintained and are still maintaining an unequal contest against the mighty British Empire;

Whereas I am informed that a certain proclamation, dated 1 September 1900, has been issued by Lord Roberts, Field-Marshal, Commander-in-Chief of the British forces in South Africa, stating that the South African Republic has been conquered by Her Majesty's troops and that the South African Republic is annexed to the British Empire, while the forces of the South African Republic are still in the field and the South African Republic has not been conquered, and the aforesaid proclamation is therefore opposed to international law;

And whereas the independence of the South African Republic has been recognized by nearly all the civilized Powers;

Whereas I deem it desirable immediately to inform all whom it may concern that the aforesaid proclamation is not recognized by the Government and people of the South African Republic:

Now I, Stephanus Johannes Paulus Kruger, State President of the South African Republic, by the advice and consent of the Executive Raad, in accordance with Article 147 of its Minutes of the 3d of September 1900, do hereby proclaim, in the name of the independent people of this Republic, that the aforesaid annexation is not recognized, but is by these presents declared null and void.

The people of the South African Republic is and remains a free and independent people and refuses to submit to British rule.

Given under my hand at Nelspruit in the South African Republic on the third day of the month of September 1900.

S. J. P. KRUGER.

Meanwhile, it became evident that the hope that we should be able to arrest the enemy's progress in the mountains, was futile, thanks to his overwhelming superiority of numbers; and, when the enemy began to advance from every side on Nelspruit, a decisive step became necessary. A council was called, consisting of the members of the Transvaal and Orange Free State Governments and a number of officers, including the Commandant General, and it resolved to send me to Europe as a delegate, to endeavor to promote the cause of the Republics. General and Vice-President Schalk Burger was to hold office as Acting State President during my absence. A proclamation was issued, giving notice of this resolution in the following terms:

Whereas the great age of His Honor the State President renders it impossible for His Honor to continue to accompany the commandos;

And whereas the Executive Raad is persuaded that His Honor's invaluable services can still be profitably employed in the interests of the land and people:

Now the Executive Raad does hereby resolve to grant His Honor a six months' furlough in order to proceed to Europe and there promote our cause. His place will be filled, in accordance with the law, by Mr. S. W. Burger, Vice-President.

S. W. Burger,
Vice-President.
F. W. Reitz,
State Secretary.

Government Office, Nelspruit, 10 *September* 1900.

If my departure from Pretoria was a bitter blow to me, my departure, under such sorrowful circumstances, from the land to which I had devoted my life was doubly bitter. I saw it swarming with the enemy, who, in his arrogance, was already declaring that the war was over and that only guerrilla bands now infested the country. I had to bid good-by to the men who had stood beside me for so many years and to leave my country and my people, my gray-haired wife, my children, my friends and the little band of lion-hearted fighters who, surrounded as they were on every side, had now to make their way through an uninhabited district to the north of the Republic, there to reorganize and recommence the struggle. But I had no choice. I must either submit to the decision or allow myself to be taken prisoner. My age prevented me from riding and it was, therefore, impossible for me to accompany the commandos further. On the other hand, it was a consolation to leave the Government in the hands of such true men as Schalk Burger, Reitz, Louis Botha and De la Rey, and I knew the loyal support which they would receive from the noble President Steyn. On the evening of the 10th September we took leave of one another at Nelspruit and I was left alone with the escort which the Executive Raad had given me for my protection.

On the next day, after spending the night at Crocodile Poort, I began my long pilgrimage to Europe, a journey the result of which neither had nor could have been anticipated. From Crocodile Poort I traveled in the private railway-carriage of the manager of the Netherlands South African Railway Company. At Hectorspruit I waited a few hours for President Steyn and a few other friends, who had come there to take leave of me, and then continued my journey to Lorenzo Marques over Komati Poort, the last station in the Republic, past the frontier station, Resano Garsea, where the director of the Portuguese railway took charge of the train. At Lorenzo Marques, the train was not stopped at the station, but shunted to a siding, so that, as darkness had already set in, I was able to reach Consul General Pott's house unobserved. It was my intention to remain there until I could embark for Europe on board the first outgoing steamer, which would have been the steamship *Herzog*, of the German East African Line. But, on the next day, the Portuguese Governor arrived and said that he had been instructed to take me to his own house as the guest of the Portuguese Government. When I showed some hesitation, the Governor declared that I must accompany him at once and that, if I refused, he must employ force. This action on the part of the Portuguese Government must undoubtedly be ascribed to the pressure brought to bear upon it by the British Government, for the Portuguese Governor governed only in name: the real governor was the

KRUGER'S FOURTH PRESIDENCY

British consul at Delagoa Bay. Governor Machado, who was probably fulfilling a disagreeable task much against his own wish, treated me with great kindness, but would not allow me to move without accompanying me. None of the members of my escort, who were also quartered at the Governor's house, was allowed to set foot in the town unless accompanied by an aide-de-camp; and even then they were not permitted to enter into conversation with any one. At first, the two gentlemen who traveled with me, as well as a few other friends, were at least allowed to visit me; but this, too, was very soon forbidden, on the ground, as we were informed, that the British consul had complained. This situation lasted some weeks, during the whole of which time I was practically a prisoner in the Governor's house, and it was there that I kept my seventy-fifth birthday. I was not allowed to receive the congratulations of the burghers who thronged the town and who were reduced to shouting good luck to me from the street outside.

The first ray of light that broke through this night of affliction was the Queen of Holland's offer to carry me to Europe on a man-of-war, an act which was appreciated in the highest degree by the whole Boer nation. Now at least all uncertainty was removed as to my being able to pursue my journey. As the ship, however, was still at some distance from

Delagoa Bay, I was not able to embark until the 21st of October, and then the *Gelderland*, whose captain and officers received me with every mark of friendship and loving-kindness, had first to take in coal. The journey from Delagoa Bay to Dar-es-Salam, where the *Gelderland* arrived on the morning of the fifth day, passed off very well. It is true that, at first, I suffered a little from sea-sickness, for the first time in my life; but I was soon able to light up my pipe again, a certain proof that the sickness was past. At Dar-es-Salam, some German officials came on board and invited me to a dinner which they wished to give in my honor. I begged, however, to be excused, in view of the sorrowful circumstances of my country. The same thing happened at Djibouti, where we arrived on the 2d of November. From here the journey was continued to Suez. Every ship that passed the *Gelderland* saluted, and I was cheered by the passengers on board those which came close enough. One French ship even went out of her course to salute the *Gelderland*, and the only exceptions were the majority of the English ships, of which, at one time, as many as five were in sight, near Sardinia. From Suez we proceeded to Port Saïd, where we stopped to take in coal. The voyage from here to Marseilles was exceedingly unpleasant, quite apart from the number of newspaper correspondents who made fruitless attempts to interview me. A storm raged which sent the waves flying over the ship; and the vessel pitched and rolled to such an extent that my sickness returned.

At the end of the voyage the captain of the *Gelderland* invited my friends and myself to an official dinner. The saloon was decorated with the Dutch colors and with a Transvaal banner, the same flag which the American school-boys had sent me, with an address, from Philadelphia. In consequence of the bad weather we arrived one day late, on the 22d of November, in the harbor of Marseilles.

A few days before our arrival, the members of the South African deputation, with the exception of Wolmarans, who was unwell, had gone to Marseilles, with Dr. Leyds and some other gentlemen, to receive me. Professor Hamel, of the University of Groningen, kindly acted as interpreter. From the deck of the man-of-war, to which the members of the deputation put out in a long-boat, one saw nothing but one mass of people, all cheering and waving their handkerchiefs. Even the steamers lying at anchor in the harbor swarmed with people.

I went on shore after cordially thanking the captain of the ship and his officers for the kindness and consideration which they had shown me. I still retain the pleasantest recollections of my voyage on the *Gelderland*. Thousands of people were shouting their greetings with the loudest enthusiasm.

The president of the Committee for the Independence of the Boers, which had been lately formed, " interpreted the feelings of all Marseilles," as he himself said when he welcomed me and added that the enthusiasm which I beheld around me would convey more to me than any words which he could utter. I declared that I gratefully accepted the welcome offered me, although, in view of the sorrow in which my country was wrapped, I had not come in order to be festively received.

" The war in South Africa," I continued, " has exceeded the limits of barbarism. I have fought against many barbarous Kaffir tribes in the course of my life; but they are not so barbarous as the English, who have burnt our farms and driven our women and children into destitution, without food or shelter. I hope that God will not abandon the Boer nation. But if the Transvaal and the Free State are to lose their independence, it shall only happen when both nations have been annihilated with their women and their children."

On the road to the hotel stood thousands of people, who cheered me continually as I passed and, during the afternoon, a number of deputations came to welcome me.

This splendid reception was a thorn in the side of the English at Marseilles, and they tried to spoil the procession by throwing coppers from the windows of a hotel among the populace, in order to raise a tumult. But this proceeding narrowly escaped having serious results, for the people, furious at this behavior, stormed the hotel, so that police protection had to be sent for.

Immediately after my arrival, I telegraphed to President Loubet to salute him and to thank him for the sympathy of his Government and people. The Prefect of Marseilles called on me on behalf of the President.

On the 24th of November, I started by special train for Paris, and was cordially cheered throughout the journey. The train stopped at one or two stations, and great crowds had gathered to welcome me. I stepped out of the train at Lyons, to receive the welcome of the crowd, and the mayor handed me a beautiful medal as a souvenir. At Dijon, where we spent the night, the drive to the hotel was accomplished to a salute of guns.

On the next morning, we continued our journey to Paris, where a solemn reception took place and several speeches were delivered. In reply to the address of the Vice-President of the Municipality of Paris, I said that, " as soon as I had set foot on Parisian soil, I had acquired fresh confidence, for the arms of the city, a ship floating on the waves, assured me that the Republics would not go under."

On the way to the hotel, immense masses of people had gathered, who cried, "Long live Kruger! Arbitration for ever!" and continually flung nosegays into the carriage. The people in front of the hotel called out for me to appear on the balcony, and I had to do so three or four times a day, before the crowds would disperse.

At four o'clock in the afternoon, President Loubet received me at the Élysée, sending me a company of cuirassiers as an escort, and immediately afterwards paid me a return visit.

During my stay in Paris, from the 26th of November till the 1st of December, I visited some of the sights, including the Eiffel Tower, the Hôtel de Ville, the International Exhibition, at which I was greatly touched to read the inscriptions on the walls of the Transvaal pavilion, containing every good wish for the Boers. In the sessions-hall of the Hôtel de Ville, where the whole Town Council had assembled, the chairman expressed the admiration of the people for the heroism of the Republics and said that, "if the Republics were silent, the nations must speak," and thus bring about arbitration.

The president of the *Conseil Général* also made a speech. In my reply, I said that, "if the Boers, who were not yet defeated, but would go on fighting much longer, could hear of the reception which had been given me in France, they would be still further strengthened in their resolve to keep up the struggle." I also thanked the press for the light which they had thrown on the English methods of warfare and added:

"If you were able to send reporters straight to the seat of war, they would stand astounded at the atrocities that are being perpetrated by England."

After receiving a series of deputations, I left Paris on the 1st of December, amid scenes of undiminished enthusiasm and escorted by the authorities and private societies, for Cologne. On the way to the French frontier, the same scenes were repeated which had marked the journey from Marseilles to Paris. At every station where we stopped, I was received by great crowds. The same thing happened in Belgium. The enthusiasm which I witnessed in France not only delighted me, but confirmed me in my hope that my journey would not be in vain.

This hope, however, was doomed to be very soon frustrated. On the evening of the same day, we reached Cologne, where an enthusiasm reigned such as Cologne had, perhaps, never beheld before. Unfortunately, an accident occurred at the railway station which cost one of the spectators his life. The crowd was such that two people fell through an opening on to the platform, and one of them broke his leg and died from the effects of the fall. Owing to the size of the crowds I had to drive by a circuitous route to my hotel. Here, shortly after my arrival,

THE MEMOIRS OF PAUL KRUGER

I received a telegram from the German Emperor, saying that His Majesty could not receive me at that time, as he had a hunting engagement. We then resolved to proceed to the Hague; but, before leaving Cologne, I received a series of deputations, who gave me every mark of sympathy. I also received the wife of the man who had died of the accident at the station and assured her of my heartfelt condolence. I did not miss the opportunity of visiting the famous cathedral.

It is really not necessary for me to say that throughout my journey through Germany and Holland I met everywhere with the same sympathy for the cause of the Boers as at Cologne. At station after station, I was received by the representatives of the different towns, in addition to corporations and societies with their banners and badges. The train drew up at the Hague in the evening, when it was already growing dusk. The precincts of the railway station and all the streets leading to the hotel at which I was to stay were closely packed with an endless crowd of cheering people. I had telegraphed to the Queen, on reaching the Dutch frontier, to offer her my homage. Immediately after my arrival at the hotel, Her Majesty's ministers called upon me, and, on the next day, I went to the Court, to wait upon the Queen and to thank her for her great kindness in

KRUGER'S FOURTH PRESIDENCY

sending a man-of-war to bring me to Europe. I was afterwards invited to dine with the Queen and Her Majesty's Consort, the Prince of the Netherlands, called on me at the hotel.

After a short delay, I paid a visit to Amsterdam, where a great reception was held in the *Paleis voor Volksvlijt* and a solemn service in the principal church. On returning to the Hague, where I had not originally intended to stay, since it was necessary that I should as soon as possible consult a good physician about the condition of my eyes, I fell seriously ill: I had probably caught a cold, which very soon developed into inflammation of the lungs. I recovered, however, and proceeded to Utrecht, where I stayed for two months and a half; during which period I underwent a successful operation on both eyes, effected by Professor Snellen and my own physician, Dr. Heymans. From there, I moved to Hilversum, where I lived for eight months, at the Villa Casa Cara, with my suite. Our stay was interrupted by a visit of some weeks to A. D. W. Wolmarans at Scheveningen and by a long-promised visit to some of the other Dutch towns. At Rotterdam, I was shown a tree which I had planted in the Zoölogical Gardens in 1884, and took a trip up the Maas, on board the *Lehmann*, which the Fop Smit Steamship Company had placed at my disposal. I was proud, on this occasion, to see the old church at

Dordrecht where the Synod of 1618 to 1619 was held which exercised so great an influence upon the Church to which I belong. I also revisited Kampen, the Mecca of the Protestant Church. In both towns my reception was of the most cordial nature imaginable.

Shortly after my return to Hilversum, I received the heaviest blow of my life. A cablegram informed me that my wife was dead. In my profound sorrow I was consoled by the thought that the separation was only temporary and could not last long; and my faith gave me the strength to write a letter of encouraging consolation to my daughter, Mrs. Malan. Wolmarans invited me to spend another fortnight with him at Scheveningen, to distract my thoughts a little. I then went back to Hilversum, where I lived in absolute retirement, interrupted only by the necessary conferences, and devoted myself entirely to the perusal of my Bible.

At the commencement of the winter, on the 10th of December 1901, I moved to the Villa Oranjelust, on the Maliebaan, at Utrecht. Here I received the news of De la Rey's brilliant victory over Lord Methuen. I rejoiced exceedingly at the victory, but, when some one observed, during the reading of the news, that it was to be hoped that De la Rey would keep Methuen a prisoner, I said:

"I could not approve of that, and I hope that

KRUGER'S FOURTH PRESIDENCY

De la Rey will release him without delay; for we Boers must behave as Christians to the end, however uncivilized the way in which the English treat us may be."

When I learnt that Methuen was released, I expressed my sincere gratification. A series of further favorable tidings arrived from home, so that the position of things seemed to justify the greatest hope.

For the rest, I had, throughout the war, replied to every inquiry from the scene of war that my confidence was still unshaken, but that it must be left entirely to the generals in the field to decide whether and how, under the stress of circumstances, they wished to alter their previous resolutions. During the peace negotiations, I had only one answer to all the questions put to me as to what I thought of peace, namely, that all would happen as God wished. And, when peace was at last concluded, I applied to the generals the Bible text 2 Cor. viii. 3:

"For to their power, I bear record, yea, and beyond their power they were willing of themselves."

Nor, in so far as I myself am concerned, will I consent to lose courage because the peace is not such as the burghers wished. For, quite apart from the fact that the bloodshed and the fearful sufferings of the people of the two Republics are now ended,

THE MEMOIRS OF PAUL KRUGER

I am convinced that God does not forsake His people, even though it may often appear so. Therefore I resign myself to the will of the Lord. I know that He will not allow the afflicted people to perish. He is the Lord and all hearts are in His hand and He turneth them whithersoever He will.

STEPHANUS JOHANNES PAULUS KRUGER
About 1865

From an old-fashioned silver-plate photograph, taken by Mr. Jeffreys, of Cape Town. It was given by Kruger (who was at the time Field Cornet of Potchefstroom) to Mr. Jeffreys's father at Potchefstroom, about the year 1865. Mr. Jeffreys believes that the old plate was a positive (instead of a negative, from which photographs are printed nowadays), consequently, the left side comes out as the right. This photograph is the only one showing the loss of President Kruger's thumb. In the other photographs he always seems to hide the left hand, and the right thumb comes out clearly in some. In this print the right hand seems to be thumbless owing to the inversion of the plate.

APPENDIX

APPENDIX A

SPEECHES DELIVERED AT THE SOLEMN INAUGURATION OF HIS HONOR S. J. P. KRUGER AS STATE PRESIDENT OF THE SOUTH AFRICAN REPUBLIC, ON THURSDAY, 12 MAY 1898.

Mr. President of the First Volksraad addressed His Honor the State President in the following words:

MR. STATE PRESIDENT,

I welcome you in the name of the First and Second Volksraad on the occasion of this solemnity, at which you have for the fourth time taken the oath of office as State President of the South African Republic.

Already fifteen years have passed since you first appeared as the head of this state. Nay, what do I say?—it is not only for fifteen years that you have served the country; you have also served it in other capacities, such as that of a member of the Triumvirate and as Vice-President, to take office later as State President. As I and many others know, the task of serving the country was laid upon your shoulders from your youth; and while you were still young it was the Lord's will to place you in a position where you could be of political service to this

APPENDIX

country. You have served the country for no short time, and you have naturally encountered many difficulties and obstacles in your path, because, as we know, man's path, as God leads him upon earth, is not one of roses. Many days of adversity came and many dark and difficult days, as all must admit; but we, as a Christian people, must ever believe that it was God's will and guidance.

Your Honor, I feel, and the Raad and all those who labor in the field of politics feel, that it is no easy task that to-day has once more been laid upon your shoulders, that of acting as the head of this young state, which has always to fight so great a struggle. I seem, however, to see clearly that our consolation lies in this, that the people of the South African Republic remain true to you and cling to you. It must of course be a great comfort to you to think of the last elections, which show how the people remain attached to your person and that they still place their entire confidence in you, because they are naturally convinced of the excellence of your government during the fifteen years that you have served the country as State President. A great proof of this is the great interest which the public shows in seeing you, who are now full of years, once more invested, by the taking of your oath of office, as State President.

I sincerely congratulate you, Mr. State President, in the name of the First and Second Volksraad, and I would add that, as Christians, we must always fix our hopes on the Lord, for, if the Lord were to leave us to ourselves, to rule the country according to our

APPENDIX

own wisdom and understanding, we should have to succumb and to yield up everything, for our own understanding does not give us the penetration required to govern the country. But there is one thing that I know and that I may say, which is that you know your God and that you daily consult your Creator, and we, as Christians, are always with you on this point, to ask the Lord for understanding, wisdom and strength. We know what it means when a man is unable to see through a single moment and often his eye becomes so dimmed that it seems as though dark clouds were hanging before it; but God has always shown us the light again and thus also shown Himself to be our Counselor, who leads us according to His counsel. This faith in God and that proved attachment of the people to your person will, I think, be your comfort on this day. May God, while lending you His aid, also vouchsafe you His grace and His blessing. The people continue to be faithful to you and to stand by you. Therefore, in the name of the First and Second Volksraad, I wish Your Honor God's best blessing, and I hope and trust that God may spare you in our midst and grant you the strength that you may require, and that my prayer may be heard so that, by God's strength, you may be enabled to fulfil your arduous task.

And we and the people also trust that God will guide you and that you will, as you always have done, protect the rights of the people, such as the independence of the country, that have been placed in your hands.

I wish Your Honor, in the name of this body,

APPENDIX

understanding, wisdom and strength. May God strengthen you and aid you in your old days to fulfil your difficult task and may we always work together in harmony. I venture, in the name of the Volksraad, to promise you that the Raad will meet and assist you, in every possible way, to support you with all its strength, as this body always does, because we know that we have placed the government of our country in trustworthy hands. Therefore I promise you the best support of the Volksraad, and I hope that the good God will grant that the work of the Volksraad and the Government may be bound together by fraternal ties, for, so long as the Executive Raad and the Volksraad act with wisdom and work together, hand in hand, like brothers, I do not doubt that the promise will be fulfilled to us: " Where true love reigns, God gives His blessing."

I have spoken.

The President of the Volksraad, then turning to the assembled multitude, spoke as follows:

INHABITANTS OF THE COUNTRY, PEOPLE OF THE SOUTH AFRICAN REPUBLIC,

I present to you His Honor Stephen John Paul Kruger, State President of the South African Republic, who has once more taken the oath in that capacity before the First Volksraad (*three cheers*). Burghers, I think this is a solemn day for you and me.

Here stands our State President. For fifteen

APPENDIX

years he has served the country in that capacity; and this year we have once more seen that the people of the South African Republic place their confidence in His Honor, as appears from the last elections (*prolonged cheers*).

Burghers, His Honor has obeyed your summons; the public has called upon him and, in his old age, he has listened to your voice, because His Honor heard in it the voice of God. His Honor has taken the oath; but what is now our duty as burghers of the country? We must support His Honor with strength, obedience, love and harmony (*cheers*).

When the people remain unanimous and when the people preserve the ties of affection that bind the Afrikander Nation, that gives His Honor strength to perform his duties of office with a more and more willing and cheerful mind; but you know that, where discord reigns, this always makes it difficult and arduous for the head of a state. Therefore I hope and trust that every burgher will take this to heart and aid His Honor not only with worldly assistance but also with his prayers to God.

Let every burgher bow down to God and beseech the Lord to give strength and force to our State President, so that His Honor may be fortified by God's hand. For we know that we owe the existence of the South African Republic to the strength of our omniscient Creator, who has guided us.

I hope, therefore, that you will be obedient and loyal to His Honor.

I have spoken (*prolonged cheers*).

APPENDIX

His Honor the State President now spoke as follows:

Mr. President of the First, Mr. President of the Second, and Honorable Members of both the First and Second Volksraad,

But first let me ask that the secretary take down my words, that my speech may not later, for one reason or another, be misunderstood.

Honorable sirs,

I stand here before you, in obedience to the voice of the people, in which I believe I recognize God's voice, in order once more, as State President, to take upon myself the government of the country.

Honorable sirs, when I look back upon my past career, knowing, as I do, by experience all the burdens and great difficulties attached to this arduous post, I cannot but frankly confess that I consider myself incapable and blind: I repeat, incapable and blind. When I look back and see how the Lord has guided the people and that God has set the people free, then I know, now that I am to govern the people, what would follow if I were to falter, for I have not only to give an account to you honorable gentlemen, but also to God, and my life is short; I shall have to appear before Him, and when I think of that, my heart fails me, and I can only pray.[1]

His promise is that to them who expect aid and strength from the Lord He will teach the plain path, and him that feareth the Lord He will guide.

---
[1] President Kruger here quoted a stanza from the Dutch hymnal. — *Translator's Note*.

APPENDIX

He who acknowledges this in his heart looks to the Lord, our faithful God of the Covenant, for light, wisdom and divine strength. He will give us everything out of His infinite wealth of mercy. Yes, I trust in that faithful God of the Covenant, because He has so clearly led us along various paths. And so I accept this post in the fear of God and in all uprightness; yes, it is my innermost desire and the wish of my heart to live for Him and to govern the people according to His will.

My earnest endeavor will be none other than to keep in view the welfare of the people and the progress, prosperity and independence of the country. Honorable sirs, I shall scrupulously watch the circumstances of the country, in which we have sometimes observed such swift and rapid progress; and in particular, I shall constantly see to it that in this inevitable progress, the independence of the country is not in the smallest degree endangered and also that not the smallest right is abandoned whose loss might undermine the independence of the country; for I should bring down a judgment on myself if our independence were violated through me. For God has so clearly led us that the blindest heathen and the greatest unbeliever must acknowledge that it was God's hand that gave us our independence.

Honorable sirs, I rely upon you as the embodiment of the legislative power to support me in these my views and, in your wisdom, to suggest measures whereby the country may be maintained in its independence and prosperity in every quarter. And in particular, I rely upon you to take into

APPENDIX

earnest consideration the needs of all the inhabitants of the country, without distinction of persons or nationality.

I have learned, with the deepest regret, that very great depression prevails in the gold-fields, mostly among the poorer and less well-to-do. I assure you of my sympathy with their fate, and I trust that this great depression may soon pass away. The Government are doing all that they can to assist the gold-fields, as is shown, first, by the decrease in the railway tariff by £200,000; secondly, by the decrease of the import duties on food and other articles that are required for the immediate use of the mines, by about £700,000; thirdly, by the order that has been issued to import natives of Mozambique as workmen, in order to assist the mines; fourthly, by the reduction in the price of dynamite. You all know that, in 1893, when the contract was concluded for the erection of the dynamite factory, dynamite was imported at about £6 per case. The company reduced this price to £5, which was gradually reduced to £4 5s. per case and has now again been brought down to £3 15s., and I hope and trust to be able to reduce the price still further. I am still engaged upon this. As I have already said at public meetings, the dynamite factory was not erected to oppress the mining industry but to support and help it, and principally the weak mines, and I hope that these will keep going until I have succeeded, for both the mining industry and the dynamite factory belong to the State and must support one another; and you may be convinced that I shall not swerve from this

APPENDIX

determination, but shall succeed in making the dynamite cheap for the mines.

I learn with deep regret that there are banks and other institutions in the gold-fields which are totally ruining the poor and less well-to-do. When, some years ago, the mines were flourishing, these people borrowed money and, I am told, on good security in order to extend their business; and now that a time of depression has come, the mortgages are being called in and they have to pay back the money, although the security is quite as good as before, and in so doing their property is sold beneath its value. If this be true, then those banks cannot be regarded otherwise than as godless and un-Christian; for they bring hunger and oppression upon the poor and force everything into the hands of the rich. Honorable sirs, we already have the diamond-fields as a warning; and, if what I am informed of is true, the Volksraad will have to take measures to protect the poor and less well-to-do and the Government will be obliged to withdraw the licenses of those banks or to refuse to renew them; for in this way they serve rather for the oppression and undermining of the poor than for their support. God sees all, and the Lord says: "Deliver the poor from the snare of the fowler." Such things may not exist among us.

Then it has also come to my ears that contracts are being made in Europe with poor workmen who do not know but that the price of food is the same here as there, so that, when they arrive, they are caught in a trap, since they are not able to live on the wages named in the contract. I hope that you

APPENDIX

will take measures that no contract made abroad will be binding here before it has been approved and confirmed by an official appointed for the purpose, with the consent of both parties, the hirer and the hired. Such fraud and deception must not exist among us, though I hope that things are not as stated.

Then, again, I am informed, honorable sirs, that companies are being floated here on properties which have not even been properly examined to see if they contain gold. Shares are sold and allotted in Europe to persons who do not know but that the ground is good and who do not discover until they come here that the property is valueless, and then the blame is cast upon the Government. The shareholders in Europe are as much entitled to the protection of the Government as the people here. I hope, therefore, that such rules will be made that no company can sell or allot its shares before the State Mineralogist or the State Engineer has examined the ground and issued his report; so that the European public may no longer be deceived and then think that it is the fault of the Government. That must be prevented.

In conclusion, let me say that there are two matters which we must keep in view, and the second of these I mention because of God's Word. The first is that you must not grant any privileges which would injure our independence; and the second, that you must not close your ears to the lamentations of the poor, whether they are friends or foreigners, but must try to snatch them from the snare of the fowler. Then God will be in our midst and bless us. Yes, gentlemen, if we stand firm, and if you support me

APPENDIX

in these matters, it will be found true that "concord gives strength," and God will be in our midst.

GENTLEMEN OF THE EXECUTIVE RAAD,

A word to you too. In the first place, I thank you sincerely for the support which you have given me hitherto,—for the support which you have given me, when necessary, in the discussion of affairs and for the support which you have given me in their execution. In the second place, I thank you, right honorable members, for all that you have done for the country and for your loyalty and your love of independence, which is such that you are ready to sacrifice your lives and properties for the independence of your country. I thank you again, and I shall rejoice if you will continue in this course, supporting me when necessary, and if you will continue loyal to your country, so that we may stand up as one man for the independence that God has given us and be ready, all of us, to sacrifice our property with the burghers who have shown that they too are willing to sacrifice everything for that object. Let us remain loyal and true, and do you pray for me, as I do for you, so that together we may work as the executive power.

RIGHT HONORABLE SIRS, MEMBERS OF THE EXECUTIVE RAAD AND LEGISLATIVE ASSEMBLY OF OUR SISTER STATE,

In the first place, I thank you for the interest which you have displayed by attending these proceedings. We are very closely allied, and you agree

APPENDIX

with me that there is nothing better than peace and amity, especially between two sister states; and when such co-operation exists, though the whole world rages God will bless us, for where love and concord reign He gives His blessing; we obtain His grace and He dwells amongst us for ever and ever.

Then, turning to the *Corps diplomatique,* His Honor spoke as follows:

DIPLOMATIC AND CONSULAR OFFICERS OF THE FOREIGN POWERS,

A word to you too. You are well aware, from my past career, that nothing is dearer to me than to live in peace and amity with foreign powers, each keeping the others' interests in view and all assisting one another as far as possible. It is my wish that this Government may so rule our State that the foreign powers will never have occasion to urge just grievances against us. I hope to continue in this way and it will always be my earnest endeavor to do so. Therefore I trust that I may receive your kind support, for then the bonds of friendship will be drawn ever more closely between us; and where this co-operation, love and friendship prevail, God grants His blessing, for there He dwells in the midst of us. I wish you every blessing, each for his own country. May peace and friendship reign! I shall not fail, whenever you bring before me the interests of the State of which you are the diplomatic representative or the consul, to support you, so that no grievances may arise against us.

APPENDIX

Now turning to the public, His Honor spoke as follows:

All of you who stand before me, give me your attention that you may understand what I wish to say to you. In the first place, I wish to speak to the burghers of the country; in the second, to the new burghers who have been naturalized; in the third, to the foreigners who do not wish to change their nationality, but who wish to live among us as foreigners.

Now then, you Burghers of the Country!

I have listened to your voices by accepting the appointment that has fallen to me by your election and again taking up the government of the country as State President. In the first place, I thank you for the confidence which you have placed in me. When I stand before you like this and look at your faces, I see many who have struggled, prayed and fought with me for the land of our abode and of our independence. Oh, then an array of thoughts comes up within me, all of which lead to one point, namely, that we must observe God's ways. To go over all these with you I have not now the time; but I trust that you will recall everything in your own thoughts and consider those ways, those proofs of the faith that God has shown us,—that He has rescued us from oppression and given us other blessings; and the ways in which God has punished us and we have been oppressed by our adversaries. Then we were weak, but unanimous, striving to obtain

APPENDIX

assistance from God. Then we performed mighty deeds. Let me go back with you in thought to Paarde Kraal, where we were weak and helpless. But the people, the Volksraad and the Executive Raad were unanimous, one in mind and one in heart, to call on God for help, and then God led us through wonders and miracles. Burghers, let it be a lesson to us what concord did, in which God always blessed us; let us therefore strive to stamp out discord, where it exists among us, and let us strive in unison to suppress the evil spirit that leads us to opposition. I say that evil spirit; and mind, I exclude no one, not even myself, when I speak of the evil spirit that tempts us to break God's words and His commandments. God's ninth commandment says: "Thou shalt not bear false witness against thy neighbor;" and it has truly become a habit among us for one brother to bear false witness against the other. Let none point with his finger at the other, but be upright: let each place his hand in his own breast, and he will find that it comes out leprous.

Let us stand in sincerity this day before God's countenance. We see that God's arm is stretched out: He is chastising us; and we shall find that everywhere we are breaking God's commandments. Let me quote an instance to you. Suppose that a father is rich and has many goods, and that his child has nothing and has to live on him; and his father gives him his goods and says: "Child, take these goods and use them, and I shall tell you when I want any of them, but do not abuse them." Then will not the father be angry when, after the son has gone

APPENDIX

away, he sends for some of his own goods, and the son will not give them up or gives only the worst? We often ask, Why does the Lord chastise us so? But is this not in order that we may return to Him? Yes, we really act towards God like one who makes a marriage contract. Our worldly goods hold us back and make us serve the world with them, while we want God to care for our souls. Let each of us, brothers, search his heart, so that we may become convinced of God's pleasure. Behold, God gives us worldly goods; but for what purpose? That we may live for the honor of God. Naked we came out and naked we shall return; we shall take nothing with us. God, therefore, gives us those goods, meat and clothes, that we may live; but also for churches, schools, the poor, etc., etc. What do we do, brothers and fellow-countrymen, what do we do? We give of our worst and commonest goods when there is need; but see what happens when there is a circus, a play, a lottery or a race-meeting: then each encourages the other and even lends the other money to pursue worldly pleasures; but, when God calls to us to put something into the poor-box to help to support the poor, there are many who go to church but put nothing in the box or select the least they have. For what do they use their goods,—God's goods? Is it not true, what God says, that we rob Him, that we take His goods from Him and give them to the world and will not serve Him with them? See, brothers and fellow-countrymen; let every one who has an immortal soul look to it. See God's hand. Pestilence holds sway among men and beasts. The

APPENDIX

locusts are eating the grass of the veldt and heavy droughts have prevailed and it grows worse from year to year and will grow worse from year to year until we turn back. God will not desert His people. Read Psalm 89.[1] The Lord will not retract that, but He chastises us to bring us nearer to Him. You will ask, "How can David say that he kissed the rod and with his heart?" Yes, if you love your father, and possess nothing, and have to live on him, when you have committed a sin and he says, "Leave my sight," you will go on your knees and say, "No, strike me but do not send me away." That is why David was able to say that when he lived in luxury he strayed from God; but that when He chastised him he returned to Him. He felt this in his heart.

Let us feel this too, that the Lord rather chastises us than rejects us. Listen to His voice and, when you hear His voice, do not harden your hearts, but let yourselves be guided; for why should you wish to die? Will you continue as you are doing? See how merciful the great God is. He says, "Return to me, you rebellious children, and I will heal your trespasses. Yes, try me," says God, "if you will not believe, and see if Heaven's windows do not open and shower down blessings upon you. I shall upbraid the devourer so that your barns may be filled and your fields filled with herds; but turn to Me, you rebellious children, and I will heal your trespasses."

Brothers and fellow-countrymen, do not think that I exclude myself. I have also much to do my-

[1] President Kruger here quoted two stanzas from the Dutch metrical psalm-book.— *Translator's Note.*

APPENDIX

self and I too am guilty in this matter; but let us confess our sins together before it is too late, and God will help us.

You New Burghers,

This last reminder was also for you and for all that have an immortal soul; but still, a brief word to you separately. I call you new burghers, who have been naturalized and have given up your nationality. You have surely understood that God says: "No one can serve two masters, or else he will hold to the one and despise the other," and therefore you have given up the country of your birth, in all honor and decency, and accepted this country as a new motherland. Endeavor now to agree with the old burghers and to live with them in harmony, for then you also will be contributing to the progress of the country. Obey the laws of the land and, if you do so, you will have contributed greatly not only to the growth and prosperity of the country but also to your own interests; and, where harmony and concord reign, there God bestows His blessing.

You Foreigners,

A word also to you who do not wish to give up your country and to be naturalized, but prefer to live among us as foreigners. If you are obedient to the laws of the land, you are welcome among us. Seek your profit and endeavor to make your fortunes: we shall help you and wish you well. Live with us, obey the laws and, in so far as possible, I assure you of my support, to the utmost of my power,

APPENDIX

even if you do not wish to become burghers of the country; and then you will be promoting not only your interests, but ours as well. If you foreigners make your fortunes and work with us, you shall enjoy the same protection of the laws as any others; and, when you go, I shall be sorry to see such good friends departing; and, should you return again to make your fortune, you will be received with open arms; we shall rejoice that you come back to us, knowing that you are true friends to us, even if you would not give up your country. Be assured that all sensible men will aid and receive you, so that you too may live in joy and gladness in our midst (*cheers*).

His Honor then turned to the judges and spoke as follows:

RIGHT HONORABLE THE CHIEF JUSTICE, JUDGES OF THE SUPREME COURT AND STATE ATTORNEY,

You are responsible for a weighty task, for, by virtue of your office, you represent the solidity of the State. It depends on you to confirm confidence in the country, but it also depends on you that confidence in the country should not be shocked. Let me first, however, stop to consider what concerns the confirming of confidence in the country; and do all of you, who stand here, note my words. Our ancestors were led hither, clearly seeing that it was God's hand. All men, in their natural state, when there is no law, lead a licentious and reckless life. When, in 1836, the people trekked across the Orange River, we came together, but it was not permitted

APPENDIX

that we should live recklessly. We took God's Word as our guide on our trek and chose rulers to prevent crime and to decide all differences. It is evident that this did not proceed from our nature, but from God's hand; and so we came to the Vaal River. I will not now speak of the other trek, for that would take too long. The people then elected a Volksraad as the highest authority in the land, as the legislative power. That body was instructed to make fixed laws, since we had only the decisions and rules of the court martial. And so the honorable Volksraad chose a commission to draw up a constitution, consisting of the late Mr. Lombard, the Landdrost of Potchefstroom, the late Mr. Boomen, the grandfather of our Predikant Boomen, and myself. To our number was added Mr. Stuart, as secretary, to assist us, and we laid down the constitution: our names stand at the foot of it.

And what is the principle that it contains? In framing Article 8 of the Grondwet, we had in mind how God had led the people and how God's Word was a guide by which we must act. Article 8 says: " The people demands the greatest possible social liberty and expects this, because it has kept its religious faith and its engagements, and because it has submitted to law, order and justice and maintained the same." Now observe whither this article points. It points to God's Word. The people demands the greatest possible social liberty: not a licentious or reckless liberty, but one based upon God's Word. That is the principle which this article contains. The people demands liberty; but it is not

APPENDIX

only a free, but also a civilized people, which does not demand a reckless or licentious liberty, but one based upon God's Word. And to what does that point? What I am about to say is important, and I cannot do better than refer to what God tells us. Moses led Israel out of Egypt and was the lawgiver and fixed the law by God's command, and what does the law say? That you shall not do what seems right in your eyes, but what God orders: that you shall do and that you shall perform; you shall do no more nor less than that. Moses selected the wisest and oldest men out of the people and appointed them to be officers and judges under him and laid down rules which could not be departed from, but left it to the judges to expound and administer the laws according to their judgment and conscience; but not to depart from the laws. That is God's commandment. The New Testament shows us the Lord and Master; but I will first say that Moses' subordinate officers were not the law-givers, and therefore had not to question whether the law was right, for that the Law-giver had to answer for. Only the Sovereign Power above Moses could alter what the Law-giver had laid down, even as God did at the rock which Moses struck with his staff; but the judges must deliver justice according to the law as they receive it, and then act as faithful servants, by administering the laws to the best of their knowledge and conscience.

So it is also with you, right honorable judges. The people by an article in the constitution has appointed a Volksraad as the highest authority in the land, the

APPENDIX

legislative body, which passes laws and resolutions, and you must administer them to the best of your knowledge and power. No one can hinder you in that, and when you administer the laws and resolutions as you receive them from the legislative body, then you confirm confidence in the country, for then all those who have received their property by decrees know that they are safe and that all laws and resolutions bearing thereupon will be maintained. Foreigners who come here and who know the laws and resolutions passed by the Volksraad and who are willing to submit to them are able to secure their rights in this way, by trusting in the court, that it will not depart therefrom, but that the laws and resolutions laid down by the highest authority in the land, under which they have obtained their rights, will not be altered by the court, neither on the left hand nor on the right hand; and then you, from the highest to the lowest judge, confirm confidence in the country. Each must act according to orders, laws and rules laid down by the legislative body that stands above him. Even if, now and again, owing to man's weakness, an article is wrongly applied and a judgment of a lower court appealed against and quashed by the High Court, no one can be reproached with this or punished for it, since he has acted to the best of his knowledge and conscience under his oath. There is no longer an appeal from the High Court; and if you, honorable judges, in your own judgment, set aside a decree of the Volksraad, you adopt this right of criticism from the Devil; but if, perhaps, from human weakness, you pronounce a judgment

APPENDIX

which is not purely in accordance with the law, but is pronounced to the best of your knowledge and conscience, then you are not indictable either before God or man. From you there is no longer any appeal, and therefore you are called " gods; " but God stands in the midst of the council of the gods and pronounces judgment upon good and evil. If you act to the best of your knowledge and conscience and remain within the law, then one day it shall be said unto you also: " Thou good and faithful servant, thou hast been faithful over a few things, I will make thee ruler over many things." Then not only shall confidence in the country be confirmed, but also in you, who stand by the law, and men will have confidence also in the highest authority in the land and it shall not be scoffed at. Then also the sovereign voice of the people will be confirmed, which alone has the right to condemn laws.

Let us return to the point of how you can shock confidence, and look back to Moses. Moses gave the law, yet could not depart from it, but had to pronounce judgment as the law prescribed. Only the supreme authority, the sovereign God alone could condemn the law; and not the subordinate. The Devil instituted the principle of criticism in Paradise and criticized God's Word, which said: " Ye shall not eat of that tree, lest ye die." But then comes the Devil and criticizes that Word, saying: " Ye shall not surely die: for God doth know that in the day ye eat thereof, ye shall be as gods, knowing good and evil." And that interpretation is over the whole earth. Thus we see, under Moses, that Korah,

APPENDIX

Dathan and Abiram assumed to themselves the right of criticism, on the principle of the Devil, and unsettled the land. Rebellion and discord arose against Moses until God destroyed Korah, Dathan and Abiram. God punished them heavily, because they had acted against truth,—against God's Word. The right of criticism is a principle of the Devil. Listen attentively to what I say and do not underrate my words. We shall one day have to appear before God, and I do not know if I shall again have the opportunity of speaking to you. It may be the last time. Let the teachers, too, hear what I say. You judges shock the whole country if you take upon yourselves the right of criticism; for those who have obtained rights under whatever law or decree of the Volksraad will then be shocked, for they cannot tell how things will go when the court has to decide, and it is able to disregard a law. Then confidence is destroyed in the country, and not only in the country, but also in the court, and the Volksraad will be despised and scoffed at. If you come to this, then you will be like the steward in the New Testament, who did not obey the orders of his Lord and Master, but acted according to his own pleasure; and as the Devil says: "Ye shall be as gods and ye shall not die." But he who arrogates this to himself is dismissed from his post. That Christ teaches us. Then confidence in the country is shocked; and, if we reflect upon this, we see that God's Word teaches us that God can dwell in the midst of us only if every one remains true in his post.

Right honorable sirs, you know that our late Chief

APPENDIX

Justice, with some of his colleagues, adopted the right of criticism and became as wanton as a fish in the water that is free to swim about as it pleases. However, he jumped out of the water, that is to say, out of the law, on to dry land. The Volksraad then passed a resolution, with reference to the laws of the land, to the effect that, if a judge refuses to submit to them, I must dismiss him. I did my best, but the late Chief Justice was as slippery as a fish that has just jumped out of the water, so that I could not master him. Then his colleague, the Chief Justice of Cape Colony, who knew the ability of our late Chief Justice, came, of his own accord, to my assistance, and we got him back into the water, that is to say, the law. Then I was glad, because I knew the ability of the late Chief Justice and did not wish to lose him. After that, the late Chief Justice again became so wanton that he jumped so far out of the water that I saw no chance of getting him back and had to let him go, the more so as he then roundly declared that he did not wish to go back to it, because he refused to acknowledge the law as I understood it. But what does the late Chief Justice say now? That it is my fault. He says that I did not keep my promise; and what I am now saying I want taken down on paper, that all the world may read it. He can call it a promise, but I do not call it a promise; but I kept my word, when I told him to revise the constitution and that I would lay it as soon as possible before the Volksraad. That was about March, in any case long before the time when the Volksraad was to sit. But

APPENDIX

now I see that, in a speech delivered in Cape Colony, he has said, if the papers report him correctly, that "as soon as possible" means "to-day." The man seems to have lost his senses. How can I bring a matter before the Volksraad in March when it does not sit till May? As soon as the Volksraad sat, I brought the matter before the Raad and that body, without delay, appointed a committee which asked the late Chief Justice to help to revise the constitution, which, however, he refused to do, notwithstanding his promise in writing. I do not take it amiss of him, however, for in my eyes he seems to have lost his senses. What does he do next? He says, in a manifesto, that if the people will not help him, he will apply to England,—that is, if I understand properly what he has written. He knows that he has taken the oath, not only as regards his office, but that his oath is binding upon him as a burgher of the country; and he knows that a burgher is not allowed to appeal to another power: if he does, he is guilty. Moreover, he himself has repeatedly declared that the suzerainty no longer exists in our internal government, and yet he flies to that. But I do not take this amiss of him now, for in my eyes he seems to have lost his senses. That is not all. He also drew a comparison saying: "Suppose the Volksraad passed a resolution depriving the people of its rights; who would then protect the people?" The late Chief Justice, however, forgets to say that what he suggests the Volksraad might do, he himself has already done. For, at the time of the claim-lottery on the Rand, he actually took away hundreds

APPENDIX

of property-rights from the public and awarded them to one or two; and there is no help for it, because the Supreme Court has the final decision. But, if the Volksraad were to take such a step, the people would come with petitions to have that step annulled. What does the late Chief Justice say further? He says that his dismissal is a violation of the convention, because he was appointed by the Interregnum; but he knows that this is not true. He was a judge in President Burgers's time, and, when the Interregnum came, Mr. De Wet was appointed Chief Justice. At least, so I am told, and I believe that it is true. When we took over the country again, the late Chief Justice went away. We sent for him to Kimberley to take office as Chief Justice, but he was not appointed as such by the Interregnum. He must have forgotten this, or I must have read wrong. What does he do next? He himself really violates the convention by the principle which he accepts; for he refuses to acknowledge any resolutions of the Volksraad that are contrary to the convention. By the convention we obtained land, but also hundreds of places were cut off by the convention for which deeds of sale had already been issued and some had even been occupied, and the convention itself lays down that the Volksraad must decide in the matter of the annulment of conveyances: so that that was against the constitution. Now, if the principle of the late Chief Justice had been maintained, then the convention would have been broken, and that we may not do, for then we should come into collision with England. That is where the maintenance of that principle

APPENDIX

would have brought us. Then those places would have had to fall back into our possession and the conveyances be restored, for the decrees of the Volksraad concerning them were in conflict with the constitution, which does not recognize them. If, therefore, that principle was correct, there would be nothing for it but for us to take up the sword to go and fight against England.

Gentlemen, I appreciate the late Chief Justice's abilities so highly that, if I thought it would do any good, I would have him confined in a lunatic asylum, for I liked him greatly, and would wait until he was cured to employ him again. His abilities were great, but he went astray when he accepted the Devil's principle, the right of criticism. Let me speak my mind to you, for the late Chief Justice has said that I dismissed him illegally. Now the whole world can hear how the matter really happened.

You other Officers and Officials, from the highest to the lowest,

On you also depends much that concerns the growth and prosperity of the country, on you who stand under orders and instructions, both verbal and written. If you scrupulously and zealously observe your duty and each of you fulfils it in his place, you promote the welfare of the country and contribute much to its progress and prosperity, and not only act in the interest of the country, but in your own interest so long as you keep to your instructions, verbal and written, each in his place. Do not undermine one another!

APPENDIX

AND YOU OF THE ARMY!

To you, right honorable Commandant General and other officers, a brief word also: from you to the State President and down to the officer lowest in rank, who all form part of the defences of our country against the enemy. If the State President receives news of a hostile invasion and does not inform you of it, that will be on the State President's head and the blood that is shed will be laid to his account and he will be punished for it; and if you, Commandant General, receive the news and do not keep watch or do not post watches, that will be on your head and the blood that is shed will be laid to your account and you will be punished. But if you have given your orders to your subordinates and they do not keep watch then the bloodshed will be on their heads and they will have to bear the responsibility and the punishment: so God's Word teaches us. Let each watch in his own department. From the Volksraad down to the lowest official, all form a machine of state with many wheels, and when each wheel works in its place with the others, concord reigns, and concord gives strength, on which God bestows His blessing. But when a wheel does not fit into the machine it must be taken out and placed on one side or shifted, as otherwise the whole machine might go to pieces. If that wheel does not fit in anywhere else, it must be placed on one side. If, however, it does fit in some other place, then, if the smallest wheel works in harmony with the largest, the machine of state may be expected to go well and everything will spread light, and on such a co-operation God's blessing rests.

APPENDIX

His Honor then turned to the clergy:

REVEREND SIRS, SERVANTS OF GOD'S WORD,

When I turn my eyes upon you, a favorite text rises to my mind: "How beautiful are the feet of them that publish peace." I say "publish peace;" I know that that is your task upon earth. The right of criticism was instituted by the Devil, for he said to Adam and Eve: "Eat of the fruit of this tree and ye shall not die and ye shall be like gods;" and in this way the Devil has led away thousands upon earth to build on their own merits and thus to oppose God's Word and to unsettle all things, so that there is no foundation; and if an eye is not kept upon this preaching, you know what the Christians upon earth, who stand by God's Word, have to fight against. I do not speak of minor points, but of the main point; and he who holds fast to that has to fight against the spirit of the air. The Devil laid hold of Cain's soul, and the latter did not accept the punishment: he placed himself on God's level, made his sacrifice, and expected God to be content with what was beautiful in Cain's eyes, and Cain sang hymns of praise to the Lord which came from nature, but which he thought were pleasing to God. But God rejected them, because God found no religion in Cain. He was outside God's words. But how beautiful are the feet of them that publish peace, like Abel. He acknowledged the judgment that fell in Paradise, that man was condemned—which the Devil brought about together with the right of criticism—and took a first-born lamb—and

APPENDIX

this refers to Christ—yes, and prayed in the spirit that the punishment which he had deserved might fall upon the Lamb, as otherwise he would suffer eternal death. God accepted the sacrifice and heard his prayer, and there we have the Father, Son and Holy Ghost. The severity of the law is not respected by men because of the Devil's right of criticism; and it is even so with Christ's work of redemption, through the Holy Ghost. Then preach these words: "How beautiful are the feet of them that publish peace." Stand firm in the struggle. The Devil goes further and respects nothing; for we read: "I will put enmity between thee and the woman, and between her seed and thy seed; it shall bruise thy head, and thou shalt bruise his heel." So at last he comes to the Son of God in the wilderness—and with the same intention he comes to the whole earth—and says to Jesus: "If Thou be the Son of God, command that these stones be made bread." But Christ says: "Man shall not live by bread alone, but by every word that proceedeth out of the mouth of God." Then he sets Christ on the pinnacle of the Temple, and the Devil says to Him: "If Thou be the Son of God, cast Thyself down from hence: for it is written, He shall give His angels charge over Thee, and in their hands they shall bear Thee up, lest at any time Thou dash Thy foot against a stone." But Christ answering says: "It is said, Thou shalt not tempt the Lord thy God." Then the Devil takes Jesus up into an high mountain and shows Him all the kingdoms of the world, saying: "If Thou wilt worship me, all this shall be Thine." But Christ

APPENDIX

says, "It is written, Thou shalt worship the Lord thy God, and Him only shalt thou serve."

See there your preaching of the Gospel, you servants of Christ, founded on God's Word, and if you preach thus, you will be a help to the State, for it rests upon God's Word, as shown in Article 8 of the constitution. The people says that it has liberty, and that is so, but based upon God's Word; and thus was this land designed by our forefathers, on the basis of God's Word, for the maintenance of law and order. That is a thing that does not proceed from men; for I myself did not understand one of the depths of that article, how God at that time led us. Reverend sirs, predikants, stand firm in the faith; for how beautiful are the feet of them that publish peace in Jesus Christ; for the Devil's doctrine of criticism says that man has become as a god and can secure his own happiness by his own lights and his own reason and his own merit, and therefore that he shall not die. No, stand firm, and preach in accordance with God's Word, for then you are truly the clergy of our people; and lead it in that road and always keep the fear of the Lord before its eyes, so that the people may walk in the right paths, both socially and religiously, and if your work is earnest and true and sincere, then will you really be a support to the state. Then there will be general harmony. "Fear God and honor the King." We shall respect you in your divine profession, in your precious labors, in your heavenly work, for how beautiful are the feet of them that publish peace. We cannot, however, protect you further than our

APPENDIX

power allows. We shall respect you and protect you, yes, even help and assist you to help to build up the church, but also not further than God's Word commands; and know that, when the earthly judge goes so far that he begins to meddle with the internal government of the church, he is inspired with the spirit of Anti-Christ, for then he usurps the place of Christ, who is the Head of the church. If the worldly power does this, it adopts the Devil's right of criticism to get that into its claws and destroy religion. God has erected this Christian state and a Christian government, which will protect the church outside us, and you too, reverend sirs; but if you go outside the body that said, " Feed my lambs, feed my sheep," you meddle with the body politic and are possessed of the spirit of the Pope, and your preaching is no longer a beautiful preaching of the Gospel. So long as each remains within his own sphere of activity, there will be a healthy co-operation, and God's spirit will rest upon us and the Lord will bless us.

Now, dear Children,

A brief word to you. You are the ones upon whom the State President keeps his eye, for I see our future church and state in your hands; for when all the old people are gone, you will be the church and state, but if you depart from the truth and stray, you will lose your inheritance. Stand firm by God's Word, in which your parents have brought you up. Love that Word. I shall endeavor with all my might to assist churches and schools, to let you receive a Christian education, so that you may both

APPENDIX

religiously and socially become useful members of church and state, and I trust that the teachers and ministers will also do their best. It is a great privilege that your Government has ordered a Christian education, and you are greatly privileged in being able to enjoy a Christian education, and not you alone, for the object is to extend it so that all may have the opportunity of receiving it and turning it to account. It is a great privilege that the Government and the legislative power have thus laid down the law as to Christian instruction. It is also a great privilege for you that the Government and Volksraad have accepted our language as the state language. Keep to that, keep to the language in which your forefathers, whom God led out of the wilderness, struggled and prayed to God and which became ever dearer and dearer to them: the language in which the Bible comes to you and in which your forefathers read the Bible, and which contains the religion of your forefathers. And, therefore, if you become indifferent to your language, you also become indifferent to your forefathers and indifferent to the Bible and indifferent to your religion; and then you will soon stray away entirely and will rob posterity of your Dutch Bible and of your religion, which God confirmed to your forefathers with wonders and miracles. Stand firm then, so that we may not trust you in vain, and keep to your language, your Bible and your religion. It is a good thing to learn foreign languages, especially the language of your neighbors with whom you have most to do; but let any foreign language be a second

APPENDIX

language to you. Pray to God that you may stand firm on this point and not stray, so that the Lord may remain among you, and posterity will honor you for your loyalty.

SCHOOLMASTERS AND MISTRESSES,

A brief word to you also. You have, as it were, become the guardians of the children in the place of the parents who have given their children to God before the pulpit to be educated for the Lord, in His service and to His honor. You have taken them over to feed them, as Christ said, like lambs, to the honor of God. You know that the New Testament says that women brought their children to Jesus. They were healthy and not sick children. The unbelievers only take them to the doctor; but none of them will send their healthy children to the doctor. Here, however, you see the women coming with healthy children to Jesus, and the disciples rebuked them, but Jesus said: "Suffer little children to come unto Me, and forbid them not, for of such is the Kingdom of Heaven." The mothers brought their children to receive the heavenly blessing on the inward vocation and to be healed inwardly. But if you, schoolmasters and mistresses, do not know the faith, how then will you bring the children to Christ through the faith? I trust, however, that you do know it. Therefore, never forget to bring the children to the Lord through the faith, and take care that religion is not left in the background and only educational subjects taught, for then you are attacking religion and it will be forgotten. For, when man proceeds only ac-

APPENDIX

cording to his nature and his knowledge, he begins to believe what the Devil has said, that men shall be as gods; and then it can be said of such a man: " The greater the mind, the greater the beast." Then he rushes from place to place. Therefore let religion not be neglected, for that is the foundation of church and state. Stand firm by the Bible and teach the children who are entrusted to you for that purpose, and it shall be said to you too: " Thou good and faithful servant, thou hast been faithful over a few things, I will make thee ruler over many things: enter thou into the joy of thy Lord and sit at My right hand."

I have spoken.

Certified as a true extract from the original minutes of the Honorable First Volksraad of the 12th of May 1898.

(Signed) W. J. FOCKENS,
Secretary to the First Volksraad.

I certify that the above is a true and faithful copy.
H. C. DE BRUIJN PRINCE.

APPENDIX B

SPEECH OF STATE PRESIDENT KRUGER IN THE FIRST
VOLKSRAAD ON MONDAY, 1 MAY 1899

*To the Right Hon. Mr. President of the First
Volksraad and to the honorable members of the
First and Second Volksraad*

GENTLEMEN,

It is a great pleasure to me once more cordially to welcome you in this your house of assembly and to give my hearty thanks to God, who rules the Universe and who has spared and saved you all, so that you may again, with His help, devote all your energies to the interests of our dear country and people.

1. In those places where different members of your honorable assembly retired last year in rotation, I have ordered new elections for members of the First and Second Volksraad. The result of those elections will be laid before you.

2. As the vacancy arising through the election of Mr. A. D. W. Wolmarans to be a member of the Executive Raad must be filled as soon as possible, I have issued a writ for the election of a new member for the village and district of Pretoria. The result of that election will be communicated to you.

3. The term of office of Mr. S. W. Burger, member of the Executive Raad, will expire by rota-

APPENDIX

tion on the 6th of this month; I therefore ask you to provide for the vacancy before that time, and I take leave to remind you that the present occupant is re-eligible.

4. I hope in this session to call your attention as early as possible to certain proposals which I wish to make to your honorable assembly with regard to the franchise, the bewaarplaatsen and the dynamite question.

5. It is a great pleasure to me to be able again to state that the Republic continues in friendly relations with foreign powers. The correspondence between our Government and the British Government, arising from the difference of opinion regarding the international relations of the Republic towards Great Britain and Ireland, is not yet finished; I trust, however, that this matter will soon be brought to a satisfactory conclusion. It is always my endeavor to do all in my power to confirm those good relations.

6. The Raad of Delegates has this year held its annual sitting at Bloemfontein. The report, with the suggestions of that body, shall be laid before you. Those suggestions, in which the Government joins, deserve your earnest attention.

7. In accordance with the resolutions of your honorable assembly touching the suggestions of the Raad of Delegates for 1898, the Governments of the Republics appointed commissions to try to make the constitutions of the two states, in so far as possible, similar. Those commissions met in the month of February last at Pretoria. The report of their deliberations shall be laid before you. A commission

APPENDIX

consisting of the Chief Justices of the two Republics has undertaken the duty of making further suggestions for the assimilation of laws in accordance with the resolutions passed in your session of 1898. This important work, however, requires long consideration and mature deliberation, and this commission has not yet quite finished a work which, when it has once been given force of law by the representatives of the people of both states, will certainly promote the welfare and the prosperity of the sister republics.

8. Negotiations have been entered into with the Orange Free State touching the payment of registration fees for goods which, by treaty, are imported free of duty into the South African Republic, this in accordance with the resolution of your honorable assembly, numbered 1,365, of the 4th of October 1898. These negotiations have led to a provisional agreement between the Governments of the two states which shall be laid before you for your approval.

9. In view of the threatening danger that the terrible sickness known as the bubonic plague might visit South Africa, at the suggestion of our Government a conference was held, at the commencement of the year, at Pretoria, consisting of representatives of the Orange Free State, Mozambique, Natal and Cape Colony, in order to frame measures to prevent the entrance and spread of the Asiatic pestilence in South Africa. The report of the labors of the conference, which is sure to be read by you with interest, will be laid before you during this session for your

APPENDIX

approval of the suggestions and proposals therein contained.

10. An invitation has been received from the Imperial German Government to dispatch a representative of the Republic to attend the International Veterinary Congress which will be held at Baden-Baden in the month of August of this year. Taking into consideration that this Congress may be of great importance to the Republic, the Government has thought fit to depute the Governmental Veterinary Surgeon as its representative, which will, I trust, meet with your approval. He will, at the same time, make use of this opportunity to study the bubonic plague and the various remedies.

11. I am able to inform you that earnest endeavors are being made and that negotiations have already been entered into for the appointment of an able financial minister for the South African Republic.

12. I am very much pleased to be able to inform you that great progress has been made this year in trade, especially in the first quarter, as appears from the increased revenue of the state.

13. I call your attention to the resolution of your honorable assembly, numbered 325 and passed on the 15th of March 1899, in the matter of the grant of a bonus to the retired member of the Executive Raad, Mr. J. M. A. Wolmarans. I must express my sincere regret that the honorable gentleman has been compelled by the state of his health to hand in his resignation, since he has always been a most useful member of the Executive Raad, thanks to his clear insight into affairs, his energy and his

APPENDIX

great love for his country, in which he always showed himself to have at heart the true interests of land and people; and I cannot omit to express to him my thanks for all that he has done, hoping that your assembly will come to a favorable decision on the request already made by me, as contained in the Government Message of the 10th of March 1899.

14. The Executive Raad has found it necessary to dispatch a commando against the rebellious natives of the tribe of Ramapulaan, under their leader M'Pesu, in the Zoutpansberg district. I cannot find sufficient praise for the courage, the skill and the sagacious prudence of our Commandant General and officers, by which they have brought this war to a satisfactory conclusion, and for the excellent and gallant behavior of our burghers, and I congratulate all of us on the rapid and thorough manner in which this revolt has been suppressed. We mourn the fact that this commando has claimed some valuable victims and our sympathy is with the survivors. The Government has decided to found a village, to be called Louis Trichardt, on the spot where the laagers stood, and I am convinced that the action of the Government meets with your approval.

15. Seeing that the Netherlands South African Railway Company has resolved to repay the sum of £2,000,000 which it had borrowed from the Government, the necessity for the conclusion of a loan on the part of the Government disappears for the present.

16. I must express, in my own name and that of the Executive Raad, our great satisfaction with the

APPENDIX

labors and transactions of our Envoy Extraordinary, Dr. W. J. Leyds, who reported to us on the occasion of his visit here.

17. It appears from various sources of information that the mining industry has made the greatest progress during the past year. The value of the gold extracted was £16,240,630, being an increase of £4,886,905 over 1897. The total value of the gold extracted in our country to the end of 1898 amounts to £70,228,603. The results of 1898 place the South African Republic considerably above any other gold-producing country, and represent 28 per cent. of the estimated produce of the whole world.

18. The Government has resolved to give effect to the former resolutions passed in connection with the coolie question, with the result that, from the 1st of July, 1899, coolies will be allowed to reside only in those streets, quarters and locations of the different towns and villages which have been set apart for their use.

19. There are many plans for public works, principally bridges and buildings, which could not be carried into execution or even discussed, because the Executive Raad was overwhelmed with so much other business and also because financial arrangements must first be made with this object.

20. In obedience to the order of your honorable assemblies, the Government has published the Draft Constitution and the Criminal Procedure Law in the *Staatscourant* for the approval of the people. Your earnest attention is invited to those important laws.

21. In obedience to your order, the Government

APPENDIX

will again lay a pensions law before your honorable assembly for discussion. I hope that this law will enjoy your earnest consideration.

22. It has been my privilege to visit certain districts and villages, and to hold meetings at the following places: Heidelberg, Rustenburg and Johannesburg. I hope, in the course of this session, to call your attention to the demands and wishes of the burghers, in so far as these have been brought to my notice.

23. The Government finds, from the various reports, that about 746,500 head of cattle have perished from the pest. To my great gratitude, however, I am able to inform you that this so dreaded disease may now be regarded as suppressed. In January last, a few cases still occurred, but only at Lydenburg, Krugersdorp and Piet Retief; and, thanks to the immediate fulfilment of the regulations contained in the proclamation and to the goodness of Providence, the disease was confined within those limits and spread no further.

24. The Government has given orders for the survey of places for irrigation purposes, and the report on the subject shall be laid before you.

25. A list of newly-appointed, resigned, suspended and discharged functionaries shall be submitted for your approval.

26. The different reports of the heads of departments shall be laid before you.

27. Different bills and modifications of the laws shall be submitted for your approval.

28. The Government has given effect, in so far

APPENDIX

as possible, to the instructions of your High Assembly, as will appear from the papers and reports that will be laid before you.

29. The Government proposes, in the course of this session, to bring before your notice different matters of greater or lesser importance for your consideration and decision.

And with this, gentlemen, I once more confidently place the interests of our dear country and people in your hands. God grant you the necessary strength and wisdom to settle the matters which you will take in hand, under His high blessing, for the welfare and prosperity of land and people.

(Signed) S. J. P. KRUGER,
State President.

I certify that the above is a true and faithful copy.
H. C. DE BRUIJN PRINCE.

APPENDIX C

TWO SPEECHES OF PRESIDENT KRUGER AT THE DECISIVE SITTING OF THE FIRST AND SECOND VOLKSRAAD OF 2 OCTOBER 1899

I

Speech delivered at the Commencement of the Sitting

HONORABLE SIRS,

To tell you what is in my mind: you know how the Lord transplanted this people to this country and led it here amid miracles; so that we should have to say, " Lord, I no longer believe in Thee," if things came to such a pass with us that now, when thousands of enemies are assailing us, we voluntarily surrendered the land which He gave us and not we ourselves. Let us trust in God and together offer up our prayers to the Lord. He is waiting for our entreaties and He will be with us. The decision rests with Him, and He will decide, not on lies, but on the ground of truth.

You are familiar with the course of events and know how the Volksraad and the people have yielded in everything that was demanded. First, it was a question of the franchise. Three times we yielded in this matter and I repeat, so that it may appear

APPENDIX

upon the minutes, that it is a lie to say that we were not willing to treat those who came from abroad as our equals.

When the Convention of 1881 was concluded, there were only a few English here; and what was it that they wanted? They were quite willing to be treated on an equal footing with our burghers, but registered themselves as British subjects; they preferred to remain foreigners rather than become subjects of this state.

You know, moreover, that, under the Convention of 1884, at the time of the Blue Mountains commando, they refused to take the field with our burghers, although by so doing they would have at once received the franchise. I brought the matter three times before the Raad and begged it to pass a resolution that they must defend the country; and the Volksraad confirmed that all who took part in the war should obtain the franchise. Then Loch came here and complained that the English were not treated as the most favored nation. I thereupon again issued another proclamation, because I thought that there might really be people to be found who wished to stand on an equal footing with our burghers; I did this, although the Convention (of 1884) expressly prescribes that they shall possess not equal political, but equal commercial rights. Now think—we are standing before the Lord and let each of us send his prayer on high to the Lord—where can they say that, with regard to trade, they were less favored than our own burghers? Nowhere. They were, in this respect, even more favorably placed than

APPENDIX

our burghers. They could take gold and anything they liked out of the country and they could even obtain political rights, but they would not have them. The High Commissioner demanded that we should extend the franchise and we had already done more; we even tried, afterwards, to treat them, the Uitlanders, on an equal footing with our burghers, but they declined.

In this respect, therefore, there is no injustice on our side. We can appear frankly before our Lord. He will decide and He decides not by virtue of lies, but according to justice and truth. Let us therefore send up our prayers to Him on high, that He may guide us, and then, if thousands come, the Lord will guide us in right and justice until, perhaps, we shall be freed once and for all from all these cares. I place myself wholly in His hands.

I will accuse no one of being a false prophet; but read Psalm 108, verse 7, which came to my mind while I was struggling in prayer. You must not read it because I say so, but because it is God's Word. It was no dream that stood before my spirit, for false dreams mislead us and I do not trouble about them: I take my stand on God's Word alone. Now read that psalm attentively and associate your prayers with that: then will the Lord guide us; and, when He is with us, who shall be against us? Therefore I say to you, go among your burghers and exhort them continually to pray in this struggle.

We so often forget what the Lord has done. I will not speak again of the War of Independence,

APPENDIX

in which the Lord so visibly and wonderfully aided us. But was it otherwise in the Jameson Raid? They aimed thousands of shells and balls at us, while we shot only with rifles; and how wonderfully was the course of the bullets ordered! Three of us fell, while the enemy had hundreds killed and wounded. And who ordered the flight of the bullets? The Lord. He spared us then, to prove to us that He rules all things. The Lord will also protect you now, even if thousands of bullets fly around you. That is my faith and also my constant prayer for myself, for the burghers and for all who fight with us. I will say once more that the Lord will guide us: He will decide and show to us that He rules and none other.

II

*The Second Speech delivered at the Sitting of
2 October* 1899

The State President spoke a second time, after the Presidents of the First and Second Volksraad had supported him in enthusiastic speeches:

It gives me great confidence to see that the Raad is with me. I know that, like myself, it believes in God's Word. If you search that Word, you will find that God, when He punishes and chastises His people, does not do so in such a way that He delivers that people wholly into the hands of its enemies. We too, when we chastise our children, do not allow others to beat them. When the people, that is, the people of Israel, fell away from God and committed idola-

APPENDIX

try, it was punished and almost fell into slavery. But you see in the Old Testament how, when thousands of enemies then come to annihilate God's people, the people trusts to God, its Creator and Redeemer.

Gentlemen, you have heard how they mock at us for appealing to the Lord. That is a blasphemy against God, and we trust therefore that the Lord will not let it go unpunished. The Lord chastises us, but He will not suffer Himself to be blasphemed.

One brief word more. Moses was a man of God, and the Lord spoke with him; but, at a time of great stress and combat, his friends had to stay up his hands, for he was but a weak mortal. Aaron had to support him in the faith. So let us too remember our generals and fighting-generals in our prayers, and unceasingly offer our prayers to God. Let us support them in their faith and let us not forget to strengthen with our prayers the men who have to conduct the Government.

APPENDIX D

OPENING SPEECH OF PRESIDENT STEYN AT THE ANNUAL SESSION OF THE VOLKSRAAD OF THE ORANGE FREE STATE AT KROONSTAD, 2 APRIL 1900

MR. PRESIDENT AND GENTLEMEN,

Although the enemy is in possession of Bloemfontein and I have been obliged temporarily to remove the seat of government to Kroonstad, I nevertheless open your usual annual session full of firm confidence in the future, and I heartily bid you welcome.

1. In spite of your efforts and the efforts of both Governments to preserve peace, a war has been forced upon the South African Republic by the British Government. And the Orange Free State has been true to her obligations, and, in accordance with your resolution, ranged herself on the side of the Sister Republic when, on the 13th of October, war broke out between the South African Republic and the British Government.

2. The Republics picked up the gauntlet with no other object than that of defending their independence, which cost our forefathers so much blood and which is so dear to us, to the uttermost. Thanks to the Almighty, our arms were blessed in a manner which not only struck the world with amazement, but far exceeded our own expectations. Although

APPENDIX

the capture of General Cronjé and his gallant burghers and the occupation of Bloemfontein were heavy blows to us, I am nevertheless glad to be able to say that our burghers are still full of courage and determined to continue to fight for the preservation of our dearly-purchased independence, and, if necessary, like so many of our dear ones, to die as brave and never-to-be-forgotten heroes. With the deepest regret I have to inform you of the decease of the Vice-president and Commandant General of our Sister Republic, Petrus Jacobus Joubert, a man in whom not only the Sister Republic, but all South Africa has lost a faithful friend, a true patriot and an upright Christian, who devoted his best years to the service of his nation. May his life serve as an example to all of us and his death stimulate us, under God's blessing, to continue the struggle which he had hitherto led with such ability in the Sister Republic and to bring it to a happy peace!

3. The enemy, not content with his greatly superior force, has sought to obtain still further advantages by a constant abuse of the Red Cross and the white flag, against which abuse I have been obliged to make a protest to the neutral Powers. Ay, the mighty British Empire has not disdained, in this conflict with two small Republics, to make use of crafty proclamations in order to divide our little people. I have pointed, in a counter-proclamation of my own, to the craftiness and danger of this communication, and am glad to be able to say that, so far as I know, comparatively few have been so cowardly and faint-hearted as to surrender voluntarily.

APPENDIX

4. In order to prevent further bloodshed and to assure the civilized world once more that it is not our intention to annex the neighboring colonies, but that we are pursuing an entirely different object, namely the defence of our liberty and our rights, His Honor the State President of the South African Republic and I have written a letter to His Excellency the Prime Minister of Great Britain with a view to the restoration of peace. But, instead of aiding us in our endeavors, he has sent us a reply which will be laid before you and which clearly shows that this war had no other object from the commencement than the destruction of the two Republics.

5. Even as I, and the Executive Raad with me, had already attempted everything in order to preserve peace, so we lose sight of nothing to-day that could serve to restore peace. The Government of the South African Republic and our own Government have therefore decided to send a commission consisting of Messrs. A. Fischer, member of the Executive Raad, C. H. Wessels, President of the Volksraad, and A. D. Wolmarans, member of the Executive Raad of the South African Republic, to Europe and America to ask the civilized Powers for their intervention for the prevention of further bloodshed. That their labors may be blessed with success is and must be the object of all our prayers.

6. By virtue of the plenary powers that have been given me, I have concluded a loan with the South African Republic.

7. It will be impossible for us to proceed to the usual debates. I would therefore propose to you

APPENDIX

to adjourn them to a later date and to discuss only those questions and decrees that shall be laid before you.

I conclude with the sincere prayer that, in the name of the Thrice Holy God, we may all be granted strength to keep up the sacred struggle for freedom and justice upon which we entered in all seriousness and to continue it energetically to the end. For God forbid that we should lightly surrender the independence which we bought with our blood. I have done.

APPENDIX E

OPENING SPEECH OF PRESIDENT KRUGER AT THE ORDINARY ANNUAL SESSION OF THE FIRST AND SECOND VOLKSRAAD OF THE SOUTH AFRICAN REPUBLIC AT THE JOINT SITTING OF 7 MAY 1900

GENTLEMEN,

I once more have great pleasure in cordially welcoming you in this house of assembly and in venturing to give thanks to God, who rules the Universe and who has protected and preserved you, so that you can once more, with His help, devote all your strength to the interests of our dear country and people.

1. Some members of your Raad have informed me that, in consequence of the war, which compels their presence with the commandos, they were unable to obey the summons to attend this meeting.

2. The war in which our country is engaged with England has, in addition to the many valuable victims which it has already exacted from among the burghers of both States, also demanded its victims from the legislative and executive bodies, in consequence of which we have to lament the deaths of our meritorious fellow-members J. H. Barnard, C. J. Tosen, J. H. Kock, and our beloved Vice-president and Commandant General P. J. Joubert. One of

APPENDIX

them died a glorious death at Derdepoort in the defence of his fatherland against wild Kaffir hordes commanded by British officers; the other from the wounds which he received at the Battle of Elandslaagte when leading our burghers; while both Mr. Tosen and the Vice-president and Commandant General were taken from us by disease, the result of privations. A word of deep-felt esteem for those dead brothers, who were snatched from us in the midst of their prosperous career, is not, I think, out of place at this time. Posterity will rate at its right value the work of our late Commandant General, whose attitude inspired even the enemy with respect and whose humane and glorious conduct assured our state a name of standing among the civilized nations.

3. New elections for the vacant seats in the Volksraad could not be held because of the extraordinary circumstances.

4. I have nominated Mr. S. W. Burger as Vice-president of the South African Republic: this nomination is provisional until the First Volksraad has found time to settle the matter.

5. As Commandant General I have appointed Louis Botha, also provisionally, until an election can be held. It was the deceased Commandant General's wish that Mr. Botha should succeed him in this important post. I am convinced that this provisional appointment has also met with the approval of the nation.

6. I am deeply touched by the proof of loyalty on the part of the people of our sister Republic, who has shown by this act that she was determined to

APPENDIX

fulfil the obligations which she had made by treaty with the people of the South African Republic. In such a glorious fashion have the old ties been confirmed and strengthened which already existed between the peoples inhabiting either bank of the Vaal River. The sister Republic clearly saw that united action was necessary; for an attack on the independence of the South African Republic also implies a threat against the independent existence of the Orange Free State. The energy and the unbounded faith in the future of the Afrikander Nation which our sister Republic displayed in her attitude have set the people and the Government of the South African Republic a magnificent example, have strengthened us in the struggle for our existence which has been forced upon us by the war with Great Britain and are of even greater moral value for the outer world and for all who follow the struggle of a small people for its existence. The least, therefore, in my opinion, that our duty towards our loyal brothers and fellow-Afrikanders in the Orange Free State demands of us is that I should, at this place of your assembly, express, as your interpreter, our sincere and deep-felt sense of gratitude. God bless them for their devotion to the cause of freedom!

7. It is a satisfaction to me to be again able to inform you that, with the exception of the Kingdom of Great Britain and Ireland, the Republic continues in friendly relations with foreign Powers.

8. While visiting the various laagers, I was also at Bloemfontein, where I agreed with His Honor the State President of the Orange Free State to send

APPENDIX

a joint dispatch to the British Government, in which, after referring to the fact that we had not sought war and desired no increase of territory, we proposed to open friendly negotiations on the basis that both Republics should be recognized as sovereign international states and receive the assurance that those of Her Majesty's subjects who had assisted us in this war should suffer no damage in person or property. From the reply of the British Government, which shall be laid before you, you will see that that Government was always and is still determined to destroy the independent existence of the two Republics.

9. Even if our legislation in past years and our negotiations with the British Government had not shown that we were ready to do everything to preserve peace, we are, now that war has broken out in spite of our efforts to prevent it, prepared to do everything and to leave nothing untried to restore peace. With this object, I have agreed with His Honor the State President of the Orange Free State to send Mr. A. Fischer, the respected member of the Executive Raad of the Orange Free State, for both Republics, Mr. C. H. Wessels, President of the Volksraad of the Free State, for his State, and Mr. A. D. W. Wolmarans, member of the Executive Raad, for our Republic, to Europe and America with the commission, in the name of the people and the Governments of the South African Republic and the Orange Free State, to petition for the restoration of peace on the basis of the independence of the two Republics.

10. The presence in our fighting lines of *attachés*

APPENDIX

who have been deputed by different states to follow the progress of the war, points to the great interest which the Governments of those states take in the methods of warfare of our Republics. At the same time I rejoice to find that the sympathy of well-nigh the whole world is on our side in this struggle for right and liberty and that different countries have sent detachments of the Red Cross as ambulances to the battle-fields to allay the pain and suffering of our wounded, while at the same time funds are being collected, not only in Europe, but also in America and Asia, to help the widows and orphans of the slain. I am, therefore, but carrying out your wishes when I here express our gratitude for those self-sacrificing actions of noble humanity.

11. I have been compelled to make a protest to the different neutral Powers against various actions which are in conflict with international law and with warfare as practised between civilized nations, as, for instance, against the abuse of the Red Cross and the white flag, the ill-treatment of the wounded on the battle-field and of prisoners of war, and the employment of natives to fight against the Republics.

12. In spite of the difficult circumstances in which the war has placed the country, I rejoice to find that the treasury has been able to meet the great expenses of the war and that the mines are developing progressively.

13. I have made use of your authorization and concluded a loan with the Orange Free State.

14. By virtue of your authorization by Resolution 1,416 of the 28th of September 1899, the Govern-

APPENDIX

ment has issued and enforced decrees as circumstances demanded. The Government trusts that its action, in so far as it relies upon those plenary powers, has received your approval, and asks for instructions that it may continue in the same way.

15. It will not be possible to dispatch the ordinary business of our annual session, and I therefore suggest to you that you should discuss only those matters which will be laid before you and adjourn all others to a later date.

And with this, gentlemen, I conclude. May the Ruler of Nations vouchsafe to gird us with strength to bring to a desired end this unequal and violent strife, upon which we have entered in His name and for our sacred right. May the burghers and officers, inspired from on high with strength and with a sense of duty both towards those brave men who have given their lives for the preservation of the fatherland and towards the coming generation that expects to receive a free fatherland at their hands, feel impelled to continue the war and to remain steadfast. And thus may the South African race, whose future was always hopeful, now at last develop into a mighty tree and prove by its actions that we are worthy of taking our place in the ranks of the nations. God in His Heaven help us to attain that end! I have done.

APPENDIX F

Speech delivered on the 7th of May by President Kruger in explanation of his Opening Speech at the Ordinary Session of 1900

Right Honorable the Presidents and Honorable Members of the two Volksraads,

Although it is not my custom, allow me to add a few words to my speech: the situation of the country is such that I make this public request to be permitted to give an explanation of my address.

You know how the franchise was insisted upon before the war began. You know that the Government yielded, after obtaining the consent of the Raad, although this body saw objections to such a course, until even the burghers made representations, as though we were about to surrender almost all our rights. The Government had in view the prevention of bloodshed. The Raad then agreed to the seven years' franchise and also that all persons who had been here for more than seven years could acquire the franchise immediately. There were then nearly 30,000 who were able to acquire the franchise at once, and so much had been yielded that, if all of these had obtained the franchise, they could have outvoted the old burghers. It was only to prevent bloodshed that we yielded so much as this. Nevertheless they were

APPENDIX

not contented, and declared that they wanted to have the franchise after five years.

Our burghers were against this, and there were also members of the Raad who would not grant it; but, notwithstanding, the Government made a proposal, because they had perceived that it was not a question of the franchise, but that this was a pretext full of pharisaical hypocrisy; for documents had been found showing that, as early as 1896, it had been decided that the two independent Republics must cease to exist. I can express myself in no other terms than by calling it a " devilish fraud." They talked of peace, while the decision had already been taken to destroy us. Even, therefore, if we had yielded more, if we had even said that the franchise could be acquired after one year's residence, that would not have been accepted. For it had appeared from documents that this people should no longer be a free people. As I stated in my speech, the Government, in order to avoid bloodshed, made a far-reaching proposal to Chamberlain and Salisbury; and what was the answer? You have read that document, and, although I cannot repeat the text of the document word for word, it amounts to this, that they are angry at ever having recognized us as an independent nation, and that, in spite of all the conventions that had been made, they will never acknowledge that this nation is independent.

Honorable sirs, I must speak out and say what I have in my mind. Psalm 83 speaks of the attacks of the Evil One on Christ's Kingdom, which must no longer exist. And now the same words come from

APPENDIX

Salisbury, for he too says, " This people must not exist," and God says, " This people shall exist." Who will win? Surely, the Lord. You now see the artifices which already at that time were being employed; also how our people was willing to surrender its rights, and that the Executive Raad went so far in yielding that we almost lost our country. It was not, however, their intention to obtain those rights: they wanted our country, which was no longer to be independent. All the rest would not have satisfied them.

Let us take note of this and observe the artful cunning which this matter implies. They wrote to the Orange Free State that they had nothing against that State, but only against this Republic. They thus hoped to separate the two Republics, whereas it has appeared from the documents that neither of the two was to continue to exist. See the deceit contained in this. For the documents show that, as early as 1896, after the Jameson Raid, this was decided upon; and yet they persisted in declaring that, if the Orange Free State would lay down her arms, that country would continue to exist. The Orange Free State then resolved not to lay down her arms, and together we began.

We were 40,000 men; but we had to guard against Kaffirs on every side, and the commandant of Mafeking had even written to us that certain Kaffir captains would assist him, and we know that, altogether, those numbered 30,000 fighting Kaffirs. That number of Kaffirs alone was almost as great as the number of our combatants, while in addition there ar-

APPENDIX

rived over 200,000 English troops. And that was what we had to fight against.

Honorable sirs, mark the dispositions of God. Is it not wonderful that 40,000 men should have to fight against hundreds of thousands and, in addition, against a nation of blacks, and that we should still be alive? Acknowledge God's hand in this. For it is remarkable that, where we come in touch with the enemy, we stand almost in proportion of ten to a hundred, and yet the Lord has hitherto spared your lives.

I will not take it upon myself to prophesy, but I will point out to you the guidance contained in God's Word. That is extraordinary. This war is a sign of the times. It amounts to this, that the Beast receives the power to persecute the Church and will succeed until the Lord says, " Hitherto, but no further." And why? Because the Church must be tried and purified, for there is much evil among us. That is why this war is an extraordinary one and a sign of the times.

And every one must be convinced that God's Word is evident in this. They say that the people must not exist, but God says, "It shall exist, but must be purified." It lies so clear and open in my mind that the day of Grace is not far off, that the Lord will show that He is the Ruler and that nothing shall happen without His consent. When He permits that punishment descend upon us, we must submit and humble ourselves, confess our sins and return unto the Lord. Then, when the whole nation stands in humility, seeing that it can do nothing, but only

APPENDIX

the Lord, then assuredly we shall at once obtain peace. But this humility does not yet lie deep enough in our hearts, and we must do our duty earnestly, as Peter says in I Peter v. verses 7 and 8: " Casting all your care upon Him; for He careth for you "; but in verse 8, however, stands: " Be sober, be vigilant; because your adversary the devil, as a roaring lion, walketh about, seeking whom he may devour." This is the point respecting which we must watch and, if we fall into unbelief, we shall bring ourselves into perdition.

I ask you, brothers, is that a right way of acting, as was done, that Kaffirs should be called up by letter, and that these, as at Derdepoort, should murder even women and children? The English declared that no Kaffirs were employed against us, but it is a fact that Montioa, with his Kaffirs, is in Mafeking and is being employed to fight against us. More than half of the people in Mafeking consist of Kaffirs, who fight against us.

Honorable sirs, you must not think that all who fight against us belong to the Beast; there are certainly hundreds of the children of God among them, who, however, are forced to act as they do from fear of the Beast; but God knows all hearts. We did not seek that the blood that lies on the ground should be shed, for we had surrendered all our rights; but when they wished to murder us, we could yield no more.

How did it go with Ahab? The mighty enemy came before the walls of the city, and the people had lost courage. Then came the prophet of God and said, " Fear not." Then God arose, and in that God

APPENDIX

we must place our trust, for He is still the same God. Let us, therefore, not live as though there were no God. He rules. In the beginning was the Word, and the Word was God, and the Word was made flesh and dwelt among us. Take note of history, which must serve us as an example. It is still the same God who led Israel from the wilderness and hardened Pharaoh's heart to the end, until at last all the first-born of the Egyptians died, whereupon Pharaoh allowed the Israelites to depart. It is still the same God who stills the winds and storms upon the sea, and his arm is not shortened.

Some ask: But does that point only to the Church in the two Republics? No. See the three youths in the fiery furnace. Did these rejoice alone? No, but God's people over the whole earth. Was it only for Daniel, what happened in the lions' den? No, but for all Christians over the whole earth. Thus the Lord often employs a small band, to whom He displays His miracles as an example for the whole Christian world.

Look at the blood that has been shed here on earth. What is the cause of it? We have wanted peace and our liberty, ever since 1836, and the Lord has given them to us, and shall the Lord ever lay His hand to a thing to withdraw it again? No, but let us humble ourselves before the Lord. There is no doubt that eventually the Lord will lead us to victory. The day of grace is not far off for His people. Let us not doubt, but remain true to God's word and fight in His name. When the water shall rise to our lips and we humble ourselves earnestly before the Lord,

APPENDIX

then shall the day of Grace have come. Let each then acknowledge that it is the Lord's hand that sets us free and none other, so that man may not glorify himself. The Lord only employs man to carry out His will.

I have laid my speech before you, and I hope that the Volksraad will not sit longer upon it than tomorrow at latest, as many of the members are burghers in the field or officers. This is not the time to discuss ordinary business, and let only those matters be discussed which I submit to you. Then I have appointed an Acting Commandant General, for I have lost my right hand, although I do not mean to imply that I have not more of such men. I have lost the late Commandant General, Messrs. Kock and Wolmarans, formerly members of the Executive Raad. The State Secretary also is a new appointment, and I alone remain of all the old members of the Executive Raad; nevertheless I find much help and support in the present members, and God too will support us; He will give us strength. Let us therefore fight in the name of the Lord to the end. For the Lord is our Commander-in-chief; He gives orders and He knows when to say, " Hitherto, but no further."

It is wonderful to see how unanimously the other Powers are on our side, and how all Europe prays for us with one voice; and shall the Lord reject those prayers? Oh no, trust in the Lord and let us persevere under Him, and He will perform miracles. Even if it goes so far that I am sent to St. Helena. For then the Lord will bring back the people and

APPENDIX

set it free; and the same judgment shall fall upon Babylon, the cause of all the blood that has been shed. We are fighting for the liberty that God gave us. I say again: If brothers from this Raad and private persons, who fought in the name of the Lord and believed, should fall by the sword, then—God's word says it—they are sacrificed on the altar to the greater glory of His name and of the glorious Church which is waiting to be revealed in this sign of the times. The Church must be tried and purified, and therefore I cannot believe that it will be permitted that we shall be destroyed by this extraordinary war. The war will last until the Lord says, "Hitherto, but no further." Keep to that and fight with me! I place myself in the hands of the Lord. Whatever He may have decided for me, I shall kiss the rod with which He strikes me, for I too am guilty.

Let each humble himself before the Lord. I have spoken.

I certify that the above is a true and faithful copy.

H. C. DE BRUIJN PRINCE.

APPENDIX G

CIRCULAR DISPATCH FROM STATE PRESIDENT KRUGER TO THE COMMANDANT GENERAL, ASSISTANT COMMANDANTS GENERAL AND OFFICERS

MACHADODORP, 20 *June* 1900.

FLINCH not and fall not into unbelief; for the time is at hand when God's people shall be tried in the fire. And the Beast shall have power to persecute Christ, and those who fall from faith and their Church will know Him not, nor shall they be allowed to enter the Kingdom of Heaven. But those who are true to the faith and fight in the name of the Lord, wearing their glorious crown of victory, they shall be received in the church of a thousand years and enter into glory everlasting. Brothers, I beseech you abandon not your faith, but hold fast by it, and so go forth and fight in the name of the Lord. Look well into your hearts. If Cowardice hiding there whispers to you, " Fly," you are blasphemers, for listening to the Tempter you deny your God, your faith is dead. Believe as you would be saved that nothing happens here below without the will of God. Victory and the sword are in His hands and He gives both to those who fight in His name. Is not our God the same God who led Israel under the power of His miracles out of the land of Pharaoh? Did He not lead them safely through the Red Sea?

APPENDIX

Did He not hide them in the thick cloud which was darkness to the enemy, but light to His children; for the column of cloud was built upon the word of the Lord, and if we trust Him as they trusted Him, it shall be our guide also through the darkness, leading our feet safely to the light. But he who ceases to believe the word of the Lord shall perish in the dark prison of his unbelief. Is not our God the same God who made water flow from a rock, refreshing all Israel? Was He not the Father of those three youths who chose death rather than deny Him? He is the same God who guarded Daniel in the lions' den. The lions harmed him not, but when the King commanded that Daniel's persecutors should be thrown into the den, the lions devoured them. Is He not the same God who walked upon the waves of the sea, and when He commanded Peter to come to Him, did not Peter, in his faith, obey? But, when the strength of his faith left him and he became afraid of the water, he sank, and the Lord took his hand and saved him and admonished him for his want of faith. Is He not our Lord to-day, the same Lord who, when the storm raged, laid silence upon the waves? Is He not the same Lord who laid His hands upon the lepers and they were healed? Is He not the same Lord our Saviour who said to His children: " Fear not, be strong of heart, I will not forsake you, for you believe in My Father and in Me." And He prophesied war and judgments of war that we might not be affrighted; for these things must be. Is not our Saviour the same Saviour who took upon Himself death and who rose the third day, re-

APPENDIX

maining for forty days longer among mankind although the world saw Him not? But they saw Him when He ascended into Heaven before their eyes, telling them to fight the good fight and He would come again. And this same God our Lord and Saviour, who has brought us here from our distant home, and given us our liberty, and performed miracles on our behalf, dare we doubt that He who commenced this work will finish it? No, what He has raised up He will not allow to fall to the ground. I repeat, He is the same God who helped Gideon and his three hundred warriors, who led and strengthened them in battle and in whose hand lies every victory. Dear brothers, dear brothers, I beseech you, lose not your faith. Depend each one upon himself and fight in the name of the Lord. I am told that every one wishes to go to his own district, in order to fight there. That will cause confusion, and the result will be bad or at least without value. Let everybody fight where he happens to be, under whatever officer he finds himself; be courageous, firm, obedient and loyal, for that means victory. Observe the reports of our Commission from Europe. Observe the proclamation of Lord Roberts in the Orange Free State, and you will see that it is nothing but a decoy-bird. According to Psalm 83 the enemies of old said that the people shall not exist in Christ's Kingdom. Salisbury and Chamberlain stand convicted by their own words: "They shall not exist." But the Lord says, "This people shall exist," and Christ is our Commander-in-chief, who leads us with His Word. Dear brothers, once more I pray you, let us not fall from

APPENDIX

faith, but follow His commands. He often leads His children through the barren desert, where it seems as if they could never get through. But if we will only trust Him, I assure you He will be our guide. He who trusts in God's guidance is under the protection of the King of Kings and safe through the darkest night. His word is truth everlasting. See Psalm 92.

Let this be read to all officers and burghers, for our present sufferings are nothing compared with everlasting glory. Let us obey our Saviour.

APPENDIX H

TELEGRAM FROM THE STATE PRESIDENT TO THE COMMANDANT GENERAL

MACHADODORP, 7 *July,* 1900.

Officers and burghers, place all your faith in the Lord. He is our highest General, who turns all hearts whithersoever He will, and He says " This danger is Mine," and the final victory is also in His hand. Now follow our fight from the beginning until to-day: see if the Lord does not still stand on our side with miracles, see how He has blessed our arms, so that as a rule so few men fall on our side and so many on the enemy's that, in spite of the great multitude of troops and guns opposed to us and the thousands of shots fired at us, the enemy's arms have not been blessed. Brothers, we must have become unbelievers and lost sight of God's authority, if we doubt that He is on our side. The enemy has until now flooded our country with his vastly superior forces, which we have not been able to repel on every side; he has not done so by force of arms, so that there is no doubt but that an end will come to this flood and that the victory will be ours. So do not flinch in the faith and do not be alarmed because some of us fall away. The Apostle Paul has already said this before me in 1 Timothy. But I look at the matter thus: Some of our burghers, who, overpowered

APPENDIX

by the enemy, were obliged to lay down their arms, I excuse, if they join again at the first opportunity, in order to go on fighting; but, when others go so far as to lay down their arms and take the oath and not return, then that, according to the Scriptures, is a falling away from God, though, to be sure, such men will say, even as the Beast, that they believe in the Lord. But the Lord says, " Show Me thy faith by thy works." And, when they then perform the works of the Beast, in order to betray their brothers, then they assume a faith which is dead. See Revelation xiv. 9, 10: " If any man worship the Beast and his image, the same shall drink of the wine of the wrath of God," and so on. Brothers, any of you who may perhaps have gone so far, turn back and humble yourselves before the Lord: He will forgive you; and then fight bravely in His name. Read this telegram to the officers and burghers at every opportunity.

APPENDIX I

Circular Dispatch from the State President to the Commandant General, Assistant Commandants General, and Officers

Machadodorp, 24 *July*, 1900.

I see by your report and many other reports that the spirit of unbelief walketh about like a roaring lion seeking to make our men lose heart. Brothers, you must understand, when you let the enemy pass you and you begin to hesitate whether you shall attack him or not, you drive the others who still remain behind, in the whole country, wherever they hear this, to hesitate and doubt in their turn; but, when you do your duty and attack him wherever he shows himself, then you inspire our men who have remained on the farms in the Republic and who hear this with courage to help in the fighting, though they and we too be but few. For the victory is not in the hand of the greater force, but in the hand of the Lord, and the Lord gives it to them who fight in His name, however few we may be. Listen to the words of the Lord: "When He forsakes the people, He blunts its sword and does not bless it;" and see, we are convinced of that, that the Lord has not blunted our sword, but, on the contrary, has blessed it wonderfully against the enemy. Wherever the enemy attacks us and fires thousands and thousands of shots

APPENDIX

at the few of us, our few shots hit many more of his men than do his of ours. Is it not the spirit of unbelief that hovers through the air, to bring us to doubt and thus to make us guilty before the Lord and to let us doubt that all is within the power of the Lord? And has it not yet become evident to you that, as I said in my former sentence, we live in a time when we are being tried by faith? He who stands firm in the Lord can say, with the Apostle Paul and with Timothy: " Be not discouraged when you see blasphemers, for some must fall away." And the Lord Jesus Himself says, in Matthew xxiv., that there shall be wars and rumors of wars: " But see that ye be not troubled, for all these things must come to pass, but the end is not yet." Remember 1 Peter v. verses 7 and 8: " Casting all your care upon Him; for He careth for you." And verse 8 says: " But be sober, be vigilant against the Devil, whom resist steadfast in the faith, for he walketh about like a raging lion seeking whom he may devour." Then see in Matthew, when the Evil Spirit took the Lord Jesus into a high mountain and said: " All these things will I give Thee, if Thou wilt fall down and worship me." Then the Lord Jesus said: " Get thee hence, Satan; thou shalt worship the Lord thy God, and Him only shalt thou serve." Brothers, mark me, that is the good fight, to win the crown. And he who cannot fight the good fight shall not win the crown. For then he falls and is joined with the evil spirit of the air, who flies with his great force over the earth. And so he receives the mark of the Beast in the forehead and will drink with the Beast

APPENDIX

of the wine of the wrath of God. Read Revelation xiv. verses 9, 10, 12, and 13. Note, in particular, verse 12, which says: "Here is the patience of the saints; here are they that keep the commandments of God and the faith of the Lord Jesus." No, no, my brothers: let him who has grown faint-hearted fly to the Lord and remain faithful to Him. And by your faithful acts you will convert thousands more to the faith, so that they may fight for the liberty which the Lord has given us. He who says that he believes in the faith of the Lord Jesus and His works and goes with the Evil Spirit, that man's faith is a dead faith, for the Lord says, "Show me thy faith by thy works." And see the promise of the Lord in Psalm 108, where He says that they who fight through God shall do so valiantly, and the Lord will deliver them and tread down their enemies. Keep courage therefore, you God-fearing band; the Lord will display His strength to your weakness. Also I will call your attention to the history of the American War of Independence, where they had to fight against hundreds and thousands, and, although their number was at length reduced to less than 2,000 men, yet they conquered and the Lord gave them back their liberty. Now each of you knows as I do how unjust and godless the war is, as we were willing to yield almost everything, if we could only keep our liberty and our independence. See Psalm 83, how the evil spirit of the air said that the valiant fighter named Israel must not exist, and the Lord says, "He shall exist." And see in our declaration, which we sent to Salisbury, that we only wished to

APPENDIX

keep our independence. Then the same spirit answered that this nation must not exist, or, to use his own words: " I will not permit your nation to continue to be a nation." Dear brothers, through God's Word I am sure of this, that the victory is ours. But let us remain true and fight in the name of the Lord, on the strength of His promise, and I request the officers often to read and re-read this notice to the burghers.

APPENDIX J

Proclamation by President Steyn against the Annexation of the Orange Free State

Whereas, in the month of October, 1899, an unjust war was forced upon the people of the Orange Free State and the South African Republic by Great Britain, and those two small Republics have, for more than eight months, maintained, and are still maintaining, the unequal contest against the mighty British Empire;

Whereas a certain proclamation of the 24th of May, 1900, alleging to be issued by Lord Roberts, Field Marshal and Commander-in-Chief of the British forces in South Africa, is published to-day and contains the statement that the Orange Free State has been conquered by Her Majesty's troops and is annexed to the British Empire, while the forces of the Orange Free State are still in the field and the Orange Free State has not been conquered, and the aforesaid proclamation is therefore opposed to international law;

Whereas it is well known that the British authorities themselves have recently admitted that the Orange Free State was excellently governed, and it therefore becomes an offence against civilization as well as an infraction of the fundamental rights

APPENDIX

of such a nation to rob it of its liberty under any pretex whatsoever;

And whereas I deem it desirable immediately to inform all whom it may concern that the aforesaid proclamation is not recognized by the Government and people of the Orange Free State:

Now I, Martinus Theunis Steyn, State President of the Orange Free State, after deliberation with the Executive Raad, do hereby proclaim, in the name of the independent people of the Orange Free State, that the aforesaid annexation is not recognized and is null, void and invalid.

Given under my hand at Reitz in the Orange Free State on the 11th day of the month of July 1900.

M. T. STEYN,
State President.

INDEX

INDEX

Aapjes River: First shot of Civil War fired at, 77

Accidents to President Kruger: Leg broken at Schoonkloof Farm, 1866, 98; thumb blown off by exploding rifle, 31; treatment of wound, 32, 33

Adendorff trek, 206; Kruger's opposition to the, and resulting loss of popularity, 207

Afrikander Party: Anti-British movement throughout South Africa—Sir A. Milner's declaration, 306; Cape Election of 1897, victory of the Afrikander Party, 269

Afrikanderdom, power of, must be broken: Sir A. Milner's policy, 258

Agriculture: President Kruger's advocacy of promotion of, 168

Alliance of the Orange Free State with the South African Republic—Negotiations for closer alliance: Failure of 1887 negotiations, 172, 173; Potchefstroom Conference, 1889—Terms of alliance concluded, 196; political alliance concluded at Bloemfontein after the Jameson Raid, 273, 275

Ancestry of President Kruger, 3 *note*

Annexation of South African Republic by Great Britain in 1877: Sir T. Shepstone's mission to Pretoria, etc., 112; annexation accomplished, 119; arrival of Sir T. Shepstone in Pretoria, 115; Burgers', President, mistakes used to justify annexation, 119, 120; Carnarvon, Lord, burghers' petition to, 129; commission appointed to discuss matters with Sir T. Shepstone, Mr. Kruger a member of, 112; confederation with British Dominions in South Africa proposed, Mr. Kruger's opposition, 113, 119; deputations to protest against annexation—Commission of delegates to Europe and America appointed to appeal for intercession of Foreign Powers, etc., 125, 130; failure to obtain intervention, 127; second deputation dispatched to England, Mr. Kruger a member of, 129; expenses, provisions for, 129; Frere, Sir Bartle, deputation's interview with, 130; Hicks-Beach's, Sir M., attitude—refusal to receive deputation, reply to memorial, etc., 131; mass meeting at Wonderfontein to report on results, 140; Executive Raad's protest, 121; "inherent" weakness argument, failure of Republic to subdue Secucuni used as pretext for annexation, 116; Secucuni's petition for peace—"Duumvirate" commission to investigate, Mr. Kruger's opposition, etc., 116, 117; Jooste's, Dr., letter on nature of opposition, Mr. Kruger's suggestion of a *plébiscite* rejected by British Government, 126; Jorissen's, Dr., opinion as to the annexation, 126; Kruger's, President, attitude, Sir T. Shepstone's misstatement, 126, 128; Kruger's, President, prevision of Sir T. Shepstone's intentions, President Burgers' disregard of President Kruger's warning, 119; *plébiscite* resolved on, 127; result of *plébiscite*, 131; Shepstone's, Sir T., opposition, 130; protest to be taken to England, President Burgers' proposal, 119; repeal

INDEX

of annexation, Boer endeavor to obtain—Arrest of Pretorius and Bok on charge of high treason, 142; Cape Colony, appeal to, 139; Cetewayo, alliance with, proposed—President Kruger's opposition, 137; Gladstone, failure of appeal to, 146; Kleinfontein meetings—Frere, Sir B., reception of, 138; Joubert's speech, 137; Kruger's, President, speech, 137; last petition to Governor of the Transvaal, 172; Orange Free State, support of request for repeal by, 139; petition to British Government proposed—Sir B. Frere's agreement to forward petition, 139; preparations for war, 146; proclamation of British Government offering self-government, Mr. Kruger's opinion on, 143; resort to force proposed, 137, 138; Kruger's, President, endeavors to maintain peace, 137; Kruger's, President, warning, 137; War of Independence (see that title); Wonderfontein meeting—Kruger's, Mr., warning to burghers, 137; popular resolution against annexation, 139; Sand River Convention, annexation a violation of, 119; Shepstone's, Sir T., declaration that he was authorized and prepared to annex the South African Republic—Mr. Kruger's protest, 119; South African War partly due to the annexation, 120; village population favoring annexation, 114; Volksraad, extraordinary meeting of, 116; Burgers', President, attempt to exclude burghers who refused to pay the Secucuni war tax, 112

Annexation of the neighboring colonies on outbreak of the war of 1899: Mr. Steyn's speech in the Volksraad, 382

Anstruther, Colonel: Death at battle of Bronkhorstspruit, 154

Appendices: A, 333; B, 368; C, 376; D, 381; E, 385; F, 391; G, 399; H, 403; I, 405; J, 409

April (Kaffir servant of President Kruger), literary attainments of, 15; Kaffir missionary's difficulties caused by, 16

Arbitration on points in dispute between Great Britain and the South African Republic—President Kruger's proposals: Bloemfontein conference, 273; Chamberlain's, Mr., rejection of proposals, 272; dispatch of 27th July, 1899, 279; foreign element other than Orange Free State, exclusion of—Condition laid down in alternative proposal to Mr. Chamberlain's joint commission proposal on the franchise question, 282, 283; Chamberlain's, Mr., dispatch of 30th August, 1899, and Mr. Reitz's reply, 284, 286; Reitz's, Mr., letter of 9th June, 1899, 275; reply, 277; ultimatum of 9th October, 1899, 304, 305

Armaments of the South African Republic—Purchase of arms and ammunition after the Jameson Raid: Defenceless condition of the Republic, 265; further purchases on discovery of Mr. Chamberlain's complicity in the Raid, 247, 248

Army of the South African Republic—Commandant General: Botha, Mr. Louis, appointment of, 309, 389; Joubert, General, death of, 309; Kruger's, Mr., address to, on his election as president (12 May, 1898), 360; war between Great Britain, South African Republic, and Orange Free State (see that title)

Balloon ascent by President Kruger in Paris, 132

Ballot: First election by ballot for the presidency of the South African Republic, 258

Bantjes, Jan: President Kruger's identity discovered to Mrs. Strigdom by, 85

Barkly West: Diamond-fields discovered in 1870, 105

Basuto War: First Basuto War—Orange Free State troubles

INDEX

with Chief Moshesh, 60; Kruger's, President, successful mediation, 61, 63

Basuto War of 1865: Council of war at Malap's Town, decision of, 96; Brand's, President, refusal to endorse—Withdrawal of South African Republic burghers, 97; Katskatsberg, fight at, number of cattle captured, etc., 97; Kruger, President, sent to assist the Orange Free Staters, 95; Malap Mountains, attack on, 96; surprise of Boer camp by Moshesh, 96

Bezuidenhout, Field Cornet: Distress laid on wagon of, 149; armed resistance to forced sale of wagon, beginning of the War of Independence, 149

Big game hunting: President Kruger's experience, 17-31

Birth of President Kruger, 3

Bismarck, Prince: Reception of Boer delegates in 1884, 177

Bloemfontein: Conference between Sir A. Milner and President Kruger at Bloemfontein, 31st May, 1899: Compliant attitude of the South African Republic and unyielding attitude of Sir A. Milner, 269-275; Kruger's, President, offers and demands, 273; Milner's, Sir A., demands, 273; conference between South African Republic and Orange Free State, with the object of bringing about a closer alliance, 259

Blue Mountains, Malapoch punitive expedition to: Efforts of British subjects to escape military service, 218, 219

Bodenstein, Field Cornet: Recapture of cattle raided by Moshesh from Orange Free Staters, 60

Bok, Mr. W. E.: Arrest on charge of high treason, 142; commission of delegates to England and America, secretary to, 129; secretary to Executive Raad, appointment as, 189; secretary to second deputation of protest against annexation, 129

Boshoff, President of Orange Free State: Boer representative in transfer of Orange Free State from British to Boers, 56; compact between Orange Free State and South African Republic, Boshoff's intended violation of, averted by President Kruger, 56-59; Pretorius's, M. W., claims on Orange Free State, alliance with Commandant General Schoeman to resist, 57; Kruger's, President, opinion on Boshoff's action, 58; retirement, 70

Botha, Mr. Louis: Appointment as commandant general, 309, 389

Boundary between Orange Free State and South African Republic: President Kruger appointed to represent South African Republic in deciding question, 85

Brand, President (Orange Free State): Basuto War, refusal to endorse resolution passed by council of war at Malap's Town, 97; Civil War, advice as to final settlement of, 92; death, 195; offensive and defensive alliance between Orange Free State and South African Republic, rejection of, 196; War of Independence, peace negotiations, 159; third proclamation, opposition to publication of, 160

British Government: Annexation of South African Republic in 1877, attitude as to—Lord Carnarvon's statements, 126; diamond-fields of South Africa, contention as to ownership (see diamond-fields); Jameson Raid enquiry, charge against the Government of withholding telegrams proving Mr. Chamberlain's complicity, 247, 248; Orange Free State, handing over to Pretorius on behalf of Boer emigrants, 56

British policy in South Africa: Chamberlain's, Mr., policy of provocation, 267-272; character

415

INDEX

of, lies, treachery, intrigue, 112, 222, 236, 242; annexation of 1877 a typical case, 126, 138

British South African Company (see Chartered Company)

Bronkhorstspruit, battle of, 153; treachery, charge of, against Boers, 154

Brown: Bewaarplaatsen allotment litigation, Chief Justice Kotzé disputing validity of Volksraad resolutions, 255; dismissal of the Chief Justice, 257; Kruger's, President, defence, 356

Bubonic plague conference: President Kruger's announcement in the Volksraad, 370

Buffalo-hunting: President Kruger's experiences, 24

Burger, Mr. S. W.: Adendorff trek, opposition to President Kruger, 207; appointment as vice-president of the South African Republic, nomination, 389; expiration of term of office, President Kruger's announcement in the Volksraad, 368

Burgers, President: Advanced views of, opposition of burghers, etc., 109; dissatisfaction among burghers with the president's government, 111; Kruger's, Mr., offer to secure re-election of, if Burgers would defend independence of the South African Republic, 115; new constitution drawn up by, 118; rejection by people, 119; railway from Lorenzo Marques to Pretoria, project of—journey to Europe to raise loan, 109; opposition of burghers, 110, 112, 118; religious views, liberality of—Mr. Kruger's disapproval, etc., 110; Secucuni war tax—attempt to exclude from Volksraad burghers who refused to pay tax, 112; Secucuni War of 1870 (see that title); Shepstone's, Sir T., mission to Pretoria—president's disregard of Mr. Kruger's warning, 119; state president, election as, 108; Kruger's, Mr., statement at inauguration of President Burgers, 108

Burgher rights: Conditions upon which a burgher of either Republic should receive burgher rights in the sister state, 260; Swaziland convention, terms of, 223

Caledon River encampment, 6

Calveyn, Chief: Rebellion in Marico district, 170

Cannibalism among Kaffirs: Evidences discovered by President Kruger during expedition to avenge Potgieter's murder, 43

Cape Colony: Annexation of the South African Republic; burghers' appeal to Cape Colony to support their request for repeal, 144; governor, appointment of Sir A. Milner, 258; Kaffir cattle raids—Boers' cattle impounded for war costs after recovery by owners, 4; Moshette—Montsioa War, volunteers from the colony, 170; slave emancipation prior to trek of 1835, 4; tariff war with the South African Republic (see tariff war)

Carnarvon, Lord (Secretary of State for the Colonies): British Government's attitude on the annexation question, statements as to, 126; petition against annexation of South African Republic addressed to, 129

Celliers, Sarel: Defeat of Matabele attack on Vechtkop Laager, 8

Cetewayo's rebellion (see Zulu War of 1879)

Chamberlain, Mr. J.: Arbitration—rejection of South African Republic proposals, 279; dispatches with the object of embittering the British people against the Republic, alleged, 248; franchise question, stages of (see titles franchise question and franchise law); home rule for Johannesburg proposed, 245; publication of dispatch in the London press before it had reached the Government of the South African

INDEX

Republic, 245; invitation to President Kruger to come to England to confer on Transvaal matters—discussion of Article 4 of the London Convention precluded, 245, 249; Kruger's, President, counter conditions, 246; Jameson Raid—Chamberlain's, Mr., gratitude to the South African Republic for handing over the culprits to the British Government, 242; complicity, charge of, 228, 248; inquiry—charge against the British Government of withholding telegrams proving Mr. Chamberlain's complicity, 247; telegrams cited in evidence of the charge, 249; London Convention of 1884—violation of, by the Government of the Republic, alleged, 279; "Second Volksraad of no practical use" contention, 199; suzerainty question—contention that the Convention of 1881 held good, 176, 279; tariff war between Cape Colony and the South African Republic—Mr. Chamberlain's ultimatum to the Republic on condition that Cape Colony bore half the cost of a war, 228; war between Great Britain, South African Republic and Orange Free State—reply to Mr. Kruger's application for peace negotiations, President Kruger's comments, 392

Chartered Company: Formation of, 194; shares given to influential people in England, 193; strategic positions necessary for the Jameson Raid, negotiations for extension of territory, 249; Swaziland Convention binding South African Republic to assist the company, 223

Chastisement and punishment, distinction between, 59

Chelmsford, Lord: Commander-in-chief in Zulu War of 1879, 133; Ulundi, victory at, 134

Chief Justice disputing validity of resolutions of the Volksraad (see Kotzé)

Chief Justice and Judges of the Supreme Court and State Attorney: President Kruger's address to, on his election as president (12 May, 1898), 350

Childhood of President Kruger, 4; cattle-herding during the trek of 1835, 5

Children: Boer custom of giving two animals to each child as his special property, 5; education of Boer children during Great Trek, 11; education, religion, etc.—President Kruger's address on his election as president (12 May, 1898), 214, 333; Kruger's, President, children by second wife, 14

Christelijk-Gereformeerde Church: Kruger's, President, membership, 75; political disabilities attaching to membership, 75; removal of disabilities, 76; union of churches in 1881 not joined by, 207

Christiania, village of: Remnant of diamond territory secured by South African Republic, 107

Churches of South African Republic: *Dopper* or Canting Church, Kruger's, President, membership in, 75; political disabilities attaching to membership in, 75; removal of disabilities, 76; State Church: Intention of substituting *Dopper* for *Hervormde* as State Church attributed to Mr. Kruger by Schoeman, 78; union between *Hervormde* and *Nederduitsch-Gereformeerde* Church in 1881, 207; abandonment of union—church property dispute, 208; conference in 1891; President Kruger's attempt to compose quarrel, 208, 209; Dopper Church remaining outside the union, 207

Civil War of 1861–1864: Commandant General Schoeman's violation of the constitution —armed opposition to Grobler's presidency, etc., 71; Aapjes River, first shot fired at, 77; abolition of Volksraad and conferring of legislative power on

27   417

INDEX

Executive Raad—General Schoeman's proposal, 71; boundary question—President Kruger appointed to represent the South African Republic, 85; council of war in Pretoria, 82, 85; fighting north of Potchefstroom—President Kruger's action, flight of General Schoeman, 80; fines collected by President Kruger, 82; fresh complications, President Kruger again called on to interpose, 74; Heidelberg district meeting, 82; Kruger's, President, amusing experience on the way to the meeting, 83-86; Jeppe, Steyn's demand for surrender of, 72; joint commission meeting near Potchefstroom, failure to secure peace, 77, 79; Kruger's, President, action previous to outbreak of hostilities, 69, 73, 74; Kruger's, President, refusal to pursue the enemy after Zwartkopje, 89; Kruger's and Fourie's, Messrs., mission to the Orange Free State to carry out terms of peace conference, 91; opposition commission nominated to see that the Government adhered strictly to the peace conference decisions, 91; peace conference after Zwartkopje, constitution and decisions of, 90, 91; Potchefstroom, fighting at—artillery duel, 79; Kruger's, President, stratagem to obtain release of prisoners taken, etc., 86, 87; Pretoria meeting—resolution to carry out Volksraad decision, 73, 74; second joint commission, President Kruger's proposals carried, etc., 81, 82; settlement—amnesty—President Kruger's proposal agreed to by the Volksraad, 90; Brand's, President, advice, 91; special court appointed by Volksraad to settle matters in dispute, 73, 74; court summoned—decision in case of Andries du Toit, 82; Schoeman's, Commandant General, action, 72, 74; second joint commission, decisions of, 81; Volksraad's decision—deposition of Commandant General Schoeman, etc., 73, 74; State Church—President Kruger charged with intention to compel substitution of *Dopper* for *Hervormde* Church as State Church—report spread by Schoeman, 78; Kruger's, President, statement to Jan Kock, 78, 79; Steyn, Johannes, appointment of, by Schoeman as commandant general, 71; Zwartkopje—defeat of Schoeman's party, 88, 89

Clergy: President Kruger's address to, on his election as president (12 May, 1898), 361

Closing the drifts (see Tariff War)

Colesberg: Swaziland Convention, conference between President Kruger and Sir H. Loch, 224

Cologne: President Kruger's reception in 1900, 325

Colonizing expedition of 1845, President Kruger's share in, etc., 13, 14

Commandant General of the South African Republic: Botha, Mr. Louis, appointment of, 309, 389; Joubert, General Piet, election of, 151; re-election in 1884, 189; Kruger, election of, 82; re-election after the Civil War, 92; Pretorius, M. W., appointment, 56

Communication of the South African Republic and Orange Free State with the outer world: Boer attempt to acquire a harbor at Durban, 9; British annexation of Sambaanland and Umbigesaland, Transvaal's last outlet to the sea cut off by, 224

Company promoting on valueless property: Preventive measures, President Kruger's speech in the Volksraad (12 May, 1898), 342

Confederation of South Africa under the British flag: Messrs. Joubert and Kruger deputed to urge Cape Parliament to opposition, 158

Constitution of the South African Republic: Assimilation of the

418

INDEX

constitution of the Orange Free State to that of the South African Republic, 370; new constitution drawn up by President Burgers, 118; rejection by the people, 118; revision of—President Kruger's promise of, 256; Kotzé, Chief Justice, opposition to President Kruger's policy—dismissed from chief justiceship, 257; Kruger's, President, defence of his action in regard to Chief Justice Kotzé, 406; Schoeman's, Commandant General, violation of (see Civil War)

Convention of 1881 (see Pretoria Convention)

Convention of 1884 (see London Convention)

Coolies: Residing only in quarters set apart for them, Mr. Kruger's announcement in the Volksraad, 373

Criticism, Right of: Kotzé, Chief Justice, adopting the "Devil's Principle"—Dismissed from office, 257 and *note*; Kruger's, President, defence, 359; law requiring judicial functionaries not to assume the right of *toetsing* the validity of the laws, 257

Cronjé, General Piet: Bezuidenhout's wagon, forced sale of—Cronjé's armed resistance to sale, 149; Jameson's surrender, 237; Massouw's entrenchments, storming of, 179; triumvirate's proclamation, printing of—Cronjé's mission to Potchefstroom, 151, 152

Customs duties dispute (see Tariff War)

Customs union for South Africa: President Kruger's refusal to consider, 203

David, Kaffir missionary to Kaffirs, 16

Delagoa Bay: President Kruger's detention at the Portuguese governor's house on the way to Europe in 1900, 318

Delagoa Bay Railway: Burgers's, President, project, 109; opposition of burghers, 109, 113; concession granted to private persons—foundation of Netherlands South African Railway Company, 177; Kruger's, President, defence of concession, 178; petitions against concession, 178; Volksraad's agreement to concession, 179; grant voted by the Volksraad to enable burghers to inspect the whole railway, 225; loan—failure of attempt to raise loan in Holland, 177; opening, 225; Portuguese Government, conditions imposed by, 203, 204; Portuguese offer to build, 177

Delvers Committee established, 182

Derby, Lord: London Convention negotiations, 175, 176; dispatch enclosing draft of the London Convention, 250

Diamond-fields in South African Republic territory: Depression among the poorer classes—Relief measures, etc., President Kruger's speech in the Volksraad (12 May, 1898), 340

Discovery in 1870, 105

Dispute as to ownership of diamond territory: Arbitration agreed to by President Pretorius, President Kruger's disapproval, 106; British Government contention that the diamond territory belonged to native chiefs Montsioa and Gasibone, 106; Christiania, village of, retained by South African Republic, 107; commission appointed by South African Republic to attend discussions of Arbitration Court—protest against Governor Keate's judgment and Pretorius's action, 107; Keate's, Governor, decision in favor of chiefs, 106; Mobilo's, Chief, evidence, 106; Pretorius's, President, resignation due to result of arbitration, 107; Kruger's, President, reception by English miners, 105

Dikketon, value of, 5

Dingaan's horde: Attack on Boer settlers in Natal, 9

INDEX

Dinizulu, son of Cetewayo: Land granted to Boers in return for assistance against Usibepu, 184

Doornkop: Surrender of Dr. Jameson to Commandant Cronjé, 237

Dopper or Canting Church: Derivation and meaning of *dopper*, 75, 76; foundation in 1859, 75; Kruger, President, a member, 75; political disabilities attaching to membership, 75; removal of disabilities, 76; tenets of, etc., 76; union of churches in 1881, Dopper Church remaining outside, 207

Dordrecht, Holland: President Kruger's visit, 328

Drifts, closing of (see Tariff War)

Durban: Boer attempt to acquire harbor, 9

Dutch language as the state language: Educational medium—President Kruger's principle, 214, *note;* Kruger's, President, address to the children on his election as president (12 May, 1898), 214, 215, 364, *note;* Swaziland convention, terms of, 222

Dynamite explosion at Johannesburg, 19 February, 1896, 244

Dynamite monopoly: Abolition of —suggestions in report of the Industrial Commission, 253; reduction in price of dynamite—President Kruger's speech (12 May, 1898), 386

Edgar case: Mr. Chamberlain's misrepresentations, 267

Education: Direction of education, successive appointment of Dr. du Toit and Professor Mansvelt, 215, 216, *note;* grants to schools in which education was not given in Dutch—law of 1892, 217, *note;* Great Trek of 1836, means taken for education of children, 11, 12; Kruger's, President, education, extent and nature of, 11, 12; Kruger's, President, views on, 168; languages, study of, President Kruger's belief in the Dutch language as the one and only educational medium, 215, *note,* 217, *note;* law of 1882, faulty execution of, 215, *note;* Paris Exhibition of 1900, distinctions won by the South African Republic at, 217, *note;* reform, President Kruger's misgivings as to grants, qualification of teachers and higher education of women, 216, *note;* religious instruction—education law of 1874, defects of, 215, *note;* Kruger's, President, speech on installation as president (12 May, 1898), 214, 366, *note;* Uitlanders, education of— erection of schools at the cost of the state, 217, *note*

Eloff, Field Cornet Sarel: Capture by Viljoen at Potchefstroom, 86; escape, 86; commandeering burghers of the Zwartruggen district, 88

Eloff, Lieutenant, taken prisoner by Dr. Jameson, 237

Elephant hunting: President Kruger's experiences, 21; race with an elephant, 27

England: Invitation from Mr. Chamberlain to visit England to confer on Transvaal matters— discussion of Article 4 of the London Convention precluded, 245, 249; Kruger's, President, counter conditions, 246; Kruger's, President, visits—first visit in 1877, 125; second visit, 129-131; third visit as member of 1884 deputation, 174; relations with the South African Republic (see titles British Government, British policy, intervention, etc.)

English lord and President Kruger, anecdote of, 6, *note*

English population of the South African Republic: Educational advantages at the cost of the state, 217, *note*

Enslin: Death by treachery at Zwartkopje, 89

Envoy extraordinary of the South African Republic in Europe: Appointment of Dr. Leyds, 264

INDEX

Europe: Delegation of President Kruger during the war of 1899-1902—departure from Pretoria, 316; Holland's, Queen of, offer of a warship, 319; journey to Europe, 320; proclamation by the Executive Raad, 316

Explosion of dynamite at Johannesburg, 19 February, 1896, 244

Farrar, Mr.: Jameson Raid, signature of Johannesburg letter of appeal, 231; sentence for conspiracy at Johannesburg and complicity in the Jameson Raid, 244

Father of President Kruger, 3; Portuguese frontier delimitation commissioner in 1844, 13

Federal Council, constitution of, for the two Republics, 262

Federation of South Africa under the British flag: Messrs. Joubert and Kruger deputed to urge Cape Parliament to opposition, 149, 158, 162

Fick, Chief Commandant of Orange Free State: Basuto war—attacks on Malap Mountains and Katskatsberg, 96; Kruger's, President, mission to Moshesh—General Fick serving as escort, 61

Field Cornet, appointment of President Kruger as, 37

Financial condition of the South African Republic in 1885, 179; gold-fields discovery, effect of, 180

Fischer, Mr. Abraham: Jameson Raid, disposal of culprits—advice to the commandants, 241; state secretary of the South African Republic—refusal of appointment, 264; war of 1899-1902, intervention of foreign powers—member of deputation to Europe, 309

Floods in the South African Republic in 1893, 216

Foreign relations of the South African Republic: Kruger's, President, speech in the Volksraad, 369; (see also titles intervention and London Convention)

Foreigners (see Uitlanders)

Forts in Chartered Company's territory built by Mr. Rhodes, 194

Foster, Mr. B.: Connection with Adendorff trek, 206

Foster, murder of, by Edgar in 1898, 267

Fouché, Field Cornet D.: Officer who prevented Dr. Jameson from turning the Boer position near Krugersdorp, 237

Fourie: Mission to the Orange Free State, 91; peace conference after Zwartkopje—delegate for Schoeman's party, 90

France: Kruger's, President, visit in 1877—failure to obtain intervention of, 125; president's reception of Boer delegates in 1884, 177; press *exposé* of English methods of warfare—President Kruger's thanks, 325; welcome to President Kruger on his journey through France in 1900, 321-325

Franchise question: Uitlanders' grievances—Bloemfontein Conference (see that title); British Government decision to formulate their own proposals for a final settlement (25 September, 1899), 291; Reitz's, Mr., inquiry as to the promised dispatch, and Mr. Chamberlain's reply, 292; Steyn's, Mr., President, correspondence with Sir A. Milner, 294, 303; British subjects refusing to take the field with the burghers in 1884—President Kruger on, 377; Chamberlain's, Mr., Highbury speech—"The sands are running down in the glass," 284; commission, appointment of, by the British Government—Mr. Chamberlain's dispatch (30 August, 1899), 284; Reitz's, Mr., reply, 286; conference between President Kruger and Sir A. Milner—Mr. Chamberlain's proposal (30 August, 1899), 285, 286; Reitz's, Mr., reply, 288; Draft Law of 1899, provisions of, 277; failure of negotiations, causes of—President Steyn's correspondence

421

INDEX

with Sir A. Milner, 298; goldfields representation in the Volksraad, proposed increase in, 281; Great Britain's demands—"Devilish fraud"—President Kruger's protest against British pharisaical hypocrisy, 395; Kruger's, President, speech in the Volksraad, 388; inadequacy of reforms—further demands by the Uitlanders' Council and the South African League, 284; intervention by Great Britain (see that title); joint commission for revision of law of 1899—Mr. Chamberlain's proposal (1 August, 1899), 279; acceptance by Government of South African Republic (2 September, 1899), 289; alternative proposal by Government of South Africa, 281, 283, 290; Chamberlain's, Mr., reply of 30th August—Mr. Chamberlain's contention that he had accepted proposal, 285, 286; lapsing of proposal—Mr. Reitz's letter of 2d September, 286; Reitz's, Mr., reply of 12th August, 280; London Convention, violation of—charge against Mr. Chamberlain, 279; Smuts's, Mr., interviews with Mr. Greene, 280, 283; withdrawal of proposal by the British Government—Greene's, Mr., letter and Mr. Reitz's reply, 289; Steyn's, President, dispatch of 27th September, 294; Kruger's, President, proposals—effect on plans of Mr. Chamberlain and Sir A. Milner, 270; Phillips's, Mr., statement that "We do not care a fig for the franchise," 232; Second Volksraad, institution of, 197; burghers' approval, 198; Kruger's, President, responsibility, 197, 199; opposition to, 198; powers of Second Volksraad, 199; Uitlanders' dissatisfaction, 199; vote for, etc., conditions of obtaining, 197, 198; seven years' franchise—retrospective franchise—Afrikander leaders' proposal, 278; Smuts's, Mr., interview with Mr. Greene on 15th August, 1899, 280, 283; yielded by the Republic—President Kruger's speech in the Volksraad, 388; Steyn's, President, mediation—correspondence between Sir A. Milner and President Steyn, 293–303; negotiations—removal of British troops from borders of South African Republic stipulated for, 300; Uitlanders' council, dissatisfaction of, 279; Volksraad—new members—permission to speak their own language, Mr. Greene's letter of 12th September, 1899, and Mr. Reitz's reply, 289, 291; opening—announcement in the president's speech, 369; war of 1899–1902 forced on the Republic, franchise question used as a pretext, 269, 270, 272

Fraser, Mr., acting British agent in Pretoria: Refusal to receive petition on Uitlander grievances, 271

Frere, Sir Bartle: Annexation of 1877—deputation of protest against annexation, interview with Sir B. Frere, 130; Kleinfontein meetings—dishonest conduct of Sir B. Frere in the matter of the burghers' petition against annexation, 138, 145; reception at, 157; open letter to Messrs. Kruger and Joubert distributed among burghers, 138; arrival in Cape Town, 118; Kruger and Joubert, Messrs., invitation to, during their mission to Cape Town, 145; invitation refused, 145; Zulu War of 1879—request to President Kruger to accompany expedition, 133; Kruger's, President, refusal, 133; frontier commission—appointment, etc., 173; Massouw declared independent, 179

Gangrene, Boer remedy for, 34

Gasibone, Chief: Diamond-fields discovered in 1870; British Government contention that terri-

INDEX

tory belonged to Montsioa and Gasibone, 105; expedition against—President Kruger assistant general—success of expedition, etc., 64-66

Gelderland: Dutch warship in which President Kruger journeyed to Europe, 319

German emperor unable to receive President Kruger owing to a hunting engagement, 326

Germany: Enthusiastic reception of President Kruger, 325, 326; Kruger's, President, visit in 1877; failure to obtain intervention, 127; reception of Boer delegates in 1884, 177; veterinary congress at Baden-Baden—South African Republic representative, President Kruger's announcement, 371

Gold-fields of the South African Republic: *Bewaarplaatsen,* change in method of allotment of—Chief Justice of the Supreme Court challenging validity of the resolutions of the Volksraad, 254; dismissal of the Chief Justice, 257; Kruger's, President, defence, 356; company promoting of valueless property—precautionary measures, President Kruger's speech in the Volksraad (12th May, 1898), 342; delvers committee established, 182; depression among the poorer classes, relief measures; warning to the gold-field banks, etc.—President Kruger's speech delivered at his inauguration as president (12th May, 1898), 340; discovery of, 179, 180; beneficial results, 180; South African War largely due to discovery, 120, 180; Johannesburg, origin of, 182; population of the Witwatersrand, character of, 181; progress of mining industry; value of gold extracted, etc., President Kruger's announcement in the Volksraad, 373; representation in the Volksraad—increased representation proposed, 281; Rhodes's, Mr., determination to secure, 195; war of 1899-1902—gold-fields the first and principal cause of, 180

Goshenland: Foundation of, 170; incorporation with Cape Colony due to Mr. Rhodes, 192

Government of the South African Republic: Charge of secret dealing with Rooigronders, 171; government resuming office, appointment of triumvirate, etc., 151; self-government offered by British Government—President Kruger's definition of, 143; war of 1899-1902—transfer of the Government from Pretoria—Machadodorp, 312; Nelspruit, 314

Great Britain: Relations with the South African Republic (see titles British Government, British policy, intervention, etc.)

Great Trek of 1836, 6; education of children during the trek, 11, 12; losses sustained by Boers, 11; Moselikatse's attack on Vaal and Rhenoster encampments, 7; resolutions enacted by emigrants —treatment of natives, etc., 6

Greene, Mr. Conyngham: Withdrawal from Pretoria on declaration of war, 306

Gregorowski, Judge: Trial of the Johannesburg reformers by, 243

Griqualand, West: Diamond-fields discovered at Kimberley, 105

Grobler, Johannes: Acting President of the South African Republic during absence of President Pretorius, 70

Grobler: Peace conference after Zwartkopje—government delegate, 90

Grobler, Piet: Consul to Lobengula, appointment as, 190; murder by Khama's Kaffirs, 191; pension paid to widow, 192

Hague, President Kruger at the, 326, 327

Hammond, Mr. J. Hays: Jameson Raid, signature of Johannesburg letter of appeal, 231; sentence for conspiracy at Johannesburg

423

INDEX

and complicity in the Jameson Raid, 244

Harris, Dr. Rutherford: Negotiations on behalf of Mr. Rhodes for extension of chartered company's territory, 229

Heidelberg: Franchise reform proposals—President Kruger's meeting, 270; gold-fields, discovery of, 179, 180; meeting during Civil War—President Kruger's meeting with the young Boer, who announced that Kruger had better not come, 83

Herholdt and Hofmeyer, Messrs.: Franchise law simplification, mission to Pretoria, 278

Hervormde Church: Resolution of council, conferring equal rights on burghers of all evangelical churches, 76; state church of the South African Republic, 74; substitution of Dopper Church as state church—intention attributed to President Kruger by Schoeman, 78; union with Nederduitsch-Gereformeerde Church in 1881, 207; abandonment of union—property dispute, 208; conference of 1891—President Kruger's failure to compose quarrel, 208, 209

Hicks-Beach, Sir M., and the Boer deputation of protest against annexation: Memorial, reply to, 130; refusal to receive deputation, 130

Hilversum, President Kruger at, 327, 328

Hofmeyer, Jan: Swaziland convention, work in securing first convention, 205

Hofmeyer and Herholdt, Messrs.: Franchise law simplification, mission to Pretoria, 278

Hogge, Major W. S. (H. M. Special Commissioner): Letter to Commandant General Pretorius requesting him to take over Orange Free State on behalf of the Boer emigrants, 55

Holland: Boer delegates of 1884, reception of, 177; Kruger's, President, visit in 1877—failure to obtain intervention, 125; Kruger's, President, life in, 326-328; Queen of Holland and President Kruger—offer of warships for journey to Europe, 319; reception of President Kruger, 326

Home rule for Johannesburg: Chamberlain's, Mr. J., proposal, 245; publication of the dispatch in the London press before it reached the Government of the South African Republic—protest, 245

Hudson: Dispute with President Kruger, as to name of South African Republic, 164

Hunting experiences of President Kruger, 17-34

Illness of President Kruger, 327

Immigration restriction: President Kruger's views on, 168

Importation of goods: Registration fees for goods imported free — provisional agreement with the Orange Free State—President Kruger's announcement in the Volksraad, 370

Independence of the South African Republic: Paarde Kraal declaration, 151; Salisbury's, Lord, reply to Boer demand during war of 1899-1902, 383, 392, 393

Independence, War of (1880-1881): Ammunition, scarcity of, among Boers, 153; ammunition taken from the English, 162; armistice, English request for, 157; Boer generals serving in, 153; Boer losses, English exaggeration of, 162; Boer plan of operations, 152; Bronkhorstspruit, battle of, 153; treachery, charge of, against Boers, 154; Heidelberg, occupation of, 152; Kaffirs called out against Boers, 153; Kruger's, President, mission to Magato's Kaffirs, 155; Majuba Hill, battle of, 155; number of Boer forces, 152; number of men engaged on either side, 162; Paarde Kraal mass-meeting—meeting forbidden, participants proclaimed

INDEX

rebels, 151; resolutions, 151; peace negotiations—Boer and British representatives, 158; British Colonial Secretary's instructions, 158; Jorissen's, Dr., third proclamation drawn up by President Kruger's order, 160; Brand's, President, opposition to publication, 160; Pretoria Convention (see that title); provisional protocol, signature of, by Messrs. Kruger and Joubert, 162; terms of, 162; Wood's, Sir E., attempt to evade signature, 160; Royal Commission—appointment and constitution, 162, 163; difficulties in composition of, 158, 159; South African Republic deprived of power of interference in native quarrels—Swaziland taken from South African Republic, 201; Potchefstroom — first shot fired, 152; preparations for war, 146; taxes, refusal to pay—armed resistance to forced sale of Bezuidenhout's wagon, 149; territory claimed by Great Britain, 159, 163, 164

Independence, War of, in the Free State: A. W. J. Pretorius's command, 37 *note*

Industrial Commission, appointment of, 252; Government measures for carrying out suggestions, 254; report, 253

Industrial resources, development of: President Kruger's views, 168

Intervention by Great Britain in the internal affairs of the Republic: Cape ministry's note—intervention unnecessary, 278, 279; condition laid down in alternative proposal to Mr. J. Chamberlain's joint commission proposal on the franchise question, 281, 284; Chamberlain's, Mr., dispatch of 30th August, 1899, and Mr. Reitz's reply, 285-288; independence of the Republic, endangered by suzerainty claim—Mr. Reitz's letter of 15th September, 1899, 289, 290; Milner's, Sir A., telegram of 31st August, 1899, urging prompt and decided action, 286; need for intervention—Sir A. Milner's dispatch to Mr. J. Chamberlain, 272; Steyn's, President, dispatch of 27th September, 1899, 294; ultimatum of 9th October, 1899—final protest by the Republic, 304, 305; violation of London Convention of 1884—charge against Mr. Chamberlain, 279

Intervention of Foreign Powers: Annexation of 1877—commission of delegates empowered to appeal for, 122; failure to obtain intervention, 126; Kruger, President, a member of commission, 122, 125; war of 1899-1902—deputation to Europe, 309

Isandlhwana, British defeat by Zulus at, 134

Jameson, Dr.: Matabele, expedition against, 195; raid (see Jameson Raid)

Jameson Raid: Advance of the raiders—Dr. Jameson ignoring all requests to withdraw, 235, 236; Chamberlain, Mr. J., charge of complicity against, 228, 230, 248, 249; committee of inquiry—charge against the British Government of withholding telegrams proving Mr. Chamberlain's guilt, 230; telegrams cited in evidence of the charge, 229, 230; deputation of reformers to Pretoria demanding permission for Dr. Jameson to enter Johannesburg, 236; excitement among the burghers—desire to shoot down the Johannesburg "den with all the rebels in it," 240; ignorance of the Transvaal authorities, 232; Johannesburg, disturbed condition of—arms and ammunition, concealment of, in the Simmer and Jack mine, 228; committee to maintain order, appointment of, 236; deputations to President Kruger in support of the Government, 235; flight of thousands of in-

425

INDEX

habitants, 234; mediation—Sir H. Robinson's offer, 236, 239; Phillips's, Mr. Lionel, attack on the Government, 231; police confined to barracks in order to avoid a collision, 234; proclamations by President Kruger stating that the conspirators constituted only a small part of the population, 235, 243; reformers' letter of appeal—undated letter handed to Dr. Jameson to serve as an excuse for invasion, 231; unconditional surrender—President Kruger's terms, 239, 241, 242; volunteer corps organized by the Reform Committee, 234; work of the Transvaal National Union in raising and maintaining a ferment at Johannesburg, 228; Kruger, President—charge of keeping a horse saddled ready for flight, 234 *note*; Krugersdorp engagement, 237; proclamation by Sir H. Robinson calling upon Dr. Jameson and his force to withdraw across the frontier, 236; punishment of culprits—Kruger's, President, proposal to hand over Jameson and his men to the British Government, 241; Chamberlain's, Mr. J., gratitude, 242; objections by the commandants, 241; penalties inflicted, 242; reform leaders at Johannesburg—arrest and trial for conspiracy, 242, 243; Rhodes, Colonel, sent to Johannesburg to represent Mr. Rhodes, 230; Rhodes's, Mr., plans and intrigues, 228; strategic positions on the frontier—negotiations for extension of Chartered Company's territory, 229

Jeppe (only printer in the South African Republic): Steyn's demand for surrender of, 72, 73

Johannesburg: Dynamite explosion of 19th February, 1896, 244; franchise reform, President Kruger's proposals, 270; home rule—Mr. Chamberlain's proposal, 245; publication of the dispatch in the London press before it reached the Government of the South African Republic—protest, 245; Jameson Raid (see that title); Jorissen, Dr., appointed as special judge, 197; Kruger's, President, visit in 1887, 182; Kruger's, President, visit in 1888, 196; insult to President Kruger, 199; riot before house where President Kruger was staying—flag of the Republic hauled down, 200; Loch's, Sir H., proposed visit, abandonment of, on President Kruger's advice, 221; municipality—President Kruger's promise of, 196, 243; origin of, 182; railways (see railways); South African League—branch at Johannesburg, formation of, 266, 267; meeting to protest against arrests for contravention of the Pass Law—hostile demonstration, 267; petitions to the Queen on Uitlander grievances, 270, 271

Jones, Policeman: Action in shooting Edgar in attempting to arrest him for murder—Mr. Chamberlain's misrepresentations, 268

Jooste's, Dr., letter in the *Zuid Afrikaan*: Annexation opposed only by a handful of irreconcilables, 126; Kruger's, President, reply—suggestion of a *plébiscite* rejected by British Government, 126

Jorissen, Dr.: Annexation of the South African Republic, 1877—attitude as to, 126; commission appointed to discuss affairs with Sir T. Shepstone, member of, 116; commission of delegates to Europe and America, member of, 122, 125; Burgers's, President, discovery of a useful servant to the state, 109; Burgers, President, supported by, 117; dismissal from state attorneyship—President Kruger's protest, 174; Independence, War of, peace negotiations of 1881—Boer representative, 158; third proclamation drawn up at President Kruger's request, 160;

INDEX

Brand's, President, opposition, 160; special judge for Johannesburg—appointment, 197

Joubert, Christian: Church union of 1881, leader of seceders from, 207

Joubert, Commandant Frans: Battle of Bronkhorstspruit, Joubert's success, 154

Joubert, Commandant: Secucuni war, retreat due to lack of reinforcements, 111

Joubert, General: Adendorff trek—opposition to President Kruger, 206; burgher volunteers in the Moshette-Montsioa war—Joubert sent to recall, 170; commandant general, election as, 151; re-election in 1884, 179; commissioners for the western border, appointment of, 171; death of, 309, 382; gold-fields discovery, reception of news, 180; Independence, War of—Boer losses, extent of, 162; provisional peace protocol, signature of, 162; Massouw, expedition against, 179; military capacity of, 154, 155; peace, maintenance of, in 1879—failure of mission to Natal, 136, 137; support of President Kruger, 135, 136; presidency of South African Republic—candidature in 1882, 167; candidature in 1888, 189; candidature in 1893, 209; second deputation of protest against annexation, member of, 129; Shepstone's, Sir T., attack on, 130; triumvirate of 1880, member of, 151

Judges of the Supreme Court: Kruger's, President, address on his election as president (12th May, 1898), 350

Judicial functionaries and criticism: Law requiring a promise not to assume the right of *toetsing* the validity of the laws, 257

Kaffir chiefs, expeditions against (see names of chiefs)

Kaffirs (see native question)

Kampen: President Kruger's visit, 328

Keate, Governor of Natal: Decision as arbitrator in the diamond-fields dispute, 106

Khama: Piet Grobler murdered by Khama's Kaffirs, 191; pension paid to Grobler's widow, 192

Kimberley: Diamond-fields discovered in 1870, 105; rebellion of mining population, 182

Klerksdorp gold-fields, discovery of, 181

Klopper, Christian: President of the South A´rican Republic Volksraad, 74

Koek, Jan: Joint commission at Potchefstroom—state church question, 78

Korannas (see Massomo, Chief)

Kosi Bay: Cession to Transvaal by Swaziland Agreement, 204

Kotzé, Chief Justice: Disputing validity of resolutions of the Volksraad, 254; dismissal of the Chief Justice, 257; Kruger's, President, defence, 356; Jorissen, Dr., dismissed by, 174; presidency, candidate for, in 1893, 209

Kraep, Jan: Secretary to Messrs. Kruger and Fourie on their mission to the Orange Free State, 91

Kruger, Caspar Jan Hendrik, father of President Kruger, 3; Portuguese frontier delimitation commissioner, 1844, 13

Kruger, Gert (uncle to President Kruger), 3

Kruger, Mrs. (first wife): Death of, 13

Kruger, Mrs. (second wife): Death of, 328; separation from the president on his departure from Pretoria, 310

Kruger, Nicholas (brother to President Kruger), 25

Kruger, Piet (son of President Kruger): Member of mission to Magato's Kaffirs, 155

Kruger, Theunis (uncle to President Kruger), 3, 21; hunting experiences shared with President Kruger—panther-killing, 29

427

INDEX

Krugersdorp: Gold-fields, discovery of, 181; Jameson Raid engagement at, 237

"Kwaaie Vrouw": President Kruger's reference to Queen Victoria, 259

Language (see Dutch Language)
Lanyon, Sir O.: Kleinfontein meeting, presence at, 138; succession to Sir T. Shepstone—unfitted for post, etc., 135

Leonard, Mr. Charles: Jameson Raid—signature of Johannesburg letter of appeal, 231; Uitlanders' grievances—manifesto, 232

Leyds, Dr.: Envoy Extraordinary of the South African Republic in Europe, appointment, 264; Kruger, President, bringing Dr. Leyds from Holland, 178; State Secretary of the South African Republic, election as, 189; re-election, 264; suzerainty question, reply of 16th April, 1898, 250; Swaziland Agreement, draft proposals—Dr. Leyds's denial that he had signed and approved draft deed, 204, 205; western border disturbances; mission of Dr. Leyds, 173

Liebenberg Vlei: Home of Kruger family, 9

Lion-hunting: President Kruger's experiences, 18, 19; canine fidelity, 20; first lion-hunt, 17; roar produced by treading on body of lion shortly after death, 19

Livingstone: Arms repaired and stored for Bechuana chief Sechel, 40

Little Free State: Permission granted to Transvaal to annex, 204

Lobengula: Matabele disturbances (see Matabeleland and Mashonaland). Relations with South African Republic consul, request for appointment of, 190; murder of Consul Piet Grobler by Khama's Kaffirs, 191; treaty placing country under protection of South African Republic, 190

Loch, Sir Henry: Interview with President Kruger at Norval's Point, 200; Pretoria visit—British demonstration offensive to the burghers, 220; Volksraad resolution, 224; Swaziland question—conference at Blignautspont, 203; draft proposals, 204; Transvaal National Union—deputation; correctness of Sir H. Loch's public attitude—charge of treachery, 221, 222; Johannesburg proposed visit, abandonment of, on President Kruger's advice, 221

Lombard, Stephanus: President of commission appointed to act in Schoeman affair, 74

London Convention, 1884: Article 4—foreign relations of the Republic, interpretation of—difference of opinion between Mr. Chamberlain and the South African Republic, 249; text of Article 4, 249 note; Chamberlain's, Mr., invitation to President Kruger to visit England to confer on Transvaal matters — discussion of Article 4 of the London Convention precluded, 245; Kruger's, President, counter conditions, 246; closing the drifts to goods from over the seas—violation of the convention, 227; deputation from South African Republic resulting in grant of London Convention, 174; England willing to receive, 174; members of deputation, 174; negotiations with Lord Derby, 175, 176; railway concession—foundation of the Netherlands South African Railway Company, 177; railway loan, failure to raise, 177; reception on the Continent on return journey, 177, 178; Robinson, Sir H., President Kruger's collision with, 176; franchise question—President Kruger's speech in the Volksraad, 376, 377, 378; intervention of Great Britain in the internal affairs of the Republic (see that title). Natives, dealings of South African Republic with—conditions of convention, 171, 172; signa-

INDEX

ture of convention, 176; Stellaland and Goshenland difficulties—Transvaal Government unable to intervene under the convention, 170, 171; suzerainty question (see that title); terms of convention, 175, 176; violation of, by the South African Republic—Mr. Chamberlain's contention—dispatch of 1897, 249; dispatch of 27th July, 1899, 279

Lorenzo Marques: Detention of President Kruger at the Portuguese governor's house on the way to Europe in 1900, 318

Lorenzo Marques to Pretoria Railway (see Delagoa Bay Railway)

Lottering (Kaffir girl): Attempt to prevent Grobler's murder, 191

Loubet, President: Reception of President Kruger in 1900, 324

Louis Trichardt, village to be so called to commemorate the expedition against the rebellious tribe of Ramapulaan—President Kruger's announcement in the Volksraad, 372

Machado, Governor, kindness of, during President Kruger's detention at Delagoa Bay in 1900, 318

Machadodorp: War of 1899-1902, transfer of the Government from Pretoria to Machadodorp, 312

Machem, Chief: Raids in Makapaanspoort district, President Kruger's successful expedition, etc., 100-102

Magato, Chief: Aid given to English in War of Independence—President Kruger's mission to Magato, 155; escape from Moselikatse, 10; President Kruger introduced to Moshesh by Magato, 61

Mahura, Chief: Diamond-fields dispute—Mahura included with Chiefs Waterboer and Montsioa in arbitration, 106; Gasibone expedition, action in—submission, appointment as chief in place of Gasibone, etc., 65, 66

Majuba Hill, battle of, 155; war of 1899-1902—"Revenge for Majuba Hill," a cause of, 120

Makapaan, Chief: Expedition to avenge attack on women and children traveling between Zoutpansberg and Pretoria, 43, 44; end of resistance — Kaffirs starved into surrender, etc., 47

Makapaanspoort: Kruger's, President, visit to Kaffir chiefs in 1868, 101; Machem, Chief, subdued by President Kruger, 100-102; capture of Kaffir women, 101; restoration in consideration of Machem's good behavior, 101

Makatese tribes: Submission to Zulu chief, Moselikatse, 7

Malan, Commandant: Conditions of Dr. Jameson's surrender, 237, 238

Malan, Jacob: Command of Aapjes River post in Civil War, 77

Malapoch, expedition against: British subjects' efforts to escape military service, 218, 219, 377

Malmanie gold-fields, discovery of, 181

Mamagali, Chief: Trial and punishment for false information leading to Potgieter's attack on Strijdpoort, 11

Mampur—Murder of Chief Secucuni: Expedition to punish Mampur, 169

Mankoroane, Kaffir chief: Montsioa, assistance to, in his war with Moshette—offer to English volunteers, 170

Mansvelt, Prof., education laws of 1882 drafted by, 216 *note*

Mapela, Chief: Kruger, President, "fetching Mapela down from his mountain," 62; Moshesh, connection with, 62; Potgieter, Herman, murder of, 42, 43; expeditions to avenge murder—President Kruger assistant general, 44, 47-49; trial, 62 *note*

Mapoch, Chief, protection of Mam-

429

INDEX

pur, Secucuni's murderer: Expedition against Mapoch, 169

Maraba's town: Expedition to recover stolen cattle, commanded by President Kruger, 48

Marabastad: Chief settlement in Zoutpansberg district, 100

Marias, Commandant Jan, officer of Schoeman's party induced to accompany President Kruger to Pretoria, 83

Maré: Boer representative in peace negotiations of 1881, 158

Marriage: Civil marriage regarded as natural rite by the Boers, 13 note

Marriage of President Kruger: First marriage in 1842 (Miss Maria du Plessis), 12, 13; second marriage (Miss G. S. F. W. du Plessis), 14

Marseilles: Welcome of President Kruger on arrival in 1900, 322, 323

Mashonaland: Mr. Rhodes's intrigues (see Matabeleland and Mashonaland)

Massouw: Moshette — Montsioa war, share in—offer of land to white volunteers, 169, 170; defeat of opponents, 170; revolt in 1885—success of Boer expedition—Massouw is killed, etc., 179

Matabele disturbances: Boer encampments, Matabele attack on, during Great Trek, 6; protection of women and children, South African Republic offer of assistance to the British Government, 233; Zeerust, defeat of Matabele by Boers, 8

Matabeleland and Mashonaland: Cecil Rhodes's intrigues to avert ascendancy of South African Republic, 190-192; annexation of territory, 194; charter granting right to certain monopolies and independent action, means used to obtain, etc., 193, 194; Chartered Company, formation of, 194; concession obtained from Lobengula, 193; gold, failure to discover, 195; Irish faction in British Parliament, attempt to unite, 194; massacre of Mashonas by Lobengula, punishment of—death of Lobengula, 195; Matabeleland and Mashonaland, intrigues to avert ascendancy of South African Republic—murder of Grobler due to Mr. Rhodes, etc., 191; Robinson, Sir H., treaty with Lobengula, 193

Meyer, Lucas: Election as president of "New Republic," 184

Menitjes: Delegates for Schoeman's party at the peace conference after Zwartkopje, 90

Methuen, Lord, Capture of, by De la Rey: President Kruger's desire for Lord Methuen's release, 328, 329

Military service: Exemption of persons not in possession of full burgher rights on payment of a certain sum of money, 220; Malapoch expedition, efforts of British subjects to escape military service, 218, 219, 377

Milner, Sir A.: Anti-British movement among the Afrikander population, alleged, 271; autocratic character of, 257; governor of Cape Colony and High Commissioner for South Africa, appointment in 1897, 257; partisanship, charge of, 269; policy—"The power of Afrikanderdom must be broken," 258; Swaziland, Bunu question—interference of Sir A. Milner, 265, 266; Uitlander grievances—conference with President Kruger at Bloemfontein, 31st May, 1899—unyielding attitude of Sir A. Milner, 273; intervention, need for—dispatch to Mr. Chamberlain, 272, 286

Mining committee established, 182

Mining industry: *Bewaarplaatsen*, change in method of allotment—Chief Justice of Supreme Court challenging validity of Volksraad's resolutions, 254; dismissal of chief justice, 257; Kruger's, President, defence, 356; company promoting on valueless property—precaution-

INDEX

ary measures, President Kruger's speech in the Volksraad (12th May, 1898), 342; Delvers Committee established, 182; depression among the poorer classes—relief measures, President Kruger's statement (12th May, 1898), 340; Industrial Commission, appointment of, 252; Government measures for carrying out suggestions, 253, 254; report, 253; progress in—value in gold extracted—President Kruger's announcement in the Volksraad, 373

Mission of President Kruger: Early prophecy, 3

Missionaries: Boer attitude towards, 40, 41

Mobilo, Chief: Evidence in the diamond-fields arbitration, 106

Montsioa, Chief: Appeal for protection to South African Republic, 171; proclamation by South African Republic of protectorate over Chiefs Moshette and Montsioa, 171, 172; British Government disallowing proclamation—proclamation recalled, 172; diamond-fields discovered in 1870—British Government contention that territory belonged to Montsioa and Gasibone, 105, 106; expedition against, in 1853—President Kruger's action, etc., 50-52; Moshette, war with, 170; suzerainty of Great Britain over Montsioa's territory declared, 172, 173

Moselele, Chief: Murders committed by, in South African Republic, 38

Moselikatse, Chief: Friendly relations with South African Republic, 190; Great Trek of 1836—attack on Boer encampments, 7; defeat by Boers at Zeerust, 8; Potgieter's expedition of 1839, failure of, 9; raids of—expedition against, 20; tyranny of, 7, 107

Moselikatse Pass: Potgieter's attack on, in 1840, 10

Moshesh, Chief: Basuto War of 1865 (see that title). Gift of saddle-horse to President Kruger, 63; Orange Free State, troubles with, 59, 60; Kruger's, President, success in negotiating peace, 61-63; polygamy, views on, 62

Moshette, Chief: Protectorate proclaimed by South African Republic, 171, 172; proclamation disallowed by Great Britain and recalled, 172; war with Montsioa—offer of land to English and Boer volunteers, 169, 170; defeat of opponents, 170; Stellaland and Goshenland founded by white volunteers, 170; Transvaal proclamation forbidding burghers to volunteer, 170; volunteers' refusal to obey, 170

Mother of President Kruger, 3

Name of the South African Republic: Name Transvaal State retained under Pretoria Convention, 164; Kruger's, President, persistence in use of name South African Republic, 164; restoration of name South African Republic by London Convention, 164

Natal: Boer attempt to treat for acquisition of land, failure of, 9; railway communication with Johannesburg, schemes for—Kruger's, President, rejection of, 182-185; scheme agreed to by President Kruger at first Swaziland Convention, 205

National Union (see titles Transvaal National Union and Reform Committee)

Native chiefs: Arms, smuggling of—Livingstone's breach of Sand River Convention, 40, 41; expeditions against (see names of chiefs). Independence, War of—aid given to English by Magato, 155; Kaffirs called out against Boers, 153; raids into Cape Colony, 3; royal commission of 1881—South African Republic deprived of power of interference in native quarrels, 170; Swaziland Convention—South African Republic debarred

INDEX

from treating with natives in North and North-West by first convention, 205

Native question: Arms for the natives—Livingstone's breach of Sand River Convention, 39, 40; Boer treatment of natives—children captured in warfare, disposal of, 47, 101; Great Trek of 1836—resolutions, etc., 6; principle followed in dealing with native tribes, 40; cannibalism, evidences discovered by President Kruger during expedition to avenge Potgieter's murder, 47; Kruger's, President, opinions on—speeches of 1882 and 1888, 41 note, 168. Labor: Difficulties in dealing with Kaffir servants, 14; industrial commission, suggestions and Government measures, 253, 254; political nature of question—President Kruger's attitude towards the natives, 41 note

Native territories (see their names)

Naturalization laws of the South African Republic, 197, 198; Bloemfontein Conference proposals, 272, 273

Nederduitsch-Gereformeerde Church: Union with Hervormde Church, 207

Nelspruit, transfer of the Government of the South African Republic during the war of 1899–1902, 314

Netherlands South African Railway Company: Foundation of, 177; repayment of loan—President Kruger's announcement in the Volksraad, 372

"New Republic," origin of—incorporation with South African Republic, 184

Niekerk, G. T. van, administrator of Stellaland, 170

Nigel gold-fields, discovery of, 180

Nyhoff, secretary to President Kruger—sleeping through Moshesh's night attack, 96

Ohrigstad in Lydenburg district, foundation of, 14

Orange Free State: Alliances with the South African Republic (see alliances). Annexation by Great Britain—President Steyn's proclamation, 409; annexation by Great Britain of South African Republic, resolution by Free State Volksraad in favor of repeal, 139; barter of territory to Boer emigrants of 1836, 6; Basuto War of 1865 (see that title). Boundary between South African Republic and Orange Free State—President Kruger appointed to represent South African Republic in deciding, 85; Civil War with the South African Republic (see Civil War). Constitution of, making as similar as possible to that of South African Republic —President Kruger's announcement in the Volksraad, 369; Gasibone expedition, share in, 64, 65; loan concluded with the South African Republic — President Steyn's announcement, 383; Moshesh's raids—President Kruger's successful mediation, 61-63; Moshette—Montsioa War, volunteers from Orange Free State for, 170; presidency (see that title); Pretorius, M. W.—claims on Orange Free State, compromise effected with South African Republic, 58, 59; election as president, 69; visit in 1860, 69; registration fees for goods imported free into the South African Republic, provisional agreement—President Kruger's announcement in the Volksraad, 370; Steyn, President (see Steyn); transfer by Great Britain to Commandant General Pretorius and the Boer emigrants, 56; Volksraad, opening speech by President Steyn, 381; war between Great Britain, South African Republic, and Orange Free State (see that title); War of Independence, A. W. J. Pretorius's command in, 37 note

Owen, C. M. (H. M. Special Com-

INDEX

missioner): Letter to Commandant General Pretorius requesting him to take over Orange Free State on behalf of the Boer emigrants, 56

Paarde Kraal Meeting: Declaration of independence, 151
Panther-hunting: President Kruger's experience, 29
Parents of President Kruger, 3
Paris: Exhibition of 1900—educational distinctions conferred on the South African Republic, 217; international exhibition of 1878—President Kruger's visit, 132; welcome accorded to President Kruger in 1900, 324
Parker, President of English Mining Republic, at the diamondfields threatening war against Pretorius, 105
Peace: Termination of the war (see war between Great Britain, South African Republic, and Orange Free State)
Peace conference after Zwartkopje: Constitutions and decisions of, 90, 91
Phillips, Mr. Lionel: Attack on the Government, speech at opening of Chamber of Mines new buildings, 231; franchise—Mr. Phillips's statement that "We do not care a fig for the franchise," 232; Jameson Raid, signature of Johannesburg letter of appeal, 231; sentence for conspiracy at Johannesburg and complicity in the Jameson Raid, 244
Pittius, Gey van, administration of Goshenland, 170
Plague: Bubonic plague conference—President Kruger's announcement in the Volksraad, 370
Plessis, Louw du: Serving the guns in battle against Secheli, 39
Plessis, Miss Gezina Suzanna Frederika Wilhelmina du: Marriage with President Kruger, 14; separation from husband and death, 310, 328

Plessis, Miss Maria du: Marriage with President Kruger, 12, 13; death, 13
Population: Number of male white population of South African Republic, 129
Portugal, attitude of, during the war of 1899-1902: President Kruger's detention at Delagoa Bay, 318
Portuguese possessions in South African frontier: Commissions of 1844 to determine, 13
Postma, Dr.: Founder of *Christelijk-Gereformeerde* Church, 75
Potchefstroom: Wedding of President Kruger, 13
Potgieter, Andries (son of Herman): Murder by Chief Mapela, 43
Potgieter, General Piet: Command in expedition to avenge murder of Herman Potgieter, 44; death—rescue of body by President Kruger, 46
Potgieter, Hendrik: Commandant and leader of the Great Trek of 1836-37; election as commandant for life, 37 *note;* expedition of 1839 against Moselikatse—failure of, 9; Kruger, President, taking part in, 9, 10; Matabele, pursuit and defeat of, at Zeerust, 8; Moselikatse Pass—storming of Kaffir town in 1840, 10; Strijdpoort—attack on Rooi Kaffirs due to false information, 11
Potgieter, Herman: Murder by Chief Mapela, 42, 43; expedition to avenge—President Kruger's exploits, 45, 46
Pott, Consul-General: President Kruger's visit on his way to Europe, 318
Presidency of the Orange Free State: Boshoff, President, retirement of, 69; Pretorius, M. W., election of, 69; Reitz, F. W., election of, 195, 196; Steyn, Judge M. T., election of, 258
Presidency of the South African Republic: Acting president during President Kruger's absence in Europe—appointment of

28   433

INDEX

General Schalk Burger, 316; ballot—first election under the new law, 1897, 258; Burgers, Thomas François, election of, 108; candidates in 1893, 209; election of 1893—violence of electoral struggle, 209; Grobler, Johannes — acting president during absence of Pretorius, 70; Joubert, General, candidatures, 167, 189, 209; Kruger, President—acting as president after the annexation of 1877, 122; candidature in 1882, 167; first candidature, 114; first presidency, 168; expiration, 185; fourth presidency, 1898, 263; speech on installation, 263, 264 *note;* inauguration—speeches (12th May, 1898)—Kruger's, President, speech, 338; requested to become a candidate, 108; second presidency, 1888, 189; third presidency, 1893-1898, 213; protest by Joubert party, 213

Pretoria: Kruger, President, departure of, 316; Loch's, Sir H., visit; British demonstrations offensive to the burghers, 220; Volksraad resolution, 219; occupation by Lord Roberts in June, 1900, 312; railway to Lorenzo Marques (see Delagoa Bay Railway); Swaziland Convention—conference between President Kruger and Sir H. Loch, 222

Pretoria Convention of 1881: Dissatisfaction among burghers—convention accepted with reservation, 163; Kruger's, President, vain appeal to Gladstone, 163; name "Transvaal State," retention of, 163, 164; suzerainty clause, opposition to, 163

Pretorius: Murder by Basutos, 95

Pretorius, Commandant General A. W. J.: Death of, 55; Independence, War of, command in—election as commandant general of Potchefstroom and Rustenburg districts, 37 *note;* Montsioa, Chief, expedition against, 50; Potgieter's, Herman, murder, avenging expedition commanded by, 42, 44; Sand River Convention, 37

Pretorius, M. W.: Election in 1858, 56, 69; resignation of, 70, 107; Robinson's candidature supported by President Kruger, 108; Volksraad resolution that state president should hold no other office, 70

Pretorius, President: Annexation —election as chairman of *Plébiscite* Committee, 127, 128; arrest on charge of high treason, 142; liberation of Pretorius by force—attempt prevented by Kruger and Pretorius, 142; release on bail, 143; Civil War—joint commission — Pretorius serving for Schoeman's party on second joint commission, 81; opposition commission, member of, 91; peace conference after Zwartkopje—delegate for Schoeman's party, 90; commandant general of the South African Republic, appointment as, 56; diamond-fields dispute, agreement to arbitration in—President Kruger's disapproval, 106; Gasibone, expedition against—appointment of President Kruger as assistant general, 64; Kruger's, President, mediation between Orange Free State and Moshesh, Pretorius sharing in, 59, 60; Orange Free State—claims to government of, 56, 57; Boshoff's, President, armed resistance, 57; compromise effected, 58; Kruger's, President, mediation, 57; election of Pretorius as president, 69; resignation of presidency, 88; peace, maintenance of, in 1879—support of President Kruger, 136; peace negotiations of 1881, Boer representative in, 158; presidency of South African Republic—election in 1858, 56, 69; resignation, 70, 107; in consequence of upshot of diamond-fields dispute, 107, 108; president of Government of South African Republic, appointment as, 56; proclamation of the British Government

434

INDEX

offering self-government to the South African Republic—reading at Nauwpoort, etc., 143; return from Orange Free State, 73; Secucuni War—Kruger's, President, recommendation of Pretorius to serve as fighting general, 111; triumvirate of 1880, member of, 151; Zoutpansberg expedition—failure to supply President Kruger with ammunition, 99

Prinsloo: Peace conference after Zwartkopje—Government delegate, 90

Proes, state attorney of South African Republic, 73

Punishment and chastisement, distinction between, 59

Queen Victoria: "*Kwaaie vrouw*," President Kruger's jest, 259

Railways: Extension of railways, President Kruger's views on, 168; Johannesburg, access to, by rail—President Kruger refusing requests of Cape Colony and Natal till Delagoa Railway should be finished, 182-184; indignation in Cape Colony, 185; Kosi Bay and strip of land ceded to South African Republic for railway construction, 204; Natal scheme for railway to Johannesburg—Kruger's, President, acceptance of scheme, 203; Swaziland Convention scheme agreed to, 205; Orange Free State railways—President Kruger's proposals, 184; acceptance of, 196; profits division proposal (see tariff war); tariff, reduction of—Industrial Commission suggestions and Government measures, 253

Ramapulaan native tribe revolt, expedition against: President Kruger's announcement in the Volksraad, 372

Red Cross abuses, alleged, during the war of 1899-1902 (see War)

Reform Committee: Arrest and trial of reform leaders in January, 1896, 243; deputation to Pretoria to demand permission for Dr. Jameson to enter Johannesburg, 236; name adopted by the Transvaal National Union, 234; Rhodes, Colonel, the only man who understood his business, 234. (See also Transvaal National Union)

Reitz, F. W.: Character of, 196; franchise question, stages of (see title franchise question); president of Orange Free State, election as, 195, 196; state secretary of the South African Republic, election as, 264

Religious advancements of South African Republic: President Kruger's views on, 168

Rensburg, Adrian van: Hunting experiences shared with President Kruger—elephant hunting, 27, 29

Rensburg, President van: Civil War—joint commission at Potchefstroom, proposals, 78; special court established by joint commission summoned by president, 82; nomination as acting state president of the South African Republic, 74

Retief, Piet, murder of, 9

Rhenoster encampment: Moselikatse's attack, 7

Rhinoceros hunting: President Kruger's experiences—adventure with cow *witharnoster*, 22, 25; thumb blown off by explosion of rifle, 31

Rhodes, Cecil: Adendorff trek, opposition to, 206; character, political creed, etc., 191-195; closing the drifts—retaliatory action as premier of Cape Colony, 227, 228; delvers committee, member of, 182; financial influence, 192; gold-fields of South African Republic, determination to secure, 195; imperialistic dreams, 190; Jameson Raid (see that title); Kruger's, President, attempt to win over, by offer of Delagoa Bay, 192 *note;* political career in Cape Colony, 192; South African Republic western frontier question, Mr.

INDEX

Rhodes's mission, 171, 173; Stellaland and Goshenland—incorporation with Cape Colony due to Cecil Rhodes, 192; Swaziland question—first convention, influence in, 206; presence at conference, 203

Rhodes, Colonel, and the Jameson Raid: Only man among the reformers who understood his business, 234; representative of Cecil Rhodes in Johannesburg, 230; sentence for conspiracy at Johannesburg and complicity in the Jameson Raid, 244; signature of Johannesburg letter of appeal, 231

Ring presented to Mr. Kruger by English friend of the Boers, 131

Roberts, Field-Marshal Earl: Bronkhorstspruit, battle of—Revival of charge of treachery against the Boers, 154; war of 1899-1902 (see war)

Robertse, Frans, wounded by first shot fired in War of Independence, 152

Robinson: Candidate for Presidency supported by President Kruger, 108

Robinson, Sir H. (High Commissioner): Johannesburg, disturbed state of—offer of mediation, 236, 239; Kruger's, President, esteem for, 176; London Convention negotiations — collision with President Kruger, 176; Matabele disturbances—reply to South African Republic's offer of assistance, 233; treaty with Lobengula, 193; suzerainty question, opinion on, 250; Swaziland, opinion as to annexation of Swaziland by South African Republic, 201, 202; War of Independence, peace negotiations, royal commission—Sir H. Robinson a member of, 162, 163

Roets, field-cornet of Heidelberg district—Friendly reception of President Kruger, 82

Rooi Kaffirs of Strijdpoort: Potgieter's attack on, due to false information, 11

Rooigrond, capital of Goshenland, 171

Roos, Tielman: President Kruger's teacher, 12

Rooyen, Van: Assistance rendered to President Kruger during battle against Secheli, 39

Rotterdam: President Kruger's visit, 327

Rowlands, Colonel: Command of Secucuni expedition, 132

Royal commission of 1881 (see independence, war of, peace negotiations)

Rustenburg: President Kruger's meeting with reference to franchise reform, 270

Salisbury, Marquis of, and the War of 1899-1902: Reply to President Kruger's application for peace negotiations—President Kruger's comments, 383, 392, 393; statement that the Republics would not be allowed to retain a shred of independence, 310

Sambaanland: Annexation by England, protest of the Transvaal, 224; incorporation with the Transvaal proposed, 203

Sand River Convention: Annexation of 1877, a violation of, 119; Kruger, President, accompanying Pretorius; Livingstone's breach of—storing and repairing arms for natives, 40

Scheveningen: President Kruger's visit to Mr. Wolmarans, 328

Schoeman, Commandant General: Agreement to assist President Boshoff, 57; Mapela expedition of 1858, command of, 48; violation of the constitution of the South African Republic (see Civil War)

Schoeman, Marthinus: Escorting President Kruger on his mission to Moshesh, 60

Schoemansdaal, village of, abandoned owing to Kaffir attacks, 99

Scholtz, Chief Commandant: Command in Secheli expedition of

436

INDEX

1849, 38; confiscation of Livingstone's arsenal, 40
Schoolmasters and mistresses: President Kruger's address on his election (12th May, 1898), 366
Schoonkloof Farm: President Kruger's accident, 98
Schutte, Commandant: Expedition against Montsioa, endeavor to dissuade Kruger from attacking, 51
Secheli Expedition of 1849: Kruger, President, Deputy Commandant—share in fighting, etc., 37, 40; Secheli's accusation against President Kruger, 39
Second Volksraad (see franchise question)
Secucuni, Chief: British claim to territory of—expedition under Colonel Rowlands, 132; murdered by Mampur, 169; Wolseley's, Sir G., subjection of, 140
Secucuni war of 1876: Annexation of South African Republic by Great Britain, failure of Secucuni war a pretext for, 114, 116; Burgers's, President, determination to accompany the commando—President Kruger's refusal to command, 110; causes of, 110; failure of main attack, 111; fighting generals recommended by President Kruger, 111; Magali, Chief, successful attack on, 111; peace, Secucuni's petition for, 112, 116; tax levied by President Burgers for maintenance of outposts—burghers refusing to pay tax, 113; Burgers's, President, attempt to exclude non-paying burghers from the Volksraad, 117; Krugers, President, opposition to tax as illegal, 113
Secucuni's town: President Kruger's thumb blown off by explosion of rifle, 31
Self-government offered to South African Republic by British Government, President Kruger's definition of, 143
Shaw, Miss Flora: Telegraphic correspondence with Mr. Rhodes, showing Mr. Chamberlain's knowledge of the Jameson Raid, 229, 230
Shepstone, Offy: Adviser to King of Swaziland, appointment, 202
Shepstone, Sir Theophilus: Annexation of the South African Republic in 1877—mission to Pretoria, etc. (see annexation); Kruger's, President, attitude on the annexation question, misstatement as to, 126; presence in Pretoria during the Secucuni war-tax dispute, 113; reply to petition against annexation—attack on Messrs. Kruger and Joubert, 130; Zulu war of 1879—request to President Kruger for assistance, 134
Simmer and Jack mine: Arms and ammunition concealed in, at the time of the Jameson Raid, 229
Sister republic (see Orange Free State)
Slaves: Emancipation by the English prior to trek of 1835, method of payment of compensation, 4
Smit, General: Independence, War of — peace negotiations — proposal to renew hostilities, 159; services in, 155; London Convention deputation, member of, 174
Smit, Nicholas: Fighting general in the Secucuni war, appointment on President Kruger's recommendation, 111
Smith, Jimmy: Presentation of American children's address to President Kruger, 311
Smuts, Mr. J. C.: Character sketch, 264; state attorney of the South African Republic, appointment, 264
Snyman, Commandant General: Civil War—order to surround Schoeman, etc., 77; nomination as commandant general of the South African Republic, 74
South African Committee: Charge against the British Government of keeping back telegrams which proved Mr. Chamberlain's know-

INDEX

ledge of the Jameson Raid, 229, 247, 248

South African League: Franchise question—alleged insufficiency of reforms, further demands, 284; Johannesburg branch—formation of, 266, 267; meeting to protest against arrests for contravention of the Pass Law—hostile demonstration, 267; petitions to the Queen on Uitlander grievances, 270, 271

Spain, King of: Reception of Boer delegates in 1884, 177

Speeches by President Kruger in the Volksraad (12th May, 1898), 338 (1st May, 1899), 368; (2d October, 1899), 376, 379; (7th May, 1900), 385—explanatory speech, 391

Speeches delivered at the inauguration of President Kruger as State President (12th May, 1898), 333

Standard Bank: Refusal to advance money to the South African Republic in 1885, 179

State Attorney of the South African Republic: Jorissen, Dr., dismissal of, 174; Smuts, Mr. J. C., appointment of, 264; State President of the South African Republic (see presidency)

State Secretary of the South African Republic: Fischer, Abraham, election of—refusal of appointment, 264; Leyds, Dr., election of, 189; re-election, 264; Reitz, Mr. F. W., election of, 264

Stellaland and Goshenland: Difficulties (see western frontier question); foundation of, 170; incorporation with Cape Colony due to Mr. Rhodes, 192

Steyn, Douw, of Bulhoek Farm, grandfather of President Kruger, 3

Steyn, Elisa, mother of President Kruger, 3

Steyn, Johannes: Commandant general, appointment by Commandant General Schoeman, 71; Jeppe, demand for surrender of, 72, 73

Steyn, President: Annexation of the Orange Free State by Great Britain—President Steyn's proclamation, 409; character sketch, 259; election as president, 258; speech at annual session of the Volksraad of the Orange Free State (2d April, 1900), 381; war between the South African Republics and Great Britain—Orange Free State, attitude of—correspondence with Sir A. Milner, 293-303; speech in the Volksraad—Orange Free State ranging herself on the side of the sister Republic, announcement (2d April, 1900), 381

Strijdom, Mrs.: Mr. Kruger's amusing experience with, 84

Strijdpoort in Waterberg district, Potgieter's attack on—Rooi Kaffirs mistaken for Moselikatse's men, 10

Supreme Court: Chief Justice Kotzé disputing the validity of resolutions of the Volksraad, 254; dismissal of the Chief Justice, 257; Kruger's, President, defence, 356, 357

Suzerainty question: Abolition of the suzerainty by the convention of 1884—South African Republic contention, 250; Derby's, Lord, dispatch, 250; Leyds's, Dr., reply of 16th April, 1898, 250; Robinson, Sir H., opinion of, 250; Chamberlain's, Mr. J., contention that the convention of 1881 held good, 250, 251, 279; Chief Justice, dismissal of, appeal to the English suzerainty—Mr. Kruger's defence of the dismissal of the chief justice, 357; condition laid down in alternative proposal to Mr. Chamberlain's joint commission proposal on the franchise question, 282, 283; Chamberlain, Mr., dispatch of 30th August, 1897, and Mr. Reitz's reply, 285, 286; independence of South African Republic endangered by British claim—Mr. Reitz's letter of 15th September, 1899, 289; Kruger's, President, statement in the Volksraad uncontradicted by

438

INDEX

England, 178; London Convention—repeal of suzerainty, 176

Swaziland: Annexation of Swaziland by South African Republic, proposal, 201, 202; Kruger's, President, efforts in favor of, 203; opposition in England, 202; Bunu—murder of Umbaba and refusal to appear before the Supreme Court at Bremersdorp, 265; armed force sent into Swaziland by Government of South African Republic, 265, 266; flight of Bunu to Zululand, 266; Milner's, Sir A., interference, 265, 266; punitive measures—agreement between the Government of the Republic and Sir A. Milner, 266, 267; convention of 1893, 205; conferences between President Kruger and Sir H. Loch at Colesberg and Pretoria, 222; terms of, 222, 223; convention of 1894, 224; clause deciding cases within the competence of the Supreme Court, addition of, 267; first convention, 205; government of Swaziland handed over to committee of Boers and Englishmen, 202; King Umbandine's request for a British adviser, 202; preliminary agreement—draft proposals, 204, 205; Kruger's, President, refusal to accept, 205; Swaziland question—Swaziland taken from South African Republic by Royal Commission of 1881, 201; transfer to South African Republic—Swazi opposition, deputation to England, 223; Winton, Sir F., interview with General Joubert, 202

Swimming the Vaal in flood, in order to visit his betrothed: President Kruger's daring, 12 note

Tariff war resulting from Transvaal Government scheme for equal division of railway profits between Cape Colony, Natal, and the Transvaal, 226; Cape Government objections, alternative proposed, 226; Cape railways reduction of tariff, 226; closing the drifts—reply of the South African Republic to the Cape wagon transport policy, 227; Chamberlain's, Mr., ultimatum to the Republic—condition that Cape Colony should bear half the cost of war, 227; London Convention, violation of, 227; Netherlands South African railway, raising tariff, 226; wagon transport from the Cape frontier to Johannesburg, 226

Tempus (President Kruger's horse): Death of, due to tse-tse flies, 29; habits of, 27

Theunissen, N. (brother-in-law): Hunting experiences shared with President Kruger—buffalo hunting, 25; rhinoceros hunt adventure—thrashing administered to Kruger for recklessness, 23

Toit, Andries du: Special court decision in case of, 82

Toit, Pastor du: Commissioner of western border, appointment, 171; education, tenure of office as director of, 215 note; flag of South African Republic hoisted over "proclaimed" territory on western border, 172 note; Jorissen's, Dr., dismissal from state attorneyship—share in, 174; London Convention deputation, member of, 174

Tortoise—"You must give the tortoise time to put out its head": Significance of President Kruger's phrase, 232, 233

Trade and commerce: Increase in —President Kruger's announcement in the Volksraad, 371; Kruger's, President, fears for independent trade—refusal to allow opening of railway connections with Johannesburg other than Delagoa Bay Railway, 182; tariff war (see that title)

Transvaal National Union: Formation of, at Johannesburg in 1892, 217; Johannesburg, disturbed state of, work of the reformers. (see Jameson Raid);

439

INDEX

Loch, Sir H., and the Union—deputation—correctness of Sir H. Loch's public attitude—charges of treachery, 221; Johannesburg, proposed visit, abandonment of, on President Kruger's advice, 221; name, alteration of, to reform committee, 234; nature and aims of, 218; punishment of leaders—interpretation of President Kruger's phrase, "You must give the tortoise time to put out its head," 232, 233; Uitlanders' grievances—manifesto, 232. (See also reform committee)

Transvaal State: President Kruger's refusal to use name—restoration of name South African Republic, 164

Trek of 1835: Black servants remaining in the Colony, 5; causes of, 3, 4

Triumvirate of 1880: Kruger, President, a member of, 151; proclamation drawn up by, 151; printing at Potchefstroom, 152

Uitlanders: Dynamite explosion at Johannesburg, Uitlanders' sympathy with the victims, 244; education of—erection of schools at the cost of the state, 217 *note;* grievances of the Uitlanders—Bloemfontein conference (see that title); British Government promises to Uitlanders—employment of force to secure demands made by Sir A. Milner, 281; Executive Raad empowered to deal with, 197; franchise question (see that title); intervention of Great Britain (see that title); Kruger's, President, attitude towards grievance complaints, 183; mining grievances, appointment of the Industrial Commission, 252; Government measures for carrying out suggestions, 253, 254; report, 253; negotiations—compliant attitude of the South African Republic and unyielding attitude of Sir A. Milner, 269, 272, 275; petitions—committee to inquire into genuineness of petitions—President Kruger's offer, 274; Queen Victoria, petitions to, drawn up by South African League—first petition—Mr. Fraser's refusal to receive petition—Mr. Chamberlain's censure, 270, 271; second petition—spurious signatures, 271; South African Republic—petition from Uitlanders to the Government declaring satisfaction with administration of country, 272; false signatures, Sir A. Milner's allegation, 274; taxation grievance—reduction of taxation, 183; "thieves and murderers"—misconception of President Kruger's speech at commemoration of declaration of independence at Paarde Kraal, 201; Transvaal National Union manifesto, 232; Kruger's, President, address on election as president (12th May, 1898), 349, 350; reform committee (see titles Transvaal National Union and reform committee)

Uitlanders Council and the franchise question: Dissatisfaction with the law of 1899, 279; inadequacy of reforms—further demands, 284

Ulundi, British victory at, 134

Umbandine, Swazi king: Request to British Government for an adviser, 202

Umbigesaland: Annexation by England, protest by the Transvaal, 224; incorporation with South African Republic proposed, 203

Union of South African Republic and the Orange Free State: President M. W. Pretorius's aim, 69, 70

United States of America: Jimmy Smith's arrival at Pretoria with school children's address to President Kruger, 311

Usibepu, Zulu chief: Defeat by Dinizulu, 184

Utrecht, Holland, President Kruger at, 327, 328

Utrecht and Wakkerstroom dis-

INDEX

tricts: British desire to keep back, 159

Vaal encampments: Moselikatse's attack, 8

Vaalbank Farm, birthplace of President Kruger, 3

Vechtkop: Matabele attack on Boer laager, 7

Venter, Commandant Piet: Boer representative in transfer of Orange Free State from British to Boers, 56; commander of Orange Free State contingent in expedition against Gasibone, 64

Venter, Koos: Mr. Kruger's offer to fight Venter on behalf of President Pretorius, 58

Veterinary Congress at Baden-Baden: South African Republic representative, President Kruger's announcement in the Volksraad, 371

Vice-president of the South African Republic, election of Mr. Kruger, 118; nomination of Mr. S. W. Burger, 386

Victoria, Queen: "Kwaaie vrouw," President Kruger's jest, 259

Viljoen, Jan: Commandant of Marico—capture of part of President Kruger's escort at Potchefstroom, 85, 86; Schoeman party in the Civil War, adherence to, 78

Village or Dorp: Meaning given to the word by Boers, 113 note

Village population, foreign element in: Petitions in favor of annexation, 113, 114

Villebois-Mareuil, Colonel, volunteer in the Boer army: Promotion to general of the Foreign Legion, 309

Villiers, Sir H. de (Chief Justice of Cape Colony): Intervention in the dispute between the judicial and state authorities of the South African Republic, 256; War of Independence, peace negotiations—Sir H. de Villiers a member of the Royal Commission, 163

Volksraad: Orange Free State—annual session, opening speech by President Steyn, 381; South African Republic—adjournment of Volksraad on declaration of war with Great Britain, 306; elections—postponement in consequence of the war, 386; Executive Raad, constitution of, 70 note; Kruger's, President, speeches in the Volksraad (12th May, 1898), 338; (1st May, 1899), 368; (2d October, 1899), 376, 379; (7th May, 1900), 385—explanatory speech, 391; resolutions contrary to the convention — Chief Justice Kotzé's criticism—dismissal from office, 254-257; Kruger's, President, defence, 358; Second Volksraad, institution of (see franchise question); session of 1866—President Kruger's accident on return journey, 98

Vorster, M. W.: Resolution to take a plébiscite on the annexation, 127

Vryburg, capital of Stellaland, 171

Vryheid district, formation of, 184

Wakkerstroom district: British desire to retain, 159

War between Great Britain, South African Republic, and Orange Free State, 1899-1902—annexation of neighboring colonies—decision of the Republic not to annex: President Steyn's speech in the Volksraad, 383; annexation of the Orange Free State by Great Britain — President Steyn's proclamation, 409; annexation of the South African Republic by Great Britain—counter proclamation, 314; armaments of the South African Republic, warlike preparations after the Jameson Raid, 247, 248; army of the South African Republic, Foreign Legion—promotion of Colonel de Villebois-Mareuil, 309; number of South African Republic and Orange Free State combatants (40,000)—President Kruger's speech in the Volksraad, 393; Boer prep-

INDEX

arations — armaments, increase in, after the Jameson Raid, 247, 248; burghers, concentration of, on borders of Natal, 292; Milner's, Sir A., correspondence with President Steyn, 297; British preparations — mobilization of army corps, 292, 302; proclamation calling out reserves, 303; reinforcements, withdrawal of—ultimatum of 9th October, 1899, 305, 306; troops concentrating on frontiers of the the Republics — explanation requested, 292; Steyn's, President, correspondence with Sir A. Milner, 292-303; ultimatum of 9th October, 1899, 304, 305; withdrawal of troops condition precedent to further negotiations, 300; British war office, intelligence department preliminary report — issue of "Military Notes," 277; causes of the war —annexation of 1877, 119, 180; English press hostility to the Republic, 269, 298; franchise pretext, 269; gold-fields discovery, 120, 180; military preparations of Great Britain, 299; circular dispatch from President Kruger to the commandant general and officers in the field (20th June, 1900), 399; (14th July), 405; conduct of the war —barbarism of the English— President Kruger's speech at Marseilles, 322; French press *exposé* of English methods— President Kruger's thanks, 324, 325. (See also sub-headings Red Cross and white flag treachery.) Dalmanutha—British attack on Botha's positions, 314; declaration of war (11th October, 1899), 306; expenses of the war—position of the South African Republic treasury, 389; Glencoe — President Kruger's exhortation to the burghers, 308; government of the South African Republic, transfer from Pretoria — Machadodorp, 312; Nelspruit, 314; intervention of foreign powers—deputation to Europe — Kruger's, President, speech in the Volksraad (7th May, 1900), 387, 388; Steyn's, President, speech in the Volksraad (2d April, 1900), 383; Kruger, President — delegation to Europe—proclamation by the Executive Raad, 316; departure from Pretoria—parting from wife, 310; life at Waterval Onder, 313; speeches in the Volksraad (7th May, 1900), 385, 391; unshaken confidence in God and resignation to His will, 329; work of advising and encouraging the burghers, 307; medical aid for the Boers from European countries, etc.—President Kruger's gratitude, 389; members of the legislative and executive bodies called to the field, number who had fallen, etc.—President Kruger's speech in the Volksraad (7th May, 1900), 385, 386, 397; Methuen, Lord, capture of—President Kruger's desire that Lord Methuen should be released, 328, 329; Modder River—De la Rey holding General French in check, 308; oath of neutrality—Lord Roberts's tempting proclamations and President Kruger's warning, 312; Orange Free State, attitude of—Kruger's, President, speech in the Volksraad (7th May, 1900), 386, 387; Steyn, President—announcement (2d April, 1900), 380; correspondence with Sir A. Milner, 292-303; Volksraad resolution (27th September, 1899), 294; peace negotiations —Kruger's, President, trust in God, 329, 330; South African Republic and Orange Free State proposals for negotiations on basis of both Republics being recognized as sovereign international states, 309, 310; Kruger's, President, speech in the Volksraad (7th May, 1900), 387, 388, 392, 393; Salisbury's, Lord, and Mr. Chamberlain's reply—

INDEX

President Kruger's comments, 392; Steyn's, President, speech in the Volksraad, 382; Poplar Grove—President Kruger's retirement owing to General French's advance, 308; Pretoria —departure of President Kruger, 316; occupation by Lord Roberts, 312; Red Cross—white flag treachery by the British, etc., alleged—Kruger's, President, protest, 389; Steyn's, President, speech on the war, 381; sympathy — world-wide sympathy with the Boer cause— President Kruger's Volksraad address, 389, 397; telegram from President Kruger to the commandant general (7th July, 1900), 403; "ultimatum" delivered to British agent at Pretoria (9th October, 1899), 304, 305; Villebois-Mareuil, Colonel de—promotion to general of the Foreign Legion, 309; Volksraad, adjournment of, on declaration of war, 306; Wolseley's, Lord, plans for conquest and seizure of the two republics, 277

Warfare, Boer methods, superiority to English methods, 133, 134

Warren, Sir Charles: South African Republic western border disturbances, Sir C. Warren's mission, 173

Waterboer diamond territories: Waterboer's claim made at instigation of the English, 106

Waterkloof: President Kruger's home as an independent member of Boer community, 12

Waterval Onder: President Kruger's life at, after transfer of the government from Pretoria, 314

Wessels, C. H.: War of 1899-1902, intervention of foreign powers —member of deputation to Europe, 309

Western frontier question: Fourteen Streams meeting, 173; commissioners appointed, 173; Rhodes's, Mr., attitude at meeting, 173; frontier fixed by the commissioners, 173; Kruger's, President, mission, 173; Montsioa's appeal to South African Republic, 171; proclamation issued by South African Republic, subject to London Convention, 172; flag of South African Republic hoisted over "proclaimed" territory by du Toit, 172 *note;* proclamation disallowed by Great Britain and recalled, 172, 173; restoration to South African Republic of territory taken by British in 1881, 175; Transvaal Government debarred from assisting Rooigronders by London Convention, 171

Willoughby, Sir J.: Officer in command of the Jameson Raid, 237

Winton, Sir Francis de: Appointment as special envoy to Swaziland, 202; Joubert, General, interview with, 202

Witwatersrand gold-fields, discovery of, 180, 182

Wolmarans, A. D. W.: Church union of 1881—leader of burghers withdrawing from, 207, 208; Executive Raad, member of— election—President Kruger's announcement in the Volksraad, 368; retirement—President Kruger's announcement in the Volksraad, 371; Kruger's, President, visits to, 88, 328; war of 1899-1902, intervention of foreign powers—member of deputation to Europe, 305

Wolseley, Lord: Annexation of the Transvaal, phrase as to irrevocable nature of, 140; Secucuni, Chief, subjection of, 140; war of 1899-1902—plans for conquest and seizure of the two republics, 277

Wood, Sir E.: War of Independence—numbers of Boers engaged, questions as to, 162; peace negotiations of 1881, 159; British representative, 158; Kruger's, President, difficulty in obtaining Sir E. Wood's signature to provisional protocol,

INDEX

160; Royal Commission, Sir E. Wood a member of, 162, 163

Zeerust, Boer victory over Matabele, 8

Zoutpansberg district: Kruger's, President, expedition against rebel Kaffirs in 1867, 99; Kruger's, President, visit in 1868—reception by Kaffir chiefs, census of Kaffirs, etc., 101, 102

Zuid Afrikaan: Publication of Dr. Jooste's letter on the nature of the opposition to annexation, 126; Kruger's, President, reply—suggestion of a *plébiscite* rejected by British Government, 126

Zulu war of 1879: British claim to Cetewayo's territory, 133; Cetewayo, capture of—rumors of British treachery, 134; Isandlhana, British defeat at, 134; Kruger's, President, offer to Sir B. Frere, 133; Kruger's, President, refusal to assist the British, 134; Ulundi, British victory at, 134

Zwartkopje, battle of, 89

CPSIA information can be obtained
at www.ICGtesting.com
Printed in the USA
BVHW032059080321
602015BV00005B/28

9 789354 419409